Artificial Intelligence
with Ada

Other Related McGraw-Hill Books

ISBN	AUTHOR	TITLE
0-07-056565-1	Sheldon	*Introduction to PC and MS DOS*
0-07-023437-X	Girard et al.	*Building Expert Systems Using PC Shells*
0-07-026909-2	Hart	*Knowledge Acquisition for Expert Systems*
0-07-037470-8	Levine, Drang	*A Comprehensive Guide to AI and Expert Systems*
0-07-037486-4	Levine, Drang	*Neural Networks: The 2nd AI Generation*
0-07-053614-7	Rolston	*Principles of AI and Expert Systems Development*
0-07-016803-2	Dickinson	*Developing Quality Systems*
0-07-042632-5	Modell	*A Professional's Guide to Systems Analysis*
0-07-024327-1	Greene	*Implementing Japanese AI Techniques*
0-07-056372-1	Shafer	*Hands-on Expert Systems: A Consultant's Guide*
0-07-031606-6	Hwang, DeGroot	*Parallel Processing for Supercomputing and Artificial Intelligence*
0-07-008600-1	Brule, Blount	*Knowledge Acquisition*
0-07-044088-3	Murray, Murray	*Expert Systems in Data Processing: A Professional's Guide*

For more information about other McGraw-Hill materials, call 1-800-2-MCGRAW in the United States. In other countries, call your nearest McGraw-Hill office.

Artificial Intelligence with Ada

Louis Baker, Ph.D.

McGraw-Hill Publishing Company

New York St. Louis San Francisco Auckland Bogatá
Caracas Hamburg Lisbon London Madrid Mexico
Milan Montreal New Delhi Oklahoma City
Paris San Juan São Paulo Singapore
Sydney Tokyo Toronto

Library of Congress Cataloging-in-Publication Data

Baker, Louis.
  Artificial Intelligence with Ada

1. Ada (Computer program language)   2. Artificial
intelligence.   I. Title.
QA76.73.A35B35 1989 006.3   88-27145
ISBN 0-07-003350-1

1234567890 DOC/DOC 8954321098

ISBN 0-07-003350-1

The editor for this book was Theron Shreve.

Printed and bound by R.R. Donnelley and Sons

LIMITS OF LIABILITY AND DISCLAIMER OF WARRANTY
The author and publisher have exercised care in preparing this book and the programs contained in it. They make no representation, however, that the programs are error-free or suitable for every application to which a reader may attempt to apply them. The author and publisher make no warranty of any kind, expressed or implied, including the warranties of merchantability of fitness for a particular purpose, with regard to these programs or the documentation or theory contained in this book, all of which are provided "as is." The author and publisher shall not be liable for damages in an amount greater than the purchase price of this book, or in any event for incidental or consequential damages in connection with, or arising out of, the furnishing, performance, or use of these programs or the associated descriptions or discussions.

Readers should test any program on their own systems and compare results with those presented in this book. They should then construct their own test programs to verify that they fully understand the requisite calling conventions and data formats for each of the programs. Then they should test the specific application thoroughly.

The programs contained in this package were developed for the JANUS ADA system. Please read the text for a discussion of conversion to other systems.

ABOUT THE SOURCE CODE
The source code for the programs contained herein is available on an IBM-PC compatible double-sided diskette by mail order. Send $29.95 (New Mexico residents add applicable tax, 5.25%) for source code in Ada to:

  Dagonet Software
  2904 La Veta Dr. N.E.
  'Albuquerque NM 87110

To Jennie

Contents

Preface   xi

1. Overview of Artificial Intelligence

Introduction   1
Interest in AI   6
Limitations and Critics of AI   7
Games: Chess as a Paradigm   11
Robotics and Vision   13
Natural Language Processing and Speech Understanding   16
What Is an Expert System?   16
A Case Study   17
The Bottom Line   20
What This Book Contains   21
References   23

2. Overview of Ada

Introduction   28
Why Ada?   28
The Ada Language   29
  General   29
Unconventional Aspects of Ada   32
  Exceptions   32
  Packages   32
  Generics   32
  Overloading   33
  Tasking   33
  Object-Oriented Programming   35
The Ada APSE   35
The Programs in This Book   36
References   36

3. Backward-Chaining Expert System Shell

Overview   37
Rule-Based Expert Systems   37
  Rule-Based Expert System Principles   37
  First-Order Predicate Logic   38
  Attribute-Value and Object-Attribute Value Systems   39

Backward and Forward Chaining   40
Exhaustive Search, Uncertainty, Confidence Factors, Fuzzy Sets   42
Unification   43
Occurs Check   45
Negation, Horn Clauses, Guarded Horn Clauses, Contraposition   45
Resolution   46
Indexing Rules   48
Negation as Failure and the Closed-World Model   49
Non-Horn Clauses and Factoring   49
Circularity Check   50
The PROLOG Cut   50
Nonlogical Predicate Terms   51
The Program   51
Basic Data Structures   51
Overview   53
Dynamic Strings   54
PACKAGE LOGIC   55
PACKAGE HASH   56
PACKAGE ANDOR   57
PACKAGES MATH, MFUNCT   57
PACKAGE READIN   57
PACKAGE BACK   59
Other Data Structures   61
Depths and Contexts   61
Examples   62
Comparison with other Backward-Chaining System Shells   63
References   63
Program Listing and Test Problem Output   65

4. Forward-Chaining Expert System Shell. Arithmetic

Overview   149
Forward-Chaining   149
Arithmetic Predicates   150
Special-Action Predicates   153
Nonmonotonic Logic   154
Heuristics, Metaknowledge   154
Comparison with OPS5   154
Compiling Rules: RETE   156
Truth-Maintenance Systems   157
Learning   158
The Program   158
Data Structures   158
Program Code   160
Examples   162
References   162
Program Listing and Test Problems   162

5. Frames

Overview   233
The Frame Concept   233
Frames and Rules   235
The Program   236
Functions   236
Representation in Core   236
Representation out of Core   237

Data Structures and Subprograms   238
  Example   240
References   240
Program Listing and Test Problem Output   241

6. Syntax and Semantics

Overview   270
UNDERSTANDING LANGUAGES   270
Syntax: Formal Language Theory   271
  Post Productions and Phase-Structure Grammar   271
  The Chomsky Hierarchy   273
  Context-Free Languages   274
  Inadequacy of Phrase-Structure Grammars   275
  Transformational Grammar   275
  Attribute Grammars and Unification Grammars   276
Semantics   277
References   279

7. Augmented Transition Network Parser

Overview   281
The ATN   281
The Program   283
  ATN Operations   283
  Dictionary   284
  Program Structure   285
  Test Problem   287
Final Remark   287
References   288
Program Listing and Examples   288

8. Conclusion

Overview   353
Pattern Recognition, Language, and Rules   353
Integration, Blackboarding   354
Extensions   354
  Contrast Programming   354
  Planning   354
  Discrete Event Simulation   355
Conclusion   355

Index   357

Preface

Is artificial intelligence, commonly called AI, just "hype"?

Some books give this impression by describing brilliant accomplishments while remaining silent as to just how these results were achieved. An article in *UNIX/WORLD* answers the question "AI: Hype or a New Technology?" with "neither . . . [but] a glorified search technique operating on a glorified database."

If the emotionally charged word *glorified* is replaced by the term *sophisticated,* we would find its definition for mainstream AI quite accurate.

The purpose of this book is to dispell the impression of AI as hype by presenting straightforward descriptions of the basic ideas that underlie these claims, complete with the computer programs in Ada that implement the methods. This should demystify the subject of AI by allowing the reader the ability to readily "get behind the wheel" and take a "test drive." Claims made for AI within this book can be easily tested by the user himself, who can then go on to build applications for himself using the computer programs here as a basis.

It is beyond the scope of this book to cover all of what is now known as artificial intelligence—which is, to paraphase Elaine Rich, the study of all the things computers cannot, at present, do well. Instead, we focus on the well-defined applications of AI rather than current research topics.

The most important of these applications is probably that of *expert systems*. We discuss and implement both forward- and backward-chaining systems. The advantages and tradeoffs between these two systems are discussed. We then discuss enhancements to the simple systems presented, such as sophisticated search strategies, and the synthesis of forward and backward chaining.

These systems are not minimal toy systems, but contain a number of sophisticated features such as the ability to use non-Horn clauses, circularity checks, and confidence factors.

Next we cover the method of frames for knowledge representation. This is an alternative to the rule-based method of the expert system and is the current successor of scripts, semantic nets, and a number of other obsolescent techniques. It is actually a hierarchical database.

The next topic is natural language processing. Human grammar is so complex, and so filled with the ambiguities avoided by the designers of artificial computer languages, that sophisticated processing methods must be used—in this case we focus on augmented transition networks as a flexible approach to dealing with "English as she is spoke." Obviously, our system will not approach human literacy, but neither does any known system. Natural language processing is still very much a research field.

The field of AI covers far more than the few topics mentioned above; in fact, entire volumes have been written just surveying the field, giving very cursory descriptions of the major results. We have limited the breadth of this work in order to permit sufficient depth for the topics covered, with complete descriptions of the algorithms and the code to implement them.

Why is this book not in LISP? Isn't that the language of choice for AI? There are a number of reasons. LISP will remain, for the forseeable future, the language of choice of AI research and development, because the LISP environment is designed specifically to favor a developer at the expense of the end-user. In particular, LISP environments eschew all economies of both computer storage and processor speed. In addition (and in spite of an effort to produce a CommonLISP standard), LISP environments are all unique, each having local implementations of the idiosyncratic features desired by the local developers. This makes it easy to develop new concepts, but impossible to standardize a production system.

Conversly, implementing an AI system in a language such as Ada or C can give significant performance improvements. Such improvements can be especially important in a real-time embedded system, which must have the fastest possible performance. The prodigal memory requirements of LISP are well known and another potential problem for embedded systems. A recent article in the 1985 SIGART Newsletter described a program to play go which was transformed by its creator from a LISP program, requiring 3 megabytes of memory on a mainframe, to an equivalent program written in C, requiring 146 kilobytes and running on an IBM-PC. Speed and efficiency also can be appreciated by users waiting for a response from the system! It is likely that, while research on AI will continue to be predominantly in LISP for the near future, applications of AI will continue to move away from LISP. The Defense Advanced Research Projects Agency (DARPA) and other DOD supporters of AI applications will tend to prefer Ada for use in military systems, for example. The Pilot's Associate and other DARPA AI projects specify that, while prototype systems may be developed in LISP, the final "deliverable" must be in Ada. This specification is to ensure portability and efficiency.

While modern LISP environments can interface with the outside world, e.g., by calling subroutines in C to access sensors or other real-time data, LISP processing is typically too slow to respond in a timely manner. LISP is fine for conversing with a researcher at a terminal, but an embedded system must operate under severe time constraints. More efficient languages, such as Ada or C, would have great advantages in such applications.

An autonomous vehicle's control program necessarily must be written in Ada if it is for DOD usage. Ada would be the language of choice for non-DOD application, if thought were given to future system integration and efficiency. Indeed, Ada has special features for concurrent processing. The computers being developed under the strategic computing initiative have large amounts of parallelism. Ada may be the best way to utilize this capability. One such parallel processor machine, the SAN-DAC, has been flight-tested. Its architecture of parallel 68000s (to be 68020s in later versions) would be well-suited to Ada or C, but much less so to LISP.

In fairness, modern LISPs are set up to allow for parallel processing, insofar as the syntax allows, but no compiler has been written to take advantage of this feature. The lack of standardization of LISP dialects would still preclude the use of LISP for any sort of production environment.

This book should also be of interest to Ada novices who wish to see a variety of data structures, dynamic strings, file handling, etc., in practical, tested code.

Many AI systems currently available have huge price tags and are sold with a "buy before you look" philosophy. Readers of this book can look before they buy such a system. They can decide for themselves just how much of AI is "hype" by rolling up their sleeves and using the programs contained in this book.

Acknowledgments

This book was prepared using Ventura Publisher (except for code listings.) I'd like to thank Stephen Parks for help in editing. I'd like to thank Meridian Software for supplying an evaluation copy of version 1.0 of their AdaVantage compiler. All code was tested on the JANUS/Ada "Ed" compiler.

Louis Baker

Chapter 1

Overview of Artificial Intelligence

Introduction

The first question any book on artificial intelligence must address is, Just what is artificial intelligence? This question ranks second to "Define the universe and give three examples" in difficulty, and not by much. Everyone seems to have a personal favorite definition. The one most cited seems to be Elaine Rich's definition of artificial intelligence (AI) as "the study of how to make computers do things at which, at the moment, people are better" [1]. Such a definition clearly limits AI to pure research, because once computers do a reasonable job on the problem, it departs the realm of AI. Typically, the term AI has been restricted to processing data which was principally symbolic rather than numerical. Disciplines often considered part of AI include natural language processing (including speech recognition and language translation and understanding), "expert systems" (see below), playing games, vision and other topics in robotics, and machine learning.

An important distinction often overlooked is that between intelligence and intellect. Gordon Pask [2] defines intelligence quite simply (and circularly!) as the ability to score well on a suitable intelligence test and intellect as "creativity in the pursuit of rational as well as imaginative ends." The former is a "logical dexterity," which probably can be expressed with suitable algorithms, although these may be extremely complex. The latter may be an ultimate goal of AI research, but it cannot be said that there is, at present, any real understanding of how to make a machine "creative." H. A. Simon has written that the General Problem Solver (GPS) program, developed by his group at Carnegie-Mellon University (Carnegie Institute of Technology at the time), had simulated insight: "GPS has had at least a modest 'Aha' experience, and if I had had a little more time to discuss the planning program, I could have told you what that 'Aha' was." [3] In this case, it appears that the "insight" was a sharp reduction of the amount of search needed, once some crucial rule was obtained.

Current AI research and applications deal not with intellect so much as intelligence—competently performing a task with a nonnumerical answer, which if produced by a human, probably would not evoke comment about the originality or brilliance of the concept. If we understood intellect, we probably could have our schools turn out Einsteins by the dozen. The goal of an intelligent machine, even within a limited domain (a very particular "intelligence test"), is not to be dismissed lightly, however. The history of AI research shows that this modest (compared to intellect) goal has been frustratingly elusive.

Initially, AI research concentrated on animal and human models. The former was closely associated with control theory, i.e., mechanisms that automatically sought and maintained an equilibrium. Singh's book [4] reviews the most significant of these models, the neutral network models of McCulloch and Pitts, Ashbey's homeostat, Uttley's machines, and Rosenblatt's Perceptron. More recently, Albus's Cerebellar Model Arithmetic Computer (CMAC) [5] joined this line of models. All these models employ a form of feedback to adjust responses to inputs. In many ways, this accommodation matches the way animal brains appear to work and may be called learning. John von Neumann did some work on neural networks [3,6], showing that they could be robust in the presence of noise or failure of some elements, with sufficient redundancy. Very recently, hardware models of neural networks have been developed as content-addressable memories (in which the data effectively serves as its own address, facilitating lookup) and for solving special-purpose problems.

These models have all been able to reproduce simple behavior, such as learning, but have not shown the ability to "scale" to truly interesting and complex behavior (see below) which could be called intelligent. Part of the difficulty is our lack of understanding of the basics of neural operation. How is memory accomplished? Are there truly two distinct types of memory, short and long term? Are these different types of memories stored by different mechanisms? How do we remember, and why do we forget? Recent discoveries, such as the role of structures in the brain's limbic system in enabling us to store memories, are valuable but do not clear up the mysteries. Are memories encoded as proteins, DNA or RNA, as changes in the synapses (if so, precisely what changes to the synapses—in membranes, or production of transmitters?), or in the establishment of new synaptic connections?

It is well established that new connections or synapses form. For example, if a kitten is raised in total darkness for the first few weeks of its life, it will never see. If one eye is covered with a patch for this period, while the other is not, it will be functionally blind in the covered eye. It will then be found during autopsy that the neural pathways from that eye never developed. Clearly, the brain and eye learn to see in the first few weeks of life, and this learning occurs through a feedback mechanism which establishes synapses. But what, precisely, is this mechanism, and is it a model for all learning or, more simply, the very special learning that occurs in the first few months of life? One hypothesis is that the repeated firing of a neuron tends to break down its wall, releasing products which attract dendrites from other neurons and facilitating the formation of synapses. In effect, the neuron is signaling that it has something interesting to say, won't someone please listen. We can speculate now and hope that further experimental work provides further enlightenment, but even if breakthroughs are made in understanding the brain, it is not guaranteed that this will lead to intelligent machines based upon neural models. The key ingredient would be to devise methods for the system to organize itself, to learn connections which enable it to see or perform other tasks meaningfully. Because the human brain has roughly a hundred billion neurons, each with an average of a hundred synaptic connections (some neurons, such as the Purkinje cells of the cerebellum, can have on the order of a hundred thousand synaptic connections), programming such a network (or a model of such a network) is simply out of the question—it must be able to program itself. It is plausible that the information known as memory is encoded in the characteristics and patterns of the synapses, rather than in the bodies of the neurons. Thus, the storage capacity of the brain can be a few orders of magnitude larger than the number of neurons. By contrast, the "fan out" of computer logic elements, embodied in Perceptrons and model neural nets, is typically countable on one hand. Some may complain that the analogy is unjust, as "fan in" is really exhibited by dendrites, and computer logic can, in principle, handle very large "fan in." True, but the point is that the complexity of each element is much greater when the element is a neuron than when it is a computer circuit. At present, the brain is the only system capable of such a feat of self-organization, and how it performs this trick is unknown. Even the behavior of a synapse is quite complex. There is a whole panoply of neurotransmitters in the brain, some believed to be excitatory while others inhibit a nerve's firing. Why so many neurotransmitters? Some synapses can be either excitatory or inhibitory, depending upon the firing rate. Nerves can have synapses on axons as well as at dendrites. All in all, we are still a long way from understanding the brain—and hence from achieving AI through this route.

The other historical route to AI was the human model. Simon and Newell [6] investigated in depth how humans approached problems, and these approaches were modeled by computer programs. Such modeling served the dual purpose of confirming the validity of the model developed, as well as providing insight into problem solving in general. The GPS model has already been alluded to above. A series of programming languages, IPL to IPL-V, was developed to express the GPS program. The key idea was *means-end analysis.* To solve a problem, the program evaluated how far it was from its goal (the "end"). It then attempted to reduce its distance from the goal by the proper choice of a "means." This produced a recursive procedure, because in general a "means" did not carry us all the way to the goal in one step. Instead, it produced an intermediate goal or subgoal, which had to be achieved by application of means-end analysis. This, in turn, might require further subgoals to be established and achieved.

This key idea of recursive generation and attempted achievement of subgoals will be encountered in AI in general, and in expert systems in particular. As a psychological model, the fundamental ideas which underlie the GPS are evidenced in much of human behavior. The idea of the brain as a machine, which is constantly trying to understand the world by reducing the differences between perception and expectation, is supported by much evidence and is consonant with models such as L. Festinger's cognitive dissonance [7] theory and Piaget's theory of learning [8]. The idea of means-end analysis in problem solving has been documented in the work of Simon and Newell and many others.

As the GPS is a paradigm of most of AI, its weaknesses are in general the weaknesses of most of the field. First, let's consider the *complexity explosion:* The process of generating and achieving subgoals (or rejecting them if we cannot find a means to achieve them) can rapidly exhaust the memory and the computational speed of any computer. Generally, unless special methods to prune the tree of subgoals to be searched are used, the complexity increases exponentially, so that a small increase in the problem size (i.e., the depth to which successive subgoal generation may progress) can cause a huge increase in the number of computations required. Heuristic methods must therefore be used for the search. These methods do not guarantee that the correct answer will be achieved. In short, even if the means-end model is in principle capable of solving a problem, a practical implementation might require exorbitant resources of time, memory, etc., to solve even a modest problem. (In more technical terms, many of the problems of interest to AI are "NP-complete" and therefore are believed to become intractable as the problem size grows [9].)

Indeed, heuristics have a built-in Catch-22. Suppose, for example, we were developing a program to play chess. Without heuristics, we would have to consider all the legal moves available to ourselves and our opponents, following each set of alternatives until someone was mated or a draw was reached. That is, we would have to consider roughly 10^{120} possible chess moves [10], an impossibly huge number. Therefore, we must stop the examination of alternative positions at some reasonable depth. This is done by using a "position evaluator," a heuristic which estimates the relative advantage of the players at any stage, based upon material differences, space controlled, etc. (See, e.g., Levy's book [11] for more details.) While this cuts the number of alternatives down to a practical level, it represents increased requirements for information, namely the knowledge embodied in the heuristic rules, as well as the costs in computer time and storage to process this additional information.

Another problem is that it was found that, however well one builds the "inference engine," i.e., the portion of the computer code which performs the means-end search, the system is only as good as the information it has to work with, and "common sense" typically requires a huge amount of background information. In translating a paper on, say, physics from German to English, it is necessary not merely to know the grammars of the two languages, or even common sense semantics, but a knowledge of the area of physics discussed in the paper. Humans can and do take a lot for granted in dealing with other humans, because they can. In an article in *Science* called "The Necessity of Knowledge," [12] it is stated that "the essence of intelligence seems to be less a matter of reasoning ability than of knowing a lot about the world." What may pass for reasoning ability may be the ability to recall relevant information swiftly. In fact, as mentioned in the preface and discussed below in greater detail, expert systems are currently sophisticated databases ("knowledge bases"). Our primitive understanding of recall in the brain limits our ability to use neural models. The individual neurons operate much more slowly than electronics, but they are able to operate independently and in parallel. This enables searching through memories to find the right one at speeds rivaling a digital computer. But what are the heuristics the brain uses?

One last problem with the GPS was that it was cumbersome. In the National Research Council's *Outlook for Science and Technology,* [13] two articles appeared discussing AI, the former, "The Science of Cognition" having H. A. Simon as a coauthor. The GPS methodology is explained as "successive cycles of programming, comparing the printouts with human performance, and reprogramming." The process of developing an expert system, as discussed in Feigenbaum and McCorduck's *The Fifth Generation* [14], is also forbidding. In Chapter 3, page 5, "The Knowledge Engineer at Work," for example, a complex process is described in which the programmer–"knowledge engineer" first immerses herself (in the cited example, H. P. Nii) in the subject, studying college texts; then goes through a cycle of interviews with the expert, programming the expert system, and revising it in light of its performance and later debriefings of the expert. There is no easy way to check whether the resulting set of rules or facts incorporated in the expert system produced are consistent or complete. Indeed, like most computer programs, maintenance never ends with initial delivery to the customer but is a continuing process for the life of the system. While all computer programs share this feature, expert systems are somewhat more difficult to maintain simply because of the lack of knowledge engineers to do the job. Furthermore, most expert systems are sold as proprietary programs with the source code closely guarded. This makes program maintenance cumbersome at best.

Most recently, a "pragmatic" school of thought appears to dominate AI. "Instead of trying to recreate the human mind, the goal of AI has become much more focused on making computers more productive," says an article by Dwight B. Davis (quoting Richard P. Ten Dyke) in the July 1986 *High Technology* [15]. All's fair, as long as the resultant program works. This approach is certainly more appropriate toward applications, assuming one has sufficiently good methods, whatever the model, to deal with the problem at hand. In this approach, AI may be defined as clever programming.

Interest in AI

Artificial intelligence has had its ups and downs over the years. Its latest halcyon period began in the mid-1980s. Frost & Sullivan, a market analyst, was quoted in the May 1988 *High Technology Business* of annual AI sales (including hardware) of $1.7 billion by 1990. Arthur D. Little's AI Group estimated that by the year 2000 AI would account for 20 percent of the computer industry, with expenditures of from $40 billion to $120 billion by then. The May 30th 1988 issue of *COMPUTERWORLD* forecast the 1989 market at $3.08 billion and the 1990 market at $4.09 billion. Lieutenant General W. E. Thurman reported that the Air Force Wright Aeronautical Laboratories funded $25 million in programs through 1986 and expect the funding to double over the next five years [16]. The impetus for this upsurge appears to be the Japanese fifth-generation program and the book by Feigenbaum and McCorduck [14], mentioned above, which that project inspired. For example, John Naughton writes [17]: "Ever since the Japanese launched their Fifth Generation research program, AI has become a fashionable obsession in Western computing circles." M. M. Waldrop [18] says that the impetus for a national effort to produce intelligent computers "is in no small measure a response to Japan." Davis's article [15] also says, "Much of the current artificial intelligence activity at U. S. computer manufacturers can be directly linked to Japan's 1982 announcement of its Fifth Generation project." Without doubt, the book by Feigenbaum and Mc-

Corduck [14] did a great deal to stimulate interest in the United States in the fifth generation and especially AI. In a review by Eric Weiss [19], this book is called "a warning, a clarion call to action, and the most recent example of an over enthusiastic promotional piece for Artificial Intelligence." The authors of *The Fifth Generation* would certainly have to agree with the first portion of this quotation, as they call for a vigorous national response to the Japanese, proposing a national center for knowledge technology. The question of just what amount of enthusiasm is justified is of course subjective.

It is perhaps worth noting that the current enthusiasm is in expectation of a breakthrough, and not a consequence of one. It is not a case of a Gold Rush due to a nugget found at Sutter's Mill, but rather a desire to avoid being left behind if the Japanese find the mother lode before we do.

In addition, the military especially see AI as a technology in which we might maintain a qualitative edge over opponents. The Vietnamese war gave us "smart" bombs; now the quest is for "brilliant" weapons. The increasing precision of guided weapons (the smart bombs, among others) had increased expected attrition rates and the perils of war. The answer is "standoff." The more intelligent the weapon, the more it can be allowed to range beyond our grasp with some hope it will perform its mission. A truly autonomous weapon could possibly win wars without bloodshed—let the robots fight it out. The countermeasures arena is a good example of the pressure toward smarter systems. With spread-spectrum and frequency agility techniques, humans are simply too slow to respond to changes in threats which must be countered. Automatic systems must be used. If my jammer is smarter than your radar, it could save my life (and cost you yours). Would a jammer that could recognize a pattern in a threat radar's changes in pulse characteristics be considered to embody AI? Almost certainly yes.

Limitations and Critics of AI

As is evident from the review cited above, not everyone shares the same sanguine view of AI research. The review by E. A. Weiss cited above contains the remark: "the authors expound the present and future wonders of AI, sometimes (as is traditional in that discipline) confusing what will be or may be with what is."

The Dreyfus brothers, Hubert and Stuart, are AI's most persistent critics. In 1965, Hubert authored a RAND Corp. report titled "Alchemy and Artificial Intelligence." This became the basis for the book *What Computers Can't*

Do: A Critique of Artificial Reason, published in 1972 and recently revised
[20]. With his brother Stuart, he wrote *Mind over Machine* in 1986 [21].

The AI community has returned the favor. S. Papert wrote an "AI Memo"
at MIT in 1968, "The Artificial Intelligence of Hubert L. Dreyfus: A
Budget of Fallacies." Pamela McCorduck's book *Machines Who Think* [22]
contains a chapter called "L'Affair Dreyfus."

The argument has its amusing aspects. In 1957 Herbert A. Simon (Newell's
collaborator on GPS) predicted that [23] "within 10 years a digital computer will be the world's chess champion." Dreyfus criticized this remark
(the exact words are in dispute), and he was invited to play chess against
MacHack, a chess-playing program of the day, which was relatively primitive by modern standards, playing at an amateur level. Supposedly, he lost
the game, and the AI community chortled over this triumph. In his latest
book with his brother, Dreyfus says MacHack had erroneously given him a
queen in the middle of the game, which he felt honor-bound not to use.
Later, this queen disappeared, and still later, MacHack gave itself an un-
deserved queen, which it used to win! Such a game is not chess. No one
involved in the controversy seems to be able to produce a transcript of the
moves made in the game. The book by Feigenbaum and McCorduck obli-
quely refers to this story on page 34 when it says: "If a philosopher argued
that a machine could never play good chess, and then somebody devised a
machine that demonstrably could, and what's worse beat the philosopher in
a match, he revised his claim to say that a machine could never play championship chess." Hubert L. Dreyfus is a philosopher by training. It is difficult to know precisely what was said and what happened, given the very
divergent reports. If a single game had been played, it is a bit extreme to
call this a "match."

Lost amid the *argumentum ad hominum* and the disputes over what precisely was said is the simple fact that three decades after Simon's predicted
world champion computer, i.e., a factor of three times Simon's estimate, no
such computer exists, nor is one foreseeable. (Hans Berliner, leader of the
team developing the Hitech machine, gave a computer chess champion by
1990 a fifty-fifty chance—this cannot be called a prediction, as he is equal-
ly correct whatever happens.) Computers can easily beat players of the likes
of Dreyfus or yours truly, but they are not on a par with the best humans.
David Levy, an international master (and so by no means the best of human
players or grandmasters), has made a career of defeating chess programs
[11].

Dreyfus's arguments are often rather esoteric and difficult, probably because of their philosophical tilt. I believe his most cogent argument pertains

to what I have referred to above as an "inability to scale." At the risk of putting words into the mouths of the Dreyfus brothers, let me explain my understanding of the argument with a concrete example. Suppose I devise a program that plays chess fairly well. How do I make it world championship class? I could try brute force—more powerful computers which compute more positions per second. This would enable me to increase the depth of the search, and so I could look ahead, say, eight moves instead of seven. But because of the complexity explosion referred to above, this approach is not attractive. If I multiply my computing speed and power by ten, this does not buy me a tenfold increase in depth, but only a very small increase. The chess-playing ability hardly improves. To get beyond the point of diminished returns, only a radical change in method will suffice. But what is that new method? The older method, which brought us to that point, provides no clue.

In the strictest interpretation, this argument is almost certainly correct. It does permit a few loopholes, however. First, where is the point of diminished returns? For chess, it is clearly below grandmaster level, but for other problems of interest it may be on a par with human performance, or even exceed that of the best human experts (consider the radar-jamming example discussed above). Second, a breakthrough in hardware, such as a massively parallel computer, could conceivably break through the complexity barrier by giving us a performance improvement of many orders of magnitude. Such a computer would have to self-organize, and we don't know how to do this yet, but that does not make it impossible for all time. Finally, a radically new and different algorithm for, say, chess is not impossible merely because it is not foreseen.

At this point, H. L. Dreyfus would argue that humans don't use rules to solve problems such as chess, at least not at the grandmaster level. This brings us to philosophical speculations rather than concrete demonstrations. Merely because we are unsure how the human brain organizes itself, or how it arrives at intuitive solutions to problems, does not mean that an algorithm cannot ultimately be devised to do so as well. Human grandmasters appear to do a sophisticated recognition of patterns from a chess game, comparing these over-the-board situations to roughly 50,000 learned patterns [24]. They therefore do not proceed by "rules," even if some books on chess tactics may teach rules, but rather intuitively, in the sense that the correct solution seems to pop into their head as an "Aha" when the match with a stored pattern is achieved. Most books on chess tactics tend to teach basic patterns, i.e., forks, pins, skewers, etc. Capablanca, when asked how many moves ahead he saw, replied "only one—but it is the right one!"

If human experts in general proceed intuitively by recognizing the problem at hand as similar to one of a huge number of stored patterns, there are a number of important consequences. First, the arduous debriefing of experts to obtain rules for a rule-based expert system might be almost useless. In such a situation, we are not learning how the expert solves problems, but rather asking him to reformulate his methods into a different methodology—rules instead of pattern matching. The difficulties of such debriefings could be explained by the simple fact that experts do not work by rules, so coming up with a rule-based system that gives the same or better performance could be a chimera. Second, we are lead to the possibility of an expert system based upon pattern matching.

A pattern-matching expert system faces a number of difficulties. If we could "upload" the 50,000 or so patterns from a grandmaster and get another 50,000 from his colleague (most of these would be redundant), we could probably wind up with a computerized grandmaster superior to each individual. But how is this debriefing to be done? Since the process of pattern recognition is subconscious to the grandmaster, how is he to recall each of the patterns he knows? Furthermore, assuming these patterns could be obtained, they are only part of the problem. How are the patterns in the game at hand abstracted for comparison with those in memory? Assuming a near match is found, what next? Are variations tried by the heuristic search methods of [11] to see if the memorized pattern is indeed useful, or is some other method used?

Finally, just how does one do the matching? Pattern recognition has been a difficult and elusive goal in AI research [25]. The brain clearly does it in parallel, and there has been suggestive progress in the area of neural networks toward a pattern recognizer [26] based upon associative memories. Such a recognizer is perhaps best modeled as a (massively parallel) statistical pattern recognition system, hunting for best matches or minimum error states. In fact the models for neural networks [6], developed by J. J. Hopfield and others, exploit the analogy with physical systems such as the Ising lattice, in which couplings between elements provide feedback and produce a system which naturally "falls" into minimum energy states. Therefore, an expert based upon pattern recognition via associative memory can be simulated in a variety of ways besides neural networks. Such a simulation could be done in a data-parallel manner and would probably have to be so performed for reasonable speed performance. Bell Laboratories has fabricated neural network matrices with 22 lines per side, which can store four 22-bit words. Off-chip amplifiers must be used [6,26]. Clearly a scale-up of many orders of magnitude is needed to store an expert's recollection. But the problem cannot yet be regarded as solved.

Even if AI systems can never surpass humans in all intelligent and intellectual spheres, there are many cases where they can be of value—where we cannot easily put a human expert (the autonomous systems discussed above), where microseconds matter (the smart jammer), where economic considerations preclude sending experts to all cites (the XCON expert system discussed below). Performance beyond that of the best human for similar problems is not required for AI to be useful. (In this context, it is perhaps noteworthy that David Levy, who has regularly bested computers at chess, is chairman of Intelligent Software.)

Games: Chess as a Paradigm

Because chess has been the focus of so much interest and controversy in AI, it is worth looking at as a paradigm for AI methods. The methods of "heuristic search" owe their development to the desire to make chess-playing computers a viable proposition.

Naive brute force clearly cannot work for chess. To examine all the possible consequences of a move, which are consistent with the laws of chess, is clearly prohibitive. If we cut the search short at any point, we need a rule, or heuristic, to do this. For example, if a course of play loses a piece, we might abandon that line of play as inferior. This, of course, would preclude positional sacrifices and the employment of the various openings known as gambits. The heuristic rule has to be more sophisticated, therefore, to evaluate the pros and cons of a situation.

By any standard, chess programs have made a great deal of progress beyond the one that beat H. L. Dreyfus. In the context of understanding the criticisms of AI made by the Dreyfus brothers, it is useful to inquire as to how much of this improvement has been due to brute force and how much due to sharpening of algorithms, heuristics, etc. Undoubtedly, both better programs and better machines have improved chess performance.

Early chess programs solved the complexity explosion problem in part with a set of heuristics called a *plausible move generator,* which sharply reduced the number of positions that had to be considered. A quantum jump in machine performance, to the level somewhat below a human master, was achieved by David Slate and Lawrence Atkin in the 1970s. They were developing a program and wanted to enter it in an upcoming competition. Faced with a deadline, they concentrated their efforts on other portions of the code and, in lieu of a plausible move generator, resorted to *full-width search* in which all moves were considered plausible. This resulted in an improvement that was quite unexpected. Soon, all chess programs employed full-width search.

Do we score this advance in the improved algorithm column or as one for brute force? The change was to the algorithm, but it moved the program in the direction of brute force rather than smarter code. Simply put, the plausible move generator was excluding the best moves—the heuristics devised for it were clearly not good enough.

In 1981, Belle appeared from (where else?) Bell Laboratories. It used custom-built hardware to achieve 120,000 positions analyzed per second. It quickly became machine champion and achieved rating equivalent to that of a human master, the first machine to do so. Belle's main competitor has been Cray Blitz, running on what is now merely one of the most powerful computers in the world. It achieves approximately the same rate of position analyses per second. These computer champions clearly exemplify the value of brute force.

A third strong competitor is Bebe, another machine with specialized hardware (bit-slice in this case) for chess analysis.

Recently, Berliner's group has produced Hitech [27], a machine which again uses specialized hardware. It analyzes roughly 200,000 positions per second and has defeated Cray Blitz.

In their next encounter, however, Cray Blitz defeated Hitech. This apparently was accomplished by changes to its "opening book." Machines play the opening moves according to a "book" given them, rather than by analyzing them move by move. The justification for this is principally that the motivation for certain opening moves is deeper than the depth such machines can search (typically, at present, about eight plies, or four full moves). In addition, it saves time to be used for thinking later in the game. The change to Cray Blitz's repertoire appears to be to force it to leave the book and start "thinking" about moves sooner. Indeed, computers playing humans typically leave the opening at a disadvantage, since opening moves are often based on strategic considerations that don't bear fruit for a long time. As in the case of *depth first search,* we have an improvement due to algorithm change rather than brute force. However, the direction of the change is not one of doing things more craftily, but rather of plodding more, sooner.

The Dreyfus brothers' latest book [21] contains a detailed critique of computer programs that play checkers and backgammon as well as chess. They conclude that these programs do not equal the skill levels of the best human players of those respective games. Samuel's checkers-playing program has the interesting attribute of learning from its losses, by altering the relative weights it gives to the various terms in its position evaluator. The present chess programs require their creators to reprogram them. Unlike human masters, who create "cooks,"(traps prepared or cooked up before the game) they cannot innovate in the opening. Neither can they play the opponent rather than the board, e.g., by introducing complications which are probably unsound when the opponent is in time trouble or nervous. On the other hand, masters such as Levy can take advantage of their opponent being a machine.

Wilcox [28] gives an interesting report on go programs. Presumably because of the greater relative weight of strategy to tactics in go compared to chess, although also in part no doubt to the lower level of effort devoted to go programs, such programs play at an amateur level.

It appears fair to conclude that machines still play far below the human level and are likely to do so for the near future at least. Furthermore, the advances in chess ability all seem to be in the brute force direction of enhanced computing power, often purchased at the price of custom hardware, rather than algorithmic subtleties. It would be very interesting to explore an approach to chess closer to the human model, in which pattern recognition is used to suggest moves, as in the thinking of human masters.

Games such as chess and go are actually poor models for most forms of conflict. Bridge, for example, is a far superior model of war. It involves both deception and reconnaissance, both of which are absent from board games. It also involves communication and cooperation with allies, also important in the real world. While there has been some AI effort at bidding, there does not seem to have been much effort devoted to playing bridge. Such work would be interesting. Does pattern recognition play a similar role with bridge masters? Could computer work devise a superior bidding system, perhaps using information theory (not AI)?

Robotics and Vision

The prestigious *Handbook of AI* [29] does not even include a section on robotics, although it does include one on vision. The two-volume MIT handbook [30], however, includes both. Therefore, while scene interpretation appears to be generally considered part of AI, robotics (manipulator design and control, for example) does not.

Vision has benefited much from the animal model line of approach. It is well-known that the retina processes the image by enhancing contrasts at boundaries [31]. This facilitates edge detection, and mathematical processing that duplicates this effect is employed in most vision systems. The human ability to recognize silhouettes and line drawings emphasizes the fact that we do not generally recognize objects from surface textures but rather from edges. This suggested the "primal sketch" theory of D. Marr as a model for visual processing. The ability to use lines (edges) also greatly reduces the amount of data to be processed, from a fully two-dimensional array to a set of lines.

Similarly, once the image data is placed on the optic nerves, half the nerve fibers from each eye cross. Behind the optic chiasma, the optic nerves carry fibers from both eyes, which come from portions of each eye which look at the same fields of view (e.g., the right optic nerve behind the optic chiasma contains fibers from the outer portions of the right eye and the inner portions of the left, each of which view objects off to the left). These fibers are then sorted out in the lateral geniculate nucleus (one on each side), with alternate layers connected to fibers from alternate eyes. Almost certainly, this involves a procedure to compare the images seen by both eyes for parallax displacement and hence judgment of distance. The adjacent anterior pair of the corpora quadrigemina [32] then control the focus (and pupil size) of the eyes. While conscious effects can affect these controls— e.g., it is known that attitude can affect pupil size (something interesting or attractive tends to enlarge the pupils)—these effects are usually subconscious. Those of us blessed (?) with myopia can watch our eyes (without glasses) try vainly to focus on a streetlamp, for example, a procedure which will not stop as long as we stare at the light, even though we know it is a fruitless endeavor.

This simple picture has been challenged. For example, consider the phenomenon of *subjective contours* (Fig. 1.1). Although there are no edges, the mind's eye supplies them [33]. Curved as well as straight edges may be interpolated, including corners (multiple lines). The process is not merely the extrapolation of edges but can be triggered by texture differences. The visual perception system clearly uses clues besides edges to identify regions. D. Marr of MIT has argued that surfaces are the fundamental objects of interest, and should be the first target of the visual system in its effort to make sense out of a scene [34]. Recognition of objects by means of surface texture rather than by edges has the advantage of robustness—the object may still be picked out of a scene with foreground objects partially obscuring it, and shadows do not have the disastrous impact of producing false edges [35]. See note 36 for a discussion of the application of such methods as part of a robot manipulator system.

Recognition of objects is still very much a research topic rather than a sphere of application. Assuming one has extracted the information in the image in the form of edges and or surfaces and their orientation, there are two basic approaches to pattern recognition: statistical (also called decision-theoretic) and syntactic [25]. The former is basically a mathematical matching. For example, one may compute correlation functions between a scene

Fig. 1.1 Subjective contours.

and a comparison set of images. Peaks in the result indicate the possible location of an image in the comparison set being in the field of view. The matching pattern is selected as the one with least distance to that seen. "Noise" can therefore be tolerated, but there is little flexibility with regards to size, orientation, etc. Syntactic pattern recognition seeks to represent objects as strings in a grammar describing object properties and finding similar strings in a processed image. It is the more ambitious and less advanced form of pattern recognition. For example, to recognize various letters, we might define symbols to represent curved- and straight-line segments of various orientations and operators for the types of vertices between these line segments (Gonzalez and Thomason [25]). The various letters would be allowed ("grammatical") strings in the grammar of these symbols. The problem of decomposing an image into these strings, as one might parse an English sentence, must first be solved and then the strings analyzed to obtain the recognized character. As might be expected, the two approaches are not completely independent, and syntheses of the methods have been attempted [37]. See Ballard and Brown [38] for a good overview of the topic of pattern recognition in visual systems and, in particular, the method of the Hough Transform for recognizing objects from their edges.

As discussed above, human experts appear, at least in some cases, to proceed by pattern recognition rather than by applying rules. For this reason, pattern matching may become an important method for expert systems as well as recognition systems. The statistical model is closer to the modus operandi of neural networks [6,26] but is probably too simplistic by itself to account for the matchings humans can perform. The problem of pattern recognition is essentially the same as memory recall, and we probably will not understand one until we understand the other.

Humans also use a lot of knowledge about the behavior of objects in the real world [39]. This often accounts for the illusions which occur when artificial objects, as those encountered in Escher illustrations, turn up.

Finally, the visual recognition process involves the flow of information across region boundaries. One obvious example is the ability to perceive a shadow for what it is and the shadowed object as a whole rather than a multiplicity. Clearly, the continuity of texture is recognized across the edge of the shadow and the difference in the brightness of the two regions discounted. A more subtle nonlocality of processing is in color vision [40]. The perceived color of a region is not merely due to the cross-ratios of the excitation of the receptors in any locality. In this way, we can perceive, say, green leaves as being of the same color throughout a variety of illuminations. The visual system seems to get an overall sense of the ambient and uses this knowledge to remove any bias due to nonwhite illumination.

Natural Language Processing and Speech Understanding

We shall have more to say on this topic in the section devoted to it in this book. Here we limit ourselves to a few brief comments.

There has been a basic dichotomy in techniques between the advocates of syntactic and semantic analysis. Of course, understanding cannot take place without both. The question is which is predominant, and by how much. Current techniques cannot mix the syntactic and semantic information easily. The result is that conventional natural language systems must assume a very special world in which meanings (semantics) can be guessed with high reliability. We will discuss below a popular method called augmented transition networks (ATN) for analyzing natural language. This method is primarily syntactic in its approach, although we will discuss how semantic information may be included in sentence analysis by using the methods of "attributed grammars."

What Is an Expert System?

Just as the definition of AI is rather nebulous, the definition of an expert system depends on whom you ask. Edward Feigenbaum defines an expert system as "an intelligent computer program that uses knowledge and inference procedures to solve problems that are difficult enough to require significant human expertise for their solution" [17]. But how do we precisely define *intelligent, knowledge,* and *difficult enough* to meet this criterion? There appears to be no unanimity on these questions. For example, D. L. Parnas, who achieved recent notoriety for suggesting that the strategic defense initiative required reliable software that would be unobtainable, noted in a letter titled "Base Distinction" [40]: "At a recent large conference I asked everyone who used the term 'knowledge base' to explain how to tell the difference between a knowledge base and a database. Most declined, saying only that they had used a common buzzword. Bob Graf-ton...said that if it worked today, it was a database, and if it was going to be great someday, it was a knowledge base." Similarly, J. de Kleer, in a review of Feigenbaum and McCorduck's popular book [14], remarks, "When Sun Tzu, who is often cited in the book, wrote...about the impor-tance of knowledge for the successful conduct of war, he didn't mean MYCIN-like rules" [42]. (MYCIN refers to a renowned ruled-based expert system discussed in [14].) Indeed, [14] stresses, perhaps unduly in the opinion of reviewer de Kleer, the role of such systems as opposed to other AI methods.

A Case Study

Consider the following problem, which I have been told has been addressed by a computer program: A tank is to move from point A to point B by the optimum route—for example, it should avoid silhouetting itself on a ridge line where it could easily be spotted. Obviously, this problem is a model for similar mission-planning scenarios, such as how an aircraft might attack a target through defended airspace.

How might this problem be solved? One approach would be as follows. First, superimpose a grid (network) over the terrain containing allowable routes. Computing power available will determine the resolution of the grid, whether it is regular or can be optimized, etc. Points A and B should be lattice points, i.e., points of intersection of lines on the grid. This first step, or something very much like it, is probably common to all conceivable methods, and will therefore not be discussed further here. We are concerned only with choosing among the possible approaches.

Next, define a metric function, i.e., a measure of "distance" (cost) for each path between lattice points. The cost function (distance function) will be high for disadvantageous routes (such as those crossing or along ridge lines), prohibitively high for impassable routes (if indeed those grid lines are retained in the problem at all), and low for good routes. The problem is then to find the path of shortest distance between A and B, where short is understood in terms of our metric function and not in terms of geometric distance. Excellent algorithms for the solution of this problem have been well known for a long time [43]. We can easily (in principle) modify our metric, for example, if speed is critical and risks need be taken to reduce transit time or if fuel supply is critical and we need to minimize its con-sumption.

This highly efficient algorithm has one drawback—the metric function as-sumes that the distance or "danger" of the path from two points is independent of how we got to the first point (it would not be difficult to use a directed graph so as to allow the metric to depend upon direction of traversal of a path). For example, a short section of path defended by a system with a slow reaction time might be relatively safe if it approached that segment by a concealed route, but that same segment could be deadly if the defenders were forewarned. This, of course, greatly complicates the problem, as the segments cannot be studied independently.

The problem now becomes one of searching for the best path (through the network or graph) from the various alternatives. This may be done through conventional AI heuristic search methods. Rich [1] discusses these under the heading "weak" methods—weak in that they do not require strong, or detailed, understanding of the specific problem or the best way to conduct the search, but rather a fair heuristic method to suggest the most promising way to search. On the other hand, they may require relatively large amounts of computer resources to search the various paths. (In a sense, weak methods are like thermodynamics, whereas strong methods, such as the shortest path algorithm for a network, are like statistical mechanics. The former are sledgehammers that will work on any problem in principle, but may be costly, while the latter are finely tuned to require minimum effort for a suitable problem. Thermodynamics will tell us generalities about systems we know few specifics about, while statistical mechanics can give us very detailed and precise information, at the cost of more detailed information to start with about the system of interest.) Weak search methods, such as hill-climbing, the Λ^* algorithm for best-first search, and branch and bound may be used to perform this search. (Branch and bound is a method that originated under the banner of "dynamic programming" and thereafter not often discussed as part of AI. It, like other heuristic search methods, often uses "greedy" heuristics. See [44] for more discussion.)

These AI searches are not necessarily the only way to proceed, however. Recently, the search method known as *synthetic annealing* [45] has attracted attention. It has been applied successfully to a number of problems, such as the traveling salesperson problem. This is a difficult (NP-complete [8]) shortest-path problem, and I would expect would be well-suited to the problem discussed here.

Synthetic annealing is an approximate method that will never give us an exact answer. The weak methods can, in principle, give us an exact answer for a given network. However, it might be more practical to use synthetic annealing with a finer mesh, and get a better answer, than with a weak search method, as the latter will almost certainly require greater computer resources for the same network. If heuristics could be included in the synthetic annealing method, it could be very attractive.

But wait! While the cost of moving from A to B might depend upon how we got to A, it should not depend upon what we will do after we have departed point B. Any metric function which did not have this property would violate causality. (We might not even make it to B.) Does this fact enable us to use a divide-and-conquer strategy, i.e., evaluating the best route to A without worrying about what comes after [44]? Perhaps we could modify the usual Dijkstra algorithm for shortest route [43,44] for this method. In general, such a greedy method would fail because the best route to an intermediate point C might cause a huge penalty to be incurred by moving from C to B. Causality does not preclude foresight. For example, if a low cost route to C permitted the enemy to observe us, the cost from C to B could far outweigh the cost of a stealthy route from A to C to B. Thus, in the most general case we are forced to rely upon some form of heuristic search or synthetic annealing as our method for the problem. However, assume that the quantities that characterize the best route are few, e.g., length, duration, earliest observation by enemy, total observed time, etc. We might extend the Dijkstra shortest-path algorithm to handle this case. Instead of a unique best route to any node, we might have to remember a number of acceptable routes—those with smallest length, or latest observation by enemy, etc. We could ignore any routes dominated by others which are better in all the categories listed. If the number of acceptable routes to any node did not exponentiate, then this modification to the network method would do very well. Only for specific metric models can we decide whether this approach is competitive or not.

Is such an algorithm an expert system? Is it AI? The computation is essentially purely numerical rather than symbol manipulation. The techniques of network analysis and dynamic programming have been well known for decades (synthetic annealing is relatively new) and don't qualify as clever programming. The expertise is represented in the coefficients embodied in the metric function. Is that function a knowledge base? These questions do not have a unique, objective answer. I suspect that to sell such a program, it would probably be called an expert and an intelligent system because of the knowledge about terrain embodied in it, however that information were used.

Such a program would not contain any tools of common appearance in AI. Typically, expert systems are currently based on the use of rules. The rules, or the data they work with, or both, may be stored in databases (knowledge bases?) of a form called frames. We will discuss these methods from inference and data representation below in a number of chapters.

In the article mentioned in the preface, it is stated, "An artificial intelligence program is basically a glorified search program operating on a glorified database" [46]. This is essentially the definition we will adopt in this book for an expert system. By this definition, the use of network theory and other numerical methods do not qualify as AI, and neither, therefore, does our method for tank navigation, however smart our coefficients are. In the chapters to follow, we will discuss different search methods and different means of representing the (glorified) knowledge database.

The Bottom Line

The problem of vaporware is not limited to one segment of the computer industry. Computer programs do appear to have more of their fair share of disappointed users, perhaps because of the impossibility of testing a program under all conceivable circumstances. The areas of AI in general and expert systems in particular seem to be minefields for the unwary, perhaps because of the popularity of the fields and the consequently high levels of expectations (and promises). The fifth-generation project is already disappointing some—the budget of the Japanese Institute for New Generation Computer Technology has been cut, "evidence of technology breakthroughs are scarce," and the project may not deliver what proponents were expecting [47].

In *AI Expert* magazine, Alex Jacobson wrote [48], "Expert systems technology...when applied to a well-defined domain of interest, can provide...computer support at performance levels equal to or better than the best human experts in the domain." Taken out of context, this may sound like hype. But the domains listed in the first ellipsis are, for example, "authorizing a credit card, diagnosing faults in a piece of equipment, scheduling fleets of vehicles...or configuring a set of machines." The expert systems may not be purely rule-based but might use network or other optimization methods (numerical computations) for part or all of the problem. In the same month, *BYTE*, in a review of the book *Expert Systems 85,* (edited by M. Merry, Cambridge: Univ. Press, 1986) one of the contributions in that volume is cited as concluding "current expert systems are not nearly flexible enough to mimic human experts" [49].

In short, how satisfied you are with an expert system will depend on your expectations. If you expected the promise implicit in the name *general problem solver* to be fulfilled, you will probably be disappointed with the results.

Capturing the expertise of the world's best chess player (or internist) will be impossible for some time to come. Such experts probably use "intuition" (pattern recognition) as discussed above, rather than rules.

On the other hand, capturing fairly mechanical knowledge, such as troubleshooting automobiles, is probably within the grasp of current technology. The key is, as Jacobson implies, the "well-defined domain." Do you really understand the problem enough to write down the rules necessary to solve it? This question, of course, is the fundamental question of all of computer programming—What's the algorithm? If you can come up with a sufficiently good (perfection is not generally necessary) algorithm, then the expert system will handle it. Viewed in this light, experts systems and AI in general are merely a branch in the continual evolution of programming, not a radical departure. AI, in general, and expert systems, in particular, are not panaceas for all problems. If one has reasonable expectations for results from a suitable (not overly ambitious) problem, they can do quite well.

What This Book Contains

We will present computer programs, written in Ada, that constitute expert systems using a variety of approaches, including ruled-based systems (forward and backward chaining), a frame "knowledge base," and an ATN parser suitable for handling natural language input. We will not in general provide various code segments for producing user-friendly elements of a system, such as graphic output, menu-driven or mouse-driven input, etc. The expensive commercial AI systems provide this lagniappe, indeed such friendly I/O probably accounts for the bulk of the code in such systems. The tools for doing such things are not specifically expert system tools, even if they happen to be written in LISP. In this book, we will concentrate on code required for the "inference engine" of an expert system. We will not discuss weak or heuristic search methods. While these are the principal components of such AI systems as game-playing programs, they tend to be very problem-specific in design. The references cited above relating to dynamic programming, synthetic annealing, and other search methods (whether or not called AI by their proponents) should be consulted by those interested in heuristic search. The rule-based systems here illustrate much of the code required for searching—for example, the backward chaining system employs depth-first search; only an heuristic evaluator, and some additional code to keep track of where we were and how "good" the heuristic function estimated things were at a point, would be required to turn this into an heuristic search method.

Because of the vaporware problem you should not let a salesperson run through a snappy demo of computerware (hard, soft, or both) as the sole prerequisite for signing on the dotted line. Try using the system yourself, before you buy. That demo might be a canned package with all bugs carefully excised and all minefields for the unwary cleared.

Know what you are getting. Often, the most expensive systems are the most closely guarded as containing proprietary information, with the result that you never really know what is being done at any point.

The programs in this book are, like the moves on a chessboard, all out in the open. If people claim they have better algorithms, let them publish their code and let the world judge. If you want to know what is happening at any point, turn on the tracing feature (see below for how this may be done). There may be bugs, and the code certainly is open to improvement. But it is very useful to know what is happening (the successful expert systems to date have been constructed by their users and not bought as shells—see below for justification of this claim). Users can add friendlier shells and editors, but the core algorithms found below should require little or no modification.

References

1. Elaine Rich, *Artificial Intelligence* (N.Y.: McGraw-Hill, 1983).

2. Gordon Pask, "A Discussion of Artificial Intelligence and Self Organization," in *Advances in Computers,* Vol. 5, ed. F. L. Alt and M. Rubinoff (N.Y.: Academic Press, 1964).

3. J. Singh, *Great Ideas in Information Theory, Language and Cybernetics* (N.Y.: Dover, 1966). See also M. Minsky and S. Papert, *Perceptrons* (Cambridge: MIT Press, 1969). This book was a rather critical review of the prospects for the Perceptron approach. The original work on Perceptrons was by F. Rosenblatt, in *Psychological Review,* vol. 5, no. 6, p. 386–408 (1956). See also his *Principles of Neurodynamics* (Washington, D.C.: Spartan Books, 1962). The book *Artificial Intelligence Techniques* by E. B. Carne (Washington, D.C.: Spartan Books, 1965) contains details on building Perceptrons and hardware models of neurons. The original work on neural nets is W. S. McCulloch and W. A. Pitts, *Bull. Mathematical Biophysiocs,* 5, pp. 115–133 (1943). A. M. Uttley's work is the article "Conditional Probability Machines and Conditioned Reflexes," in *Automata Studies,* ed. C. E. Shannon and J. McCarthy (Princeton, N.J.: University Press, 1956), pp. 253–275.

4. J. S. Albus, *Brains, Behavior, and Robotics* (N.Y.: BYTE Books/ McGraw-Hill, 1981).

5. For recent work on practical implementations and applications of neural networks, see "Bell Labs models parallel processor on neural networks," *Mini-Micro Systems,* August 1986. For a discussion of content-addressable memories based upon a nonlinear neural network, along with an analysis, see "Nonlinear Neural Networks," by J. L. van Hemmen and R. Kuhn, *Physical Review Letters,* 57, 7, p. 913–16, Aug. 18, 1986, and the references cited therein. Recent interest in neural networks was given a strong fillip by the work of J. J. Hopfield, *Proc. Nat. Acad. Sci.,* (US) 79, 2554 (1982) and 81, 3088 (1984), which exploited an analogy with Ising lattices to develop a theory for such networks in terms of a Hamiltonian function. "Remembering" is analogous to a phase transition (condensation) of the lattice, when the input goes from random (high temperature) to a specific, lower entropy or temperature state.

6. H. A. Simon, "Simulation of Human Thinking," (with coauthor A. Newell), in *Computers and the World of the Future,* ed. M. Greenberger (Boston: MIT Press, 1962).

7. L. Festinger, *A Theory of Cognitive Dissonance* (N.Y.: Harper & Row, 1957).

8. R. G. Fuller,"Solving Physics Problems—How Do We Do It?" *Physics Today,* September 1982, p. 43.

9. For a rather technical discussion of NP-complete problems, including a long list of such problems, see M. R. Garey and D. S. Johnson, *Computers and Intractability* (San Francisco: W. H. Freeman, 1979).

10. C. E. Shannon, "A Chess-Playing Machine," *Scientific American,* February 1950, and in *Computers and Computation,* ed. by R. Fenichel and J. Weizenbaum (San Francisco: W. H. Freeman, 1971).

11. David Levy, *The Joy of Computer Chess* (Englewood Cliffs, N.J.: Prentice-Hall, 1984).

12. M. Mitchell Waldrop, "The Necessity of Knowledge," *Science,* Mar. 23, 1984, pp. 1279–1282.

13. National Research Council, *Outlook for Science and Technology: The Next Five Years* (San Francisco: W. H. Freeman, 1982).

14. E. A. Feigenbaum and P. McCorduck, *The Fifth Generation: Artificial Intelligence and Japan's Computer Challange to the World* (N.Y.: Signet New American Library, 2d ed., 1983).

15. Dwight B. Davis, "Artificial Intelligence Enters the Mainstream," *High Technology,* July 1986, p. 16.

16. DM data projections in *Aviation Week and Space Technology,* Dec. 10, 1984, p. 24, and Mark Lewyn, "Artificial Intelligence Developing," *USA Today,* Apr. 30, 1986, p. 1. Gen. Thurman's remarks were quoted in *Aviation Week and Space Technology,* Nov. 3, 1986, p. 151.

17. J. Naughton, "Artificial Intelligence: Can DEC Stay Ahead?" *HARDCOPY,* July 1986, p. 113.

18. M. W. Waldrop, "Artificial Intelligence (I): Into the World," *Science,* 223, 24 Feb. 1984, p. 802.

19. Eric A. Weiss, "The Fifth Generation: Banzai or Pie-in-the-Sky?" *Abacus,* Winter 1984, p. 56.

20. H. L. Dreyfus, *What Computers Can't Do* (N.Y.: Harper & Row, 1972).

21. S. Dreyfus and H. L. Dreyfus, *Mind over Machine* (N.Y.: Free Press, 1985).

22. P. McCorduck, *Machines Who Think* (San Francisco: W. H. Freeman, 1979).

23. Simon's quotation is to be found in *Science Digest,* June 1986, p. 74, "The Machine Who Would Be King," (column by Dr. Crypton). This article contains a popular review of the history of computer chess.

24. H. A. Simon, *The Sciences of the Artificial,* 2d ed. (Cambridge, Mass.: MIT Press, 1981), p. 106.

25. O. C. Selfridge and Ulric Neisser, "Pattern Recognition by Machine," *Scientific American,* August 1960, and *Computers and Computation,* ibid. reference 9. For a more recent review, see K. S. Fu, *Applications of Pattern Recognition* (Cleveland: CRC Press, 1982). Also, see R. C. Gonzalez and M. G. Thomason, *Syntatic Pattern Recognition* (Reading, Mass.: Addison Wesely, 1978).

26. Erik Larson, "Neural Chips," *Omni,* Nov. 1986, p. 113.

27. For information on Hitech, see H. J. Berliner, *SIGART Newsletter,* April 1986, p. 22 and Berliner and Ebeling, *Artificial Intelligence,* vol. 28, Feb. 1986.

28. B. Wilcox, Reflections on Building Two Go Programs, *SIGART Newsletter,* October 1985, #94, p. 29.

29. *Handbook of Artificial Intelligence,* ed. by A. Barr, P. R. Cohen, E. A. Feigenbaum (Los Altos, Calif: W. Kaufmann, 1981, 1982).

30. *Artificial Intelligence: An MIT Perspective.* ed. by P. H. Winston and R. H. Brown (Cambridge: MIT Press, 1979).

31. R. P. Feynman, R. B. Leighton, and M. Sands, *The Feynman Lectures on Physics* (Reading, Mass.: Addison-Wesley, 1963), Vol. I chapter 36. See also R. H. Masland, "The Functional Architecture of the Retina," *Scientific American,* 225, 6 (December 1986), p. 102. A discussion of the layered structure of the lateral geniculate nucleus may be found in D. H. Hubel and T. N. Wisel, "Brain Mechanisms of Vision," *Scientific American,* 241, 3 (September 1979), p. 150. See also B. Gillam, "Geometrical Illusions," *Scientific American,* 242, 1 (January 1980), p. 102.

32. H.Gray, *Anatomy* (N.Y.: Bounty Books, 1977), p. 675. See also R. H Wurtz et. al, "Brain Mechanisms of Visual Attention," *Scientific American,* 246, 6 (June 1982), p. 124.

33. G. Kanizsa, Subjective Contours, *Scientific American,* 234, 4 (April 1976), p. 48.

34. D. Marr, *Vision* (San Francisco: W. H. Freeman, 1982). See also the article "Vision by Man and Machine" by T. Poggio in *Scientific American*

250, 4 (April 1984) p. 106, and "Computer Vision," W. M. Waldrop, *Science,* 224, 15 June 1984, p. 1225.

35. W. E. Grimson, *J. Assoc. Computing Mach.,* 33, 4, Oct. 1986, pp. 658–686.

36. B. K. P. Horn and K. Ikeuchi," Mechanical Manipulation of Randomly Oriented Parts," *Scientific American,* 251, 2 (August 1984), p. 100.

37. K. S. Fu, *IEEE Trans. Patter. Anal. Machine Intell.,* PAMI-8, May 1986, p. 398 (reprint of article in PAMI-5, March 1983).

38. D. H. Ballard and C. M. Brown, *Computer Vision* (Englewood Cliffs, N.J.: Prentice-Hall, 1982).

39. D. D. Hoffman, "The Interpretation of Visual Illusions." *Scientific American,* 249, 6 (December 1983), p. 154.

40. E. H. Land, "The Retinex Theory of Color Vision," *Scientific American,* 237, 6 (December 1977), p. 108, and "Experiments in Color Vision," *Scientific American,* 223, 5 (May 1959), p. 2. See also Land, *Proc. Natl. Acad. Sci. USA* 83, pp. 3078–3080 (May 1986) and the references therein.

41. D. L. Parnas, Comm. ACM 29, October 1986, p. 930.

42. J. De Kleer, *Artificial Intelligence,* 22, p. 222 (March 1984).

43. S. E. Dreyfus, *Oper. Res,* 17, 395, May-June 1969. Reprinted in *Large-Scale Networks: Theory and Design* (ed F. T. Boesch), IEEE Press, 1976. Algorithms may be found, for example, in E. Horowitz and S. Sahni, *Fundamentals of Data Structures in PASCAL* (Rockville, Md.: Computer Science Press, 1978, 1984), p. 292ff. Note that the program presented merely computes the shortest path distance—listing the nodes on that shortest path is a bit more work.

44. For discussions of branch and bound methods see, e.g., A. E. Aho, J. E. Hopcroft, J. D. Ullman, *Data Structures and Algorithms* (Reading, Mass.: Addison-Wesley, 1983). For a discussion of dynamic programming, and a discussion of branch and bound search as applied to integer programming, see D. T. Phillips, A. Ravindran, J. Solberg, *Operations Research: Principles and Practice* (N.Y.: John Wiley, 1976). Dynamic programming was developed by R. Bellman and his associates (including S. E. Dreyfus and R. Kalaba); references may be found in the book by Phillips et. al.

45. A FORTRAN code for solving the traveling salesman problem is given in W. H. Press, B. P. Flannery, S. A. Teukolsky, W. T. Vetterling, *Numerical Recipes* (Cambridge: University Press, 1986). References to the orginal papers by S. Kirkpatrick and associates may be found in that book.

46. R. Anderson and R. Greenberg,"UNIX and AI—A Beautiful Marriage," *UNIX/World,* August 1986, p. 26.

47. K. Sorensen, "Fifth Generation: Slow to Rise," *InfoWorld,* June 9, 1986, p. 35.

48. A. Jacobson, "Just Another Commerical Software Technology?" *AI Expert,* November 1986, p. 7.

49. P. E. Hoffman, Book Reviews, *BYTE,* November 1986.

Chapter 2

Overview of Ada

Introduction

The primary purpose of this chapter is to provide a reading knowledge of the Ada programming language. In addition, we review the advanced and singular features of Ada. There are many texts on programming in Ada and it is not our purpose to supplant these. Among the best are books by Barnes [1] and Haberman and Perry [2]. However, a programmer familiar with other languages should be able, with the aid of this chapter, to understand the programs discussed. It should be unnecessary, although desirable, to have a text on Ada handy when reading this book.

Why Ada?

First of all, you may not have much choice. The U. S. Department of Defense, in an attempt to control software costs, sponsored the development and application of the Ada language. Numerous directives reinforce this stance. For example, directive 3405.2 (3/30/87) requires Ada for all computers in weapons systems, while 3405.1 (4/2/87) makes Ada the single, common computer language for all Defense computer resources.

Secondly, Ada does have attractive features which can make its use desirable. Its various features for supporting modular programming make it ideally suited to large programming projects in which various programming teams must develop code which cooperates with the other teams' codes but cannot corrupt them. Its strict typing will be familiar to PASCAL programmers. FORTRAN and C programmers will find that many more programming errors are caught by the compiler, with the result that once the code successfully compiles, it is closer to working than in more permissive languages. Ada's support for real-time computing should be of great use in writing embedded systems.

The Ada Language

General

Ada is not case sensitive (unlike C). The variables lou, LOU, Lou are all the same. On convention, advocated by Barnes, is that reserved keywords (Ada has 63, unlike FORTRAN which has none) are written in lower case, while variables are written in upper case letters. Ada achieves economies in keyword count by using some keywords in very different circumstances. Statements are terminated, as in C, with the semicolon. Because ; is a terminator and not a separator, there will often be places where PASCAL would not require a semicolon whereas Ada does. Ada supports recursion.

All variables must be declared to be of a specified type (e.g., integer). They may be assigned initial values in their declaration, or be declared as a constant. The type is checked for agreement between subprogram calls, assignments, etc.; this may be circumvented through the use of Unchecked_Conversion, but this should be used very carefully. The user can define new types, including records which are similar to structures in C, and enumeration types. He can also define subtypes. Most often, these are restricted ranges of a type. Thus the code fragment (we will indicate keywords with boldface type in this chapter)

```
ARRAY_SIZE: constant := 100;
subtype ARRAY_INDEX is type INTEGER range 1..ARRAY_SIZE;
DATA: array(1..ARRAY_SIZE) of REAL;
INDEXER: ARRAY_INDEX;
```

would enable us to use the variable INDEXER as the index of the array DATA. If INDEXER were ever assigned a value outside of the legal range, an exception would be raised (see below). There is overhead involved in this method of automatic array bounds checking. Its virtue is that the user can write the exception handler.

The user is provided with a predefined language environment which provides the enumeration type BOOLEAN, the types INTEGER, FLOAT and DURATION (which are implementation dependent), as well as the types CHARACTER and STRING. Subtypes of the integers NATURAL and POSITIVE are also predefined. Note that attempting to enter a type FLOAT number as .5 or 1., either as a constant in a program or as typed input for a program, will result in an error. Ada demands leading and trailing zeros, so you must enter 0.5 or 1.0 respectively to keep the system happy. You could also use forms such as 5.0e–1 or 5.0E–1, or

2.71828_18284_59045 if you desire, so Ada has some flexibility. You can even enter numbers in other bases, from 2 to 16 inclusive, by prefacing the number with the base and enclosing the number within # signs. Thus seventeen may be written as 2#10001# or 16#11# or 17 or even 5#32# if you so desire.

The BOOLEAN type is a predefined enumerated type that can be TRUE or FALSE. Along with the usual Boolean operators such as or, and, not, there is the exclusive or xor operator (A **xor** B is the same as (A or B) and (not (A and B)). The short-circuited operators **and then** and **or else** are also supported. To evaluate A **and then** B, first A is evaluated. If it is false, the expression cannot be true, so the remainder of the expression is not evaluated further. The value FALSE is returned. Similarly, if A is TRUE in the expression A **or else** B, there is no need to evaluate B. Instead, the value TRUE is returned. The short-circuited expressions may be used either for greater efficiency or when A is a "guard" to prevent the evaluation of B when that might cause an error condition. If the evaluation of B has side effects, care must be used. It is interesting to note that the Ada standard requires parentheses where logical expressions might otherwise be ambiguous. Thus, A or B and C would be rejected by the compiler; you would have to write A or (B and C), or (A or B) and C, depending upon what was intended.

The assignment operator is := as in PASCAL, and the comparison operators are = (equal), /= for not equal, etc. The exponentiation operator is **, as in FORTRAN, but the exponent must be an integer. Pointers can be defined as Access types, the usage being similar to PASCAL (but without the ^). A typical example might be

```
I: Integer;
type ILIST;
type IPTR is access ILIST;
type ILIST is record
        IVALUE: Integer;
        NEXT: IPTR;
end record;
       .......
IP:= new IPTR;
IP.IVALUE:=27;
```

which will assign to the pointer IP the location of memory suitable for containing a node in a linked list of integers. Note how we first have to declare type ILIST in order to define an access type to point to it. Only then can it give the specifics of the type, which contains pointers to itself. This is a bit more cumbersome than as in C.

Storage allocated as above may be released by a call to Unchecked_Deallocation. Garbage collection is implementation dependent.

Ada supports the usual structures for looping (iteration) and flow control. A typical conditional block might look like

```
if  A < 0  then
.....
elsif A = 0 then
     .....
else
     ...
end if;
```

Note the singular spelling "elsif." The case statement is similar to C's switch statement but more verbose

```
case INDEX is
        when 0 => ...;
        when 1..10 => ... ;
        when others => null;
end case;
```

Note the ability to specify a range, the need to use an explicit null statement, and the => operator.

The basic loop is of the form:

```
loop
     ...
     if ... then exit; end if;
     ...
end loop;
```

Here the exit command causes us to leave the loop. One can control looping further by replacing the first line with

```
for INDEX in 1..ARRAY_SIZE loop
```

or

```
while INDEX  < Array_Size loop
```

The last statement requires INDEX to be initialized beforehand to a legal value, of course.

Finally, the goto statement still exists for special circumstances. Statement labels (for **goto** targets) are of the form <<LABELID>>.Omit the brackets about the label in the goto itself.

Unconventional Aspects of Ada

Exceptions

Ada permits the user to define exceptional conditions, and to allow a user-specified code section to take control if such conditions or the predefined standard exceptions occur. Predefined conditions include Constraint_Error, which could be raised by an out-of-bounds subscript, Storage_Error, when an attempt to allocate new memory fails, and Numeric_Error, when an error such as a division by zero occurs. There is some debate as to the proper use of exceptions—whether they should be defined only for truly anomalous error conditions or whether they should be used freely.

Packages

Ada supports modular programming with the package construct. A package is a set of subprograms whose communication with the outside world may be strictly controlled. Variables can be typed 'Private' or 'Limited Private' to restrict what a calling program can legally do with them. The former allows calling programs to use the :=, =, /= operators on such variables. These operations must be defined as functions within the package. The latter declaration is even more restrictive. The package may define the = operator (which implicitly defines the /= operator as well). The user has the freedom to create as many variables of a limited private type as desired. Perhaps a revised Ada might treat us to a "super limited" type! in which this freedom is restricted.

Generics

Generic package specifications allow the use of similar code to handle different data types. A typical example is the implementation of a general stack handling package, which is instantiated anew for each different type of data to be stacked. Another example is a generic integration routine, which is instantiated for a specific function to be integrated. Depending upon implementation, this might require entirely new code differing merely in the pointer to the function representing the integrand (Ada does not have a mechanism for passing a function name as an argument in a subprogram call).

You will meet a generic package instantiation in most Ada programs because the input/output routines must be instantiated for each type of variable that will require reading or writing.

Thus, a statement such as

package INT_IO **is new** INTEGER_IO(NUM=>INTEGER);

is needed if we wish to read or write integers. The system- defined package INTEGER_IO is instantiated as INT_IO to read or write integers.

Overloading

Function and procedure names and some operators may be overloaded. This means that the same name may be given to different functions if they can be distinguished by differences in their argument lists. Among the operators that may be defined are the arithmetic operators "*","+","/", "—", and the equality test operator "=". Defining the equality relationship implicitly defines the "/=" operator, which may not be explicitly defined. Note that the assignment operator := and the arithmetic comparisons such as =,>,>=, etc., may not be overloaded.

Tasking

Whole books have been written on concurrent processing in Ada—see those by Shumate [3], Nielson and Shumate [4], and Burns [5]. Ada supports concurrent processing by a mechanism called the rendezvous, which takes place between two tasks. This is a high-level mechanism based upon C. A. R. Hoare's ideas [6]. There is a significant difference in that Hoare's method the communication was symmetric, with each task having full knowledge of the other, while in an Ada rendezvous there is an asymmetry between the caller and the callee [7]. The rationale for the high-level implementations is that lower level mechanisms for parallel processing, such as the semaphore of Dijkstra, are more easily circumvented by the user, with possibly disastrous results. While tasking provides many useful features, the user as always must insure deadlock does not occur. Tasking on current generation Ada compilers and machines involves a large overhead, and often simple time-slicing methods are used on single-processor machines, resulting in inefficient machine usage. I have seen a multi-processor machine whose Ada compiler made no effort to distribute tasks among processors and appeared to time-slice. Perhaps later releases of the compiler will improve on this. For this reason, tasking is not implemented in the programs in this book.

Tasks may be treated syntactically in a manner similar to constants— there can be arrays of tasks created, for example. Tasks are otherwise similar to procedures. One declares a **task** with entries, and then specifies the task body with an **accept** statement for each **entry**. There are various control structures to "guard" these **accept** statements, i.e., to prevent them from achieving a rendezvous unless conditions are right, and to select between the possible rendezvous which might occur. The **delay** statement allows one to specify pauses between the acceptance of a subsequent rendezvous, for example. Tasks activate automatically, in that they can begin a rendezvous as soon as the begin statement of the parent unit is reached. Once a task type is defined, a pointer to such a type can be defined, and a new task can be created with the **new** operator. Such tasks become active when the statement **new** is executed. In this manner, one can create an unlimited number of tasks of a given type.

Interrupts are treated as a task with a specified entry address, e.g.

```
task INTERRRUPT is
    entry HANDLE;
    for HANDLE use at 16#01fff#;
    end HANDLE;
```

This example specifies an interrupt at a hexidecimal address; the precise interpretation is machine-dependent. This is discussed in the Ada standard under representation clauses. The standard does specify that interrupts are to have higher priority than other user-defined tasks. However, unlike hardware interrupts, tasks are not preemptive, so interrupts implemented as tasks can behave quite differently from true hardware interrupts. The Ada mechanism for interrupt handling probably means that a significant amount of overhead will be required to handle interrupts, which is somewhat disconcerting in a language developed for use in embedded, real-time systems. There is no special treatment for non-maskable interrupts, for example, which microprocessors typically attempt to handle with an absolute minimum of overhead (some do not even expend the time to acknowledge such interrupts). If the Ada standard is revised, the area of tasking in general and real-time processing such as interrupt handling in particular, will be the area most modified. The January 22, 1988 *Government Computer News* ran a front-page article titled "Revisions to Ada Standard Expected After Reviews." The article went on to discuss possible changes in real-time processing. The changes to the syntax will probably be minimal. Most concerns expressed were about implementation details, such as the non-preemptive nature of tasking. Ada defines a pragma PRIORITY which can be used (in an implementation-dependent manner) to set the priority of a task. This priority is not dynamic, i.e., cannot be altered during execution. In addition, an "emergency" cannot preempt an executing task. It is plausible that a mechanism closer to the hardware interrupt will be a feature of any revised Ada.

OBJECT-ORIENTED PROGRAMMING

"Object-oriented" programming is currently in vogue. There are a variety of definitions, ranging from so restrictive as to include only one language, Smalltalk-80, to a definition sufficiently liberal to include a BASIC program which implements frames. An article by Buzzard and Mudge [8] discusses how object-oriented Ada is. (See also articles by Lane Wegmann [9] and L. Baker [10].) If we accept the general consensus that "object-oriented" is a characteristic of languages (and not specific programs) and refers to how well that language supports manipulation of "objects," then Ada is an excellent object-oriented language. G. Pascoe [11] gives four criteria for judging languages as object-oriented: information hiding, data abstraction, dynamic binding, and inheritance. Ada is perhaps the premier language for object orientation by the first criterion, gets very high marks for the next two, and supports inheritance through subtypes and generics. Packages support to a high degree the intimate connection between data and the operations allowed on that data, particularly through the use of private and limited private types, although lacking the flavor of Smalltalk message passing. The ability of objects to supply their own procedures in Smalltalk, and the similar abilities of LISP, will be missed when a frames data structure is implemented below. The mechanism of **Generic** is not a fully satisfying substitute. On the whole, however, Ada should get good grades from an object-oriented programmer.

The Ada APSE

In addition to standardizing the language, some effort has gone into standardizing the programming environment. This is the APSE, or Ada Programming Support environment. All system-specific code is supposed to reside in the KAPSE (Kernel APSE). The CAIS (Common APSE Interface Set) defines the appearance of the KAPSE to the outside world [12]. The remainder of the APSE is to be written in Ada and the same at all installations. The MAPSE, or Minimal APSE, is to contain an editor, compiler and linker, debugger, configuration manager, and JCL ("Job Control Language" or command) interpreter. The configuration manager is akin to the UNIX MAKE facility, but automatic, and insures that obsolete compilation units are not used. The JCL interpreter controls the user interface. There are independent APSE development efforts by the three armed services (AIE, ALS, ALSN). Most commercial Ada systems include a MAKE facility or some form of configuration manager.

The Programs in This Book

The programs in this book were generally developed on the validated version 2.0.1 of the JANUS/Ada ED pack. They should run on any validated Ada compiler, subject to the compiler's limitations as to symbol table size, mathematical library contents, etc. Some programs have been tested on Meridian's ADAVantage system.

References

1. J. G. P. *Barnes, Programming in Ada* (Reading, MA: Addison-Wesley, 2nd edition, 1984).

2. A. N. Habermann and D. E. Perry, *Ada for Experienced Programmers* (Reading, MA: Addison-Wesley, 1983).

3. Ken Shumate, *Understanding Concurrency in Ada* (N.Y. : Intertext/ McGraw-Hill, 1988).

4. Ken Shumate and Kjell Nielson, *Designing Large Real-Time Systems in Ada* (NY:Intertext/McGraw-Hill, 1988).

5. A. Burns, Concurrent Programming in Ada (Cambridge: University Press, 1987).

6. C. A. R. Hoare, *Communicating sequential processes, Comm. ACM*, **21**, August 1978, pp. 666-677.

7. J. D. Ichbiah, et. al., *Rationale for the Design of the ADA Programming Language*, available from the ACM.

8. G. D. Buzzard, and T. N. Mudge, *IEEE Computer*, p.11, March 1985.

9. L. Wegman, *J. Pascal, Ada, and Modula-2*, vol. 5, p.5, May/June 1986.

10. L. Baker, *AI Expert*, April 1987, p.38.

11. G. Pascoe, *BYTE*, p. 139, August 1986.

12. R. Munch, P. Oberndorf, E. Ploedereder, R. Thall, *An Overview of DOD-STD-1838A (proposed), The Common APSE Interface Set, Revision A, ACM SIGPLAN* vol. 24, No.2, Feb. 1989 / *ACM SIGSOFT* vol. 13, No. 5, Nov. 1988, p. 235.

Chapter 3

Backward-Chaining Expert System Shell

Overview

In this chapter we introduce the concepts of a rule-based expert system and present a backward-chaining example of such a system's shell. In the next chapter we will consider forward and mixed chaining, as well as present code for handling arithmetic expressions as part of such a system.

Rule-Based Expert Systems

Rule-Based Expert System Principles

Expert systems are perhaps the most visible brand of AI. This is in part because they are the most mature segment of AI and are closest to practical application. Their legacy to automated theorem proving is clear, as is the legacy of PROLOG (Logic Programming) to such systems. Rule-based, or production, systems are essentially sophisticated pattern matchers. As such, they serve as a paradigm for other AI applications. In a subsequent chapter we will process language input in which the syntax serves as grammatical rules for what is a modification of the expert system shell discussed here. The concept of *syntactic pattern recognition* goes beyond expert system shells or natural language processors. For example, the ARIADNE program for deducing protein structure has been recently discussed as an example of pattern-directed inference, e.g., rule-based expert systems [1].

Readers unfamiliar with symbolic logic should review an elementary book, such as that by Hodges [2]. The books by Kowalski [3], Gallier [4], and Chang and Lee [5] are more advanced and specifically directed to computer applications, with the last the easiest to read. The article by Brown [6] is a very good overview of the necessary concepts. Advanced results such as Church's theorem may be found in Mendelson [7]. It should be noted that logicians appear to eschew a common notation and terminology, but rather enjoy inventing their own versions of each. Therefore, be careful about assuming that the same term or symbol encountered in different places means the same thing.

We discuss in this and the following chapter the construction of a rule-based expert system shell. Besides the user interface, the principal component of such a shell is the inference engine, the portion of the code which derives conclusions from the stored knowledge and the supplied facts. We present one such engine in this chapter and another in the next. In the next chapter we also discuss various alternative forms of expert systems as well as enhancements to this one.

The easiest way to explain rule-based systems is to present an elementary example—here we will discuss an animal identification system of ancient lineage. This example of a simple rule-based expert system (both rules and inference engine) was first presented, in LISP, in Horn and Winston's first edition [8]. Next, Duda and Gaschnig [9] presented a BASIC version, and Morgenson [10] presented a Modula-2 version.

Knowledge is stored in the form of a "production system," a set of if...then... rules. In the most limited system, these rules allow the use of the conjunction *and* in the antecedent or *if* portion of the rules, e.g.

    if lays_eggs and flies then is_bird

or

    if has_feathers then is_bird.

In order to draw conclusions, i.e., to prove that the animal in question is, say, an ostrich, one has to establish facts such as "has_feathers." These may be viewed as implications of the if...then... form in which the fact is the consequence (the portion of the rule following the "then") and the antecedent is empty or true in all cases. The facts may then be considered as additional rules to be added to the knowledge base for the problem at hand.

First-Order Predicate Logic

So far, a restricted form of first-order predicate logic has been used. Propositional logic, or Boolean algebra, is concerned with expressions involving conjunction (and), disjunction (or), negation (not), implication (if...then...), and atomic variables that may be either true or false. Predicate logic is essentially propositional calculus with quantifiers added. The two quantifiers of interest are the universal quantifier *all* and the existential quantifier *there exists*.... As Herbrand noted, often the universal quantifier can be dispensed with. For example, the statement "all men are mortal" is equivalent to "if x is a man, then x is mortal." The term *first-order* comes from Bertrand Russell's theory of types. A sentence or proposition is of the next higher type from the highest type of any variable it contains, where atomic variables are to be considered of type zero. Thus, first-order logic propositions deal with atomic variables of type zero. These variables are given as true or false. If a variable were to be assigned to the truth value of some proposition, any proposition containing it would be of (at least) second order, etc. By restricting ourselves to first-order logical expressions only, we avoid many of the self-referential paradoxes of logic, such as the Cretan antinomy: "This statement is false." First-order logic is still a very rich system. While Gödel showed that true formulas in first-order logic can all be proved, Church showed that no algorithm can (in finite time) determine if a formula is true or false. If the latter is the case, the method might run indefinitely [3]. Furthermore, first-order logic is NP-complete [11]; that is, it is likely that there is no generally efficient means to establish that a set of rules is consistent.

It is an interesting aside that the proofs of Gödel and Church rely on a self-referential circularity to produce a contradiction. This is done through the mechanism of "Gödel arithmetization" by which a formula is represented by a number. Then statements can be made about the number rather than about the formula. This enables self-referential contradictions to be formulated within the framework of first-order logic.

Attribute-Value and Object-Attribute-Value Systems

The simple animal expert system discussed above had no explicit variables. All statements were assumed to be about the same, unspecified variable. Such expert systems are called *attribute-value (A-V) systems,* since there is a single object, the animal in question in this case, for which we specify a list of attributes and their associated values. In this case, all the attributes take on the logical values true or false. A-V systems are clearly rather limited, but it is perhaps too hard to dismiss them as toy systems; M.1 from Teknowledge is an A-V system, and at $5000 it would be a rather pricey toy.

The *object-attribute-value (O-A-V) system* allows us to specify different objects, each with sets of attributes and values. Such systems require the inference engine to deal with variables. Such systems will have more overhead but will also have greater flexibility. They can, for example, be used to search databases in a sophisticated manner, which an A-V system cannot. The systems developed here are O-A-V systems which can accept the A-V syntactic rules if desired.

In the systems developed below, variables are distinguished by having as the first character either *?* or *w*. Logical predicate terms are in the form of a string with the symbols terminated by spaces (or the end of the predicate term itself). For example, if we define the predicate "father $?x$ $?y$" to mean

"?x is the father of ?y," then an inquiry (goal) of the form "father who John" will search the rule base (database, knowledge base, etc.) to determine the name of John's father (remember, who is a variable). Similarly, "father John who" will tell us John's children.

There are a number of frame-based expert system shells. These differ from the production systems presented here principally in the use of frames to permit a richer connection between the objects, including the rules themselves, in the database. For example, rules or objects can be grouped hierarchically and inherit various properties. For more details, see the chapter on frames. The inference engines for such systems are essentially the same as for production systems. Frame-based systems, and systems such as OPS5 which are object-oriented, can act like O-A-V systems without explicit variables by searching through the frame for matching values. This is discussed further in the next two chapters.

There are also a number of approaches which use set and graph theory. The facts and rules are represented as an interconnected network (graph), and deductions obtained by, for example, searching for a covering of the nodes of the graph which would include the new fact to be deduced. The same principles apply to the production systems discussed here, although the search methods are typically more elaborate (and costly in terms of resources). There are some similarities with using an indexed rule base (see below).

As it is possible to write "spaghetti code," it is possible to write spaghetti rules. The use of frames and other methods to organize rules makes a rule-based system easier to maintain and debug.

Backward and Forward Chaining

Given a database of rules (the knowledge base) and a set of facts relevant to the problem at hand, e.g., lays_eggs, etc., we are faced with the problem of putting together the facts with the rules which can use them to draw conclusions. Generally, the strategies for putting the facts and rules together fall into two classes: backward and forward chaining. In backward chaining, we hypothesize a conclusion and attempt to verify that this conclusion is correct. We attempt to establish that all the antecedents needed to "fire" a rule which has our conclusion as a consequent are true. This procedure is recursive in that at any point, the proposition to be established can be treated as the hypothesized conclusion, and its demonstration is attempted. This approach derives from the theorem-proving efforts of early AI workers.

In forward chaining, we start by attempting to match given facts with rule antecedents, proceeding toward conclusions by establishing intermediate facts, and attempting to match these with antecedents to fire rules.

Hybrids of these two methods are possible, as well as other approaches more akin to developing a network or graphical representation of the rules and their associations, and developing paths along the graph. These will be discussed in the next chapter.

It is to be noted that very loose definitions of forward or backward chaining are sometimes used by software vendors who wish to claim that their products do both (see the next chapter for a specific example).

Given the choice of forward or backward chaining, there is still a lot of flexibility in the specifics of the search strategy. For backward chaining systems, the popular methods are depth-first and breadth-first searching. Other methods are called "heuristic" and require additional information. In depth-first search, if we find a rule which could establish our antecedent (i.e., it has a consequent which matches our antecedent) and if all of its antecedents are confirmed, we pursue the proof of its antecedents one by one, giving up only when there is no hope of establishing its validity. We then try the next rule whose consequent matches our antecedent, and so on. In breadth-first search, we enumerate all the rules whose consequents match our antecedent. Then, for each of these, we do the same for their antecedents, etc., terminating any path when it cannot be verified (i.e., when no relevant facts or rules can be found).

PROLOG uses depth-first backward chaining, as does the system presented here. It should be clear that a breadth-first search can generate a huge data structure, a tree of yet-to-be proved antecedents to be confirmed. Consequently, it is generally far more prodigal in storage than a depth-first search. However, as discussed by Gallier [4], breadth-first search can have some advantages, depending upon how the chaining is performed.

The choice of forward versus backward chaining is problem-dependent. Clearly, if there are only a few possible conclusions, backward chaining is probably preferable. On the other hand, backward chaining tends to appear relatively purposeless to humans who have to supply the facts by responding to machine queries, and can be a poor choice if there are many conclusions to check. If knowledge of the facts can quickly exclude conclusions from consideration, it should be used.

Exhaustive Search, Uncertainty, Confidence Factors, Fuzzy Sets

Numerous design decisions remain to be made. First, should we stop after a solution is found, or should we make an exhaustive search to see if there are others? The latter course might be prohibitively costly in time.

So far, we have naively assumed that everything is either true or false. How do we deal with uncertainty? Any practical expert system should be able to deal with real-world inputs that are often ambiguous. The generally accepted answer is the use of confidence factors, numbers which quantify the degree of certainty to associate with facts and deductions. Typically, these are implemented in terms of an exhaustive search with a floor confidence value. As soon as the confidence associated with a particular thread of reasoning drops below the floor, that thread is dropped as implausible and assumed false.

The expert systems of this book assume that the facts and rules each have an associated confidence factor. Two functions, PROBAND and PROBOR, are used to compose these factors. At present, these implement a simple Bayesian model, which interprets the confidence factors as classical probabilities between 0 and 1. Thus, $PROBOR(x,y) = x + y - xy$, $PROBAND(x,y) = x*y$. There are numerous virtues of this simple model. The probabilities remain between 0 and 1. They are monotonic, i.e., $PROBOR(x,y) > PROBOR(x,0)$ if $y > 0$, so that an alternate line of reasoning which confirms a fact or predicate term already established can only increase the confidence. Finally, $PROBOR(a,PROBOR(b,c)) = PROBOR(probor(a,b),c)$ (and similarly for PROBAND) so that the order in which a fact is established and later confirmed is immaterial in setting the confidence factor. While Bayesian probabilities do not uniquely possess these properties, they provide an intuitive example of confidence factors which do.

A popular alternative to the Bayesian approach is the *fuzzy set* approach, originated by L. Zadeh. In this case, the "or" function has the interpretation of a set union operation with $PROBOR(x,y) = max(x,y)$ and $PROBAND(x,y) = min(x,y)$ being interpreted as the intersection of the fuzzy sets. The complement of x is $1 - x$ as in the Bayesian model. For more details on fuzzy sets, see [12]. Proponents of fuzzy sets argue that the Bayesian approach assumes that the uncertainties are due to random effects, while in fact the uncertainties are due to imperfect knowledge. (Such an assumption underlies the derivation of the "or" and "and" formulas through the assumption of equal a priori probabilities.) Therefore, the Bayesian results are not really appropriate.

I. J. Good [13] discusses the estimation of probabilities from a Bayesian viewpoint, in contrast to the fuzzy set approach. At present, there is no consensus on which approach is better, or how to estimate probabilities, confidence factors, etc., in either method. Fuzzy sets are claimed to be a better model of human subjective probability estimates. Even if this were so, it does not clearly establish them as a superior form of reasoning to the Bayesian approach.

One (minor) advantage of the Bayesian approach is that if a conclusion is supported by two or more alternative lines of reasoning and one is subsequently retracted, the confidence factor can be easily calculated from the Bayesian expression for probor as $(C - x)/(1.0 - x)$, where C is the confidence factor before retraction and x is the confidence of the retracted chain of reasoning. In fuzzy set theory, the confidence factor C is unchanged if x is less than C (and hence equal to the maximum confidence factor of any supporting line of reasoning), but must be recomputed if it is not.

A variety of packages are provided for different methods of computing confidence factors—see the code.

One other possibility is so-called modal logic, which refers to logics with more than the two values true and false. An example of these many-valued logics are Post Algebras, which are analogous to Boolean algebra for two-valued logic [14]. The most popular modal logics are based on the work of Clarance I. Lewis [15]. Such logics contain an operator P or M which may be interpreted as "it is possible that." Lewis wished to avoid the problems associated with the "material" implication operator $\Rightarrow$ of Boolean algebra and so defined "strict implication" $p \dashv q$ which is false if p is true and q is false and otherwise indeterminate. The symbol for strict implication is called the "fishhook." See Hughes and Cresswell [16] for a discussion, and McDermott [17] for applications to AI. There does not appear to be a consensus at present as to the utility of modal logics or which version of modal logic is best.

Unification

In order to draw deductions, we must form a chain of relevant rules and facts. In backward chaining, for example, given the hypothesis is_cow, we must find rules which can lead to such a conclusion, e.g., if ungulate and moos, then is_cow, and then continue chaining by finding rules such as if chews_cud, then ungulate, etc., finding rules or facts (by interrogating the user if necessary for facts if they are not in the rule base). Thus, we have to match the consequents of some rules with the goal or the antecedents of other rules (recall facts behave as consequents of rules without antecedents).

The mechanism known as unification in AI is in reality pattern matching with variable substitution. The assignment of variable values which achieves such a match (assuming one is possible) is called the binding of that variable. Note that expressions or other variables may constitute bindings. Thus, unification is a rather sophisticated form of matching.

For example, if we are attempting to unify the two predicate terms "father John who" and "father John George," we proceed in a left-to-right fashion, first matching the atoms father and then John. We then tentatively attempt to bind the variable who to the atom George. This will be successful if who is either unbound or already bound to George. That binding might be indirect, i.e., who might be bound to $?x$ which is bound to George. Conversely, if $?x$ is bound to who, we must be sure that when who is bound to George, $?x$ behaves as if it were so bound as well.

For efficiency, a technique know as *structure sharing* is used. In brief, this simply means we use pointers to variables and atoms, rather than maintain a list in which all the binding information is explicitly copied. Such an alternative is naturally called structure copying.

For further efficiency, the bindings are stored in a hash table. When we want to look up a variable to determine if it is bound, we "hash" it; i.e., we compute an address for the binding information in the table from the name of the variable itself. In principle, this is (almost) independent of the number of variables, and hence an O(1) search. If the variables were stored alphabetically as, say, a binary tree, the search would take O(log n), where n was the number of variables. The use of a hashing function with its O(1) search timing yields so-called linear time unification.

The various provisos and caveats in the preceding paragraph are due to the fact that in any finite binding table, with a sufficiently large number of variables in use, there are bound to be "collisions," i.e., circumstances in which different variables hash to the same table location. This may be handled in a number of ways. The method used here is called *bucket hashing* and is generally considered one of the best ways of dealing with such an eventuality. (Other methods exist, such as linear probing.) In bucket hashing, each table address is considered to be a linked list (bucket) of all variables that hash to that address. That list is then searched for the correct variable name. Obviously, when there are many collisions, the speed of a hashed search degenerates to the speed of the search of the linked list rather than O(1), and the unification timing no longer scales linearly in the number of variables.

Occurs Check

If a variable occurs more than once in a predicate term, it obviously must be bound consistently. In some circumstances, this can cause a circularity and consequent problems for the unification algorithm [18]. Normally, this test is omitted in PROLOG because it is time-consuming and unnecessary for most rule bases. We offer the user the option of specifying such a test.

Negation, Horn Clauses, Guarded Horn Clauses, Contraposition

It is well known in symbolic logic that the statement "if a then b" is logically equivalent to (not a) or b, i.e., $\sim a$ v b in typical notation. It is useful to rewrite implications such as "if a and b...then c" as $(\sim a)$v$(\sim b)$...v(c). Note that only disjunctions—ors—are needed. Each rule, when rewritten in this form, is called a clause. Each component of the clause, such as c or $\sim b$, we will call a predicate term. There is a great divergence in the literature on this nomenclature, with these predicate terms or terms called literals [4] or letters [7] by different authors. Each term is composed of a number of symbols or atoms, which may be variables, constants, or functions.

Simplifications arise if we specify that, written in implication form, there are no negated terms, i.e., the statement is of the form

$$\text{if a and b and ... then c}$$

Such statements containing (at most) one possible conclusion are commonly called Horn clauses in AI contexts [3]. In clause form, at most one non-negated element can appear. Such statements play a major role in systems such as PROLOG. Horn clauses with exactly one negated element are called definite Horn clauses. The nonnegated element, which is typically the consequent, is then called the *head* of the clause. (In some books [3], and in Alfred Horn's original paper [19], the opposite definition is used, namely that a Horn clause has at most one negated element in a set of disjunctions.)

You may encounter the term *guarded Horn clause* in the literature, particularly in regard to the Japanese fifth-generation project. These are merely Horn clauses with additional information appended and are intended for use in parallel processing systems. The guard information, like guard clauses in Ada, is designed to prevent contradictions from arising when different clauses are bound by different processors.

The implication "if a then b" and the implication "if not b then not a" may both be written $(\sim a)$ v b and are therefore logically equivalent. The latter is called the contrapositive of the former. If we allow our inference engine to attempt to match (unify) all clauses in a rule, i.e., we treat the head as just another predicate term and allow terms to be negated at will, then we "automatically" have an inference engine which understands the rule of contraposition.

Resolution

J. A. Robinson developed the resolution principle [20] in 1965 for automated theorem proving. It is easily applied to rule-based expert systems. Consider the hypothesized goal as a "theorem" to be proved, given the "axioms" of the rule base. We attempt to show that the inverse of the goal is false. Let the goal be g (which, in general, will be the conjunction of a number of subgoals, say $g[1]$ and $g[2]$ and ...). Then its negation is $\sim g$ or the disjunction $\sim g[1]$ v $\sim g[2]$ v... . If any of the $g[i]$ are negated, say $g[1]=$ $\sim h$, then we simply use the usual double negation rule such that $\sim g[1]$ is replaced by h, and then we prove g by proving each of the $g[i]$. We attempt to unify the goal with rule predicate terms. We require that exactly one of the terms be negated (this may be tested quite efficiently using the exclusive or xor operator of Ada). This process is repeated for the other terms in the rules, which are treated as subgoals. Because we unify two terms at a time (one from each clause), the process is called binary resolution. When we have no further predicate terms left, we have established the contradiction and hence the subgoal.

An illustration will clarify this process. We hypothesize the goal is_cow. We thus attempt to disprove ~is_cow. This term will resolve with a term which is not negated and which is_cow can unify with. Such a rule could be "if ungulate and moos, then is_cow" because such a rule in disjunctive form would be written ~ungulate v ~moos v is_cow, and the predicate term is_cow is negated in the rule but not the (negated) goal. The resolvent clause is then ~ungulate v ~moos. The literal is_cow and the literal ~is_cow have been resolved and deleted. If is_cow is viewed as a fact, then the consequence of such a fact being true would be ~(~ungulate v ~moos), which is equivalent to: ungulate and moos. We now have to deal with the two subgoals. The subgoal ~ungulate will unify with any rule with ungulate as a head, i.e., of the form if ... then ungulate. If the fact ungulate is given, then we have no further subgoals to establish the required contradiction, and we can now proceed to establishing the contradiction of ~moos.

This can all be implemented by pushing the goals and subgoals on a stack. The order of attempted unification used in PROLOG and the backward-chaining system here is the depth-first search described above, which follows naturally from such a stack. PROLOG specifies that for an implication of the form "if a and b then c" treat a as the first subgoal to be established and then b. This may be achieved by pushing first b, then a onto the goal stack. Recursion naturally is used, as each subgoal can be handled in a similar manner. A breadth-first search could also be easily handled by a recursive program, although the goal stack would be different since it would contain alternative solution paths (subgoals) instead of subgoals, all of which must result in contradictions upon unification for the conclusion to be established.

"Standardizing apart" is another trick used to implement resolution efficiently, much as structure sharing is used to reduce the effort required to perform the unification needed as part of resolution. Suppose we attempt to unify two rules which happen to have variables with the same name, such as the rules

if father ?x ?y and father ?y ?z then grandpa ?x ?z

if grandpa ?x ?y and father ?y ?z then great_grandpa ?x ?z

Clearly the ?z of the first rule will have to bind to the ?y of the second, and not be confused with the ?z of the second. It would not do to require different names for different rules, as a conclusion might require the multiple use of a rule. We might have a rule

if grandpa ?x ?y and grandpa ?y ?z then great_great_grandpa ?x ?z

which might use the first rule of this section twice to establish a great_great_grandpa from facts of the form father ... . The solution is to consider each variable name to be actually the symbol in the formula along with an integer called the depth or the context of that variable. Each time a new rule is invoked, a new context is generated. This maintains the necessary uniqueness of different variable names.

It is often proved that resolution is "complete," i.e., that if the rule base can establish a fact, resolution will establish it (see Nilsson [21]). What is meant of course it that resolution will establish it in finite time for a finite rule base. What is not, however, pointed out is that if the system is queried to establish a fact which it should not be able to establish, it may not terminate in a finite length of time reporting that the fact is not provable given the rules at hand. This is a fundamental limitation on such systems. Church's theorem [4,7] establishes that this limitation cannot be circumvented, but must be lived with. Therefore, there is no perfect or ideal inference engine, even in principle, but rather different approaches which mitigate such problems. Logic is not all powerful!

Consistency, also called soundness or correctness, is the inability of resolution to decide that a fact is both true and false. It is also demonstrated by Nilsson and others. We can take some solace in this fact.

There are a variety of methods of performing resolution. See Kowalski [3] for further information on alternatives. See the discussion of factoring below for further information on completeness. Resolution on Horn clauses is simplified by the fact that as each clause contains only one positive (non-negated) term at most, the resolvent will contain at most one such term (since one is "canceled" by a negative term, it can unify with to produce the resolution). Thus, resolving Horn clauses gives rise to Horn clauses. PROLOG, because of depth-first search, sacrifices completeness [4,22].

No sound, complete recursive method can exist for second-order logic [23]. This explains in part the use of first-order logic in expert systems.

"Intelligent backtracking" systems typically modify depth-first search by storing additional information so that, if a search has failed at a current root node, the search can be resumed further up the tree than the immediate predecessor (parent) of that node when appropriate. There is an obvious tradeoff in the sophistication (and cost in memory and time) of such a system versus the improvement due to the avoidance of fruitless search paths. See, e.g., Kuman and Lin [24].

Indexing Rules

For increased efficiency, a technique known as indexing is used. This creates a linked list for each predicate, specifying what rule predicates have a chance of unifying with it. There are a variety of ways to do this, with the compromise between the sophistication of the indexing to exclude rules and the overhead in developing and storing the index. In the expert systems of this chapter and the next, we index on the first symbol of the predicate only. That is, all predicates with the same first symbol are associated via a linked list if they have opposite negation values. Clearly, if both or neither are negated, when represented in disjunctive form, they cannot possibly unify.

Negation as Failure and the Closed-World Model

In the *closed-world model,* it is assumed that all relevant information about the universe is contained in our rule base. Thus, if something cannot be proved to be true, it may be taken to be false.

A natural assumption which is made in PROLOG and other systems is the "negation as failure" mechanism [23]. To determine the truth value of "not P," evaluate P. If P cannot be proved true, then by the closed-world assumption, it may be taken to be false, and consequently not *P* may be taken to be true.

These assumptions are particularly useful in PROLOG or other systems which rely on Horn clauses, because of the limited ability of such clauses to handle negated predicates.

Non-Horn Clauses and Factoring

When non-Horn clauses are permitted, it is necessary to augment resolution with "factoring" [3,4,5]. Fortunately, this is relatively easy. Before pushing predicate terms onto the goal stack, we attempt to unify them with the term which has already been unified with the goal. If the unification succeeds, there is no need to push the term onto the stack. Any bindings generated by that unification are retained, and we proceed to the next predicate term. We permit the user to specify whether or not factoring is required—it represents another overhead burden which can be avoided if, for example, Horn clauses are used exclusively.

Our inference engine is not complete if non-Horn clauses are present. It was felt that the additional computational burden was not justified. It would not be difficult to implement a form of OL-resolution with the inference engine presented here [5]. One could also perform tests for tautological statements and for the subsumption of clauses by other clauses. Again, it was felt that the costs outweighed the benefits.

Why bother with non-Horn clauses and give up completeness? After all, as Kowalski notes, "Any problem which can be expressed in logic can be reexpressed by means of Horn clauses" [3]. For example, the implication

> if is_precipitating, then is_raining or is_snowing

converts into the clause ~is_precipitating v is_raining v is_snowing. (That is, it converts if we assume, as we do for simplicity, that the "or" is inclusive, i.e., that it might be raining and snowing simultaneously. Additional rules would be needed if the "or" were to be forced to be exclusive, i.e., is_raining-> not is_snowing, i.e., ~is_raining v is_snowing, as well as the converse is_snowing-> not is_raining or is_snowing v ~ is_raining in clause form.) The clause is currently a non-Horn clause (with our definition), but might be rewritten as the set of rules

> if is_precipitating and not_snowing then is_raining
> if is_precipitating and not_raining then is_snowing

(with additional rules relating is_snowing and not_snowing). This should make clear just what the practical burden is of doing that reexpression. It is well known that PROLOG can give "strange" answers to some problems—we will discuss an example published by Jerardi below. The inference engine presented here correctly treats such problems without need for the user to reexpress his problem. In doing so, fewer rules need to be explicitly written. In short, the rules' behavior is closer to predicate logic expressions than, for example, rule behavior in PROLOG. The contrapositive of a statement does not have to be explicitly written for the system to be able to use it. (The automatic contraposition does not rely on the ability to handle non-Horn clauses, but typical inference engines, such as PROLOG interpreters, do not seem to support such automatic contraposition.)

Circularity Check

We have already noted that proving the consistency of the rule base is an NP-complete problem and, therefore, generally not computationally feasible. This, along with Church's theorem, suggests we should have the option of some protection against an infinite loop of rule evaluation. Again, this is an overhead burden which can be omitted or invoked, depending upon user specification. Note that we cannot have perfect protection without sacrificing completeness. However, it seems more likely that we can set up rules which will be effective without a complete inference engine than it is that we can set up rule bases which are not inconsistent or will not cause an infinite loop.

Actually, one can elude Church's theorem if the predicate terms are constrained to have no more than one variable. Such rule bases would not be of much utility.

The PROLOG Cut

PROLOG implements a predicate called the cut, and indicated by the exclamation point (!). It signals that backtracking should not proceed beyond where the cut is set. It may be used, for example, to indicate that if we have gotten this far, we are on the right track and should not abandon what we have assumed so far. The reader will note that the use of the cut operator may increase the confidence factor, compared to the analogous run without cut. In effect, the cut certifies with complete confidence (i.e., 1.0) that the answer is correct to that point.

G. Gentzen's "cut elimination theorem" [4,31] is unrelated to the PROLOG cut operator.

Nonlogical Predicate Terms

It is useful to permit predicate terms to be other than logical expressions. For example, a tax adviser system might need to compute your tax liability both with and without itemizing before recommending how to file your taxes. This requires the ability to compare numbers, i.e., evaluate the logical value of tax_itemized tax_not_itemized, and the ability to compute the values of numerical variables such as tax_itemized based upon other numbers (income, etc.). In addition, it is often useful to have side effects to rule evaluation. Such side effects can include the assignment of numerical values to variables, for example, as the result of the computation of expressions. The system presented here recognizes such predicates by the " sign as the first character. The predicate might then be sent, verbatim, to a user routine for evaluation. In the next chapter, we give a package which recognizes predicates beginning with "m and treats these as mathematical operations—either variable assignments or comparisons. Because of storage limitations, it was useful to make the lexical analyzer parse the arithmetic expressions as well, so all predicates, even nonlogical predicates, are separated into blank-delimited symbols by the input routines.

The nonlogical predicate terms are indexed like any other term. This makes it easy to chain rules as desired. For example, any predicate term beginning with "t will evaluate to TRUE, as one with "f... will evaluate to FALSE. We could then connect two rules within the index by including a term, say "t27, in each. With appropriate "demons" we can achieve any desired action or side effect or effect dynamic rule selection.

While logical variables have only the scope of their rule (they standardize apart from a variable with a similar name in another formula), mathematical variables are globally visible. This property could be useful if global variables are needed.

The Program

Basic Data Structures

The two basic data structures which will constantly appear in different guises are the linked list and the tree. Only a very brief review of their properties can be given here. If the user is unfamiliar with them, I would recommend running a version of the program with profuse print statements to enable a trace of the program during execution.

Figure 3.1 illustrates the structure of a linked list. Each element includes a pointer (access type to the record of the list) to the next element. The remainder of the record contains the information relevant to that element. The tail element has a null value for this pointer. Note that while it is easy to traverse the list from the head to the tail, the reverse is not simple. For this reason, it is sometimes useful to have a doubly-linked list in which each list element has pointers to its predecessor as well as its successor. The simple type of list we have discussed here is called a singly-linked list

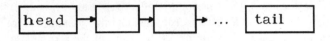

Fig. 3.1 A linked list.

when such a distinction is necessary. We will use such lists for containing rules in use. In the "bucket" hashing method, the bucket is actually a linked list.

A stack is a list in which we restrict allowable operations to the head element. The addition of an element to the stack creates a new head. Such a stack is often called a push-down stack, and the addition of an element is done by an operation called *push*. To remove the head element, the *pop* operation is used. The stack is sometimes called a last-in, first-out (LIFO) queue. When the term queue is used without qualification, it usually refers to a first-in, first-out (FIFO) queue. The term *queue discipline* refers to the type of queue (LIFO or FIFO). Stacks naturally implement recursion, and we will use them for storing subgoals, for example.

The tree is illustrated in Fig. 3.2. A restricted class of tree, the binary tree, is shown. In a tree, each "parent" node may be linked to at most two "child" nodes. All nodes must have parents except for the single "root" node. By convention, trees in computer science grow downward from the root. The nodes which have no children are called "leaves." The particular binary tree used for the symbol table is a search tree. The rule in constructing a binary search tree is that the left child of a node, if any, must precede the parent in the search order, while the right child must follow it. This enables an efficient search procedure, because at each node, if the target has not been found, we can rule out half the remaining tree as a candidate for searching. Except in pathological cases, to search a binary tree with N elements takes on the order of lg N (lg is the base 2 logarithm) visits to nodes to make comparisons.

Grady Booch's [25] book discusses these data structures, among others, and is one of the few to present Ada code for manipulating them. Horowitz and Sahni [26] is a good overview of data structures.

Overview

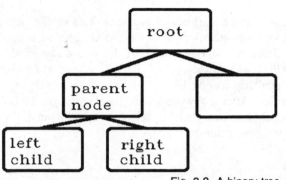

Fig. 3.2 A binary tree.

The code presented here was developed by stepwise refinement from a simple A-V system prototype, based on the Modula-2 system of Morgenson [10]. The implementation of unification and the cut operator are based on the approach of Nakamura [27], while structure of the inference engine is in part inspired by the PROLOG interpreter discussed by Shafer [28].

The program is composed of eleven packages. These are:

STRNG	Dynamic string processing
LOGIC	Definition of record types for logic data structures
HASH	Hash table for binding storage
ANDOR	Confidence factor calculations
MFUNCT	Mathematical functions
MATH	Mathematical predicate calculations
STACK	Basic POP and PUSH for stacks
CLAUSERD	Input and lexical analysis of rules, etc.
RULEIND	Index rules with rules and facts
BACK	Inference engine

The dynamic string package STRNG can be of general use. Many Ada compilers provide library packages for dynamic strings (i.e., variable-length strings), as does Booch's book [25]. The ANDOR packages are provided with multiple bodies to permit the use of a variety of models for confidence factors. The MFUNCT body may be modified by the user to permit the reference of any number of functions. All that the user need do is change the package body, recompile that body, and relink the program. None of the other modules need be recompiled. This independence is one of the virtues of packaging.

Variables with the suffix PTR are access types (pointers).

Note the with...; use...; at the start of the packages. This enables us to use routines from the libraries specified, with the use declaration simplifying the call structure. Thus, to use PUT in TEXT_IO would require the user writing TEXT_IO.PUT without the use declaration. As long as there are no ambiguities from similarly named library routines with similar argument lists, PUT will suffice. After a few constants (implicitly type INTEGER) are declared, we instantiate two generic packages for the input and output of integers and floating point numbers.

Dynamic Strings

One omission from Ada is support for strings which are constructed during program execution. Such strings are clearly vital for any application involving the processing of text, AI, or compilers, etc. There are many possible approaches a user can take to writing such a package, depending upon the desire to optimize for speed, storage, etc. Due to the modularity of Ada, one can easily have a set of packages, with different package bodies optimized differently but with the same package specification. We have constructed here a simple string package which is optimized for speed at the expense of storage. For use on microprocessor-based systems, this is probably the correct choice. More sophisticated systems can easily be designed. Strings are terminated by a designated character, in this case "$". Thus, strings are stored as in the C language, but with the terminator as in the external representation of BASIC strings. The terminator may of course be easily changed, e.g., to the null character used by C. Strings are limited in length to 255 characters, as in BASIC, but again this can easily be changed. We do not store a character count as the first element of the string, as in BASIC or Booch's [25] dynamic string package, as this would limit the flexibility of the method if at some later point very long strings had to be accommodated (for example, using a single byte to store the count, as in BASIC, would set 255 as the absolute limit).

The package defines a type LONGPHRASE for the conversion of large strings and type PHRASE which will be the principal form of storage for dynamic strings. Various other types are defined for use by the lexical analysis and inference engine routines.

SUBPROGRAM	PURPOSE
PHRASE_LENGTH	Returns character count of a PHRASE
PRINT	Writes to standard output
LONGPHRASE_TO_PHRASE	Copies a portion of a LONGPHRASE to a PHRASE
STRING_TO_PHRASE	Copies a STRING to PHRASE or LONGPHRASE
PHRASE_TO_STRING	Copies a PHRASE to a blank-padded STRING
COMPAREPHRASES	Compares PHRASEs, returns lexical order
FIND_PHRASE	Searches for a substring in a PHRASE
HASHKEY	Generates a hash index from a PHRASE and an integer

Note that some of these routines come in a variety of forms—which when invoked are controlled by the argument list. Various other useful routines, such as searching for substrings, can be imagined. We do not claim that our package is the best possible but merely that it is sufficient for the purposes of this book, namely basic lexical analysis of character input.

This package could have easily been defined as a generic package, e.g.

```
generic
STRINGLENGTH, LONGPHRASE_LENGTH, HASHLENGTH :
POSITIVE;
package STRNG is
```

and then instatiated in another package with code of the form:

```
package DYNAMIC_STRING is new STRNG(50,250,256);
```

This greatly complicates matters and reduces the efficiency of the program, since now a "component with a non-simple type" (in the words of the JANUS/Ada compiler) is created, which takes more code and memory. We follow its advice and avoid such objects.

PACKAGE LOGIC

We next define various record types. Type BINDING is to be used for storing bindings in the bucket-hashed binding table. Thus, the field NEXT is used for the linked-list implementation of the buckets. The types SYMPTR and PREDICPTR are defined in the dynamic string package. All types ending with PTR are pointers. Type SYMPTR points to the atomic symbol (variable or function name or constant) which is stored in lexicographic (alphabetized) order on a binary search tree. PREDICPTR is a pointer to a definition of each predicate term which is stored as a linked list of the symbols along with indexing information. The various integers are contexts or depths used in "standardizing apart" (see above on unification). Information on the depths of the predicates resolved upon to generate the binding (FATHER and MOTHER) is retained primarily for diagnostic purposes. POP and PUSH are used to access some lists as stacks.

Type IN_USE is used for a linked list of rules in use and is employed in the circularity check. Type GOALS is a stack for the goal predicate terms, including subgoals. Because we allow non-Horn clauses, each goal predicate term may be negated, such information being included on the goals stack. That information is stored on input for goals, rules, and facts (which are treated as rules without antecedents in this system) in arrays for each predicate term.

In some of the record types we employ, variant parts could be defined to save storage on some occasions. This would entail additional costs in time and complexity, however. This complication was therefore eschewed, but it could be retrofitted with relatively little effort.

There are some types and record fields which will be used by the other programs, such as the forward-chaining system of the next chapter. We have chosen to make LOGIC general enough to handle these, so that it is reusable. We have also chosen to avoid the complication of variant records.

PACKAGE HASH

A hash table stores information by using the "key" of the data to be stored as the location of the data in the table. This key is first hashed or converted to a number for efficiency. As noted above, such a hashed storage is necessary for efficient search and retrieval of variable bindings during unification. The code presented here uses so-called bucket hashing, in which "collisions" (different keys which hash to the same table location) are stored in a linked list associated with that location. This collision-handling strategy tends to degrade more gracefully than linear probing or other strategies.

Note that our hashing function HASHKEY, located in the dynamic string package, is simplistic and is intended for illustrative purposes only. In actual practice, one would probably want to use Ada's Unchecked_Conversion function to change characters into integers, assuming, of course, one implemented an expert system shell which interpreted rules.

Hashing is of interest for our shell because it is an interpreter of rules and facts represented as ASCII strings. For a "compiled" system, such as would be used in an embedded real-time system, variables could be named uniquely so that there would be no collisions; their names would be pointers to their binding lists, so no hash table would be needed; and even standardizing apart would be unnecessary.

PACKAGE ANDOR

This small package contains two functions, PROBAND and PROBOR, to compute the confidence factors of composite goals. A separate package permits the independence of the inference engine from the model used. Three package bodies are provided for confidence factors based on Bayesian probabilities, fuzzy set theory, and MYCIN-like factors. The examples in this book will use the first of these.

PACKAGES MATH,MFUNCT

The package MATH provides facilities for dealing with mathematical expressions, including parsing those expressions and calculating them. Unlike logical variables, which are local to a clause because of standardizing apart, mathematical variables are global and will remember assigned values. They may therefore be used as global flags. The next chapter fully discusses this package and the use of mathematical predicates.

Package MFUNCT contains the interface between the package MATH and function libraries. Thus, the MATH package need not be recompiled if the function library set is altered and new functions are added. A basic set of functions is included for illustrative purposes. Users may have to alter library names, etc., to suit their situation.

PACKAGE READIN

The main program BACK calls GETRULES, in package READIN, to input the rules and queries, and then DIAGNOSE to obtain possible deductions. GETRULES first queries for user options, such as whether the occurs check and the circularity check should be performed. It asks whether an exhaustive search is desired. If not, it will stop at the first successful solution to the goal. Otherwise, it will perform a full search through the rule base. If a goal can be established a number of ways, its confidence factor will accordingly reflect this increased confidence. Because only in the exhaustive search mode is the confidence reliably computable (otherwise it is merely a lower bound), confidence factors are not of much concern otherwise. We have the user specify a floor confidence value. If the confidence of a chain of reasoning falls below this value, the chain is discarded as unproductive.

GETRULES then calls READCLAUSE to input these rules and to perform the lexical analysis. Predicate terms are stored as a linked list via MAKEPRED. The individual symbols representing constants, variables, and functions are stored in a binary tree for fast reference in lexicographic order by MAKESYM. See the type SYMBOL in the STRNG package. The record includes, in addition to a character string array for the symbol and pointers to the left and right children in the binary tree, a pointer to the index list used to index the rules on the basis of the first symbol in the predicate. The left child will have symbols preceding the present symbol in lexicographic (alphabetic) order, the right child will have symbols which follow. In this manner, the tree may be searched for a given symbol in time proportional to the logarithm of the number of symbols present, assuming the tree is fairly well balanced. Methods to balance such trees are well known [29] and will not be given here. If the symbols encountered are randomly distributed in lexicographic order as they are encountered, the resulting tree should be well balanced.

The INDEX record contains the identity of the rule and which predicate within that rule, to which the indexed predicate might unify, additional information to be used by the forward-chaining system, and a pointer to the next index entry.

The rule syntax is an extension of that used by Morgenson [10]. In his expert system shell, which was A-V, predicates were single symbols delimited by commas. The keywords if and then were not recognized as such and stored as elements in the internal representation of the rule. In order to handle O-A-V systems with functions of variables, we made the blank a delimiter between symbols. We still require that a rule end with a comma, in order to allow rules to extend over multiple lines (this can be problematical in some Ada systems depending upon the input package specifics). We recognize "if" and "then" as keywords, along with "and," "or," and "not." Thus, one can enter rules such as

if moos,chews_cud and gives_milk then cow or god_knows_what,

if,not,moos,gives_milk,then,goat,

The lexical analyzer permits predicates with an arbitrary number of symbols, i.e., functions with an arbitrary "arity." The first symbol is assumed to be the function name, the subsequent symbols the variables or constants. It does not at present permit nesting of functions, i.e., functions as arguments of functions. This may be accomplished, of course, with a preceding predicate term. Thus, for example, consider sees ?x (feet ?x)

(a predicate term intended to assert that a person sees his own feet) used in Charniak and McDermott [15] as part of an illustration of the "occurs check" discussed above. Note that it requires a unary function feet to return not a logical value (true or false) but rather, in effect, a variable bound to the feet of the individual bound to ?x. An equivalent construct might be

feet ?x ?y, sees ?x ?y

where the first term is interpreted to bind the variable ?y as the feet of individual ?x. This limitation is similar to that of restricted binary logic [30], except that we do not restrict the arity to 2 (binary predicates).

The nonlogical predicates start with the symbol " and are called quoted predicates in the code. It was originally intended to pass these exactly as input to the processing routines. It was found to be desirable to allow the lexical analyzer to parse these as well by separating them into symbols, instead of writing largely redundant code to do the lexical analysis for, say, mathematical expressions. See the next chapter for details of how mathematical predicates are handled.

There are a number of ways a "smart editor" or smarter lexical analyzer could increase the efficiency and flexibility of the expert system. Some are discussed in the next chapter. It was felt better for this book to put the effort into the inference engine instead of the user interface, as the latter is more in the realm of conventional programming than AI techniques.

PACKAGE BACK

The main procedure of the inference engine is DIAGNOSE. It performs a few housekeeping chores such as pushing the goals (after negating each term) onto the goal stack. A goal may have multiple terms, which are in effect "anded." Thus, a solution (a set of variable bindings) must satisfy all the goal terms. If the goal terms are $g1$ and $g2$, then the terms $\sim g2$ and $\sim g1$ are pushed o..to the goal stack. Such input goals have zero depth as their context. As $\sim g1$ is now on the top of the stack, it is the first goal to be addressed by verify. If success is achieved, then $\sim g2$ remains on the goal stack and is processed in the same manner. It takes care of the indexing of the rules among one another via RULESINDEX and similarly indexes each goal to potentially useful rules with GOALINDEX. These two procedures comprise package RULEIND. Then VERIFY is called, and results printed.

VERIFY is the heart of the inference engine. It recursively calls itself in an attempt to generate and establish subgoals. Auxiliary routines used are located principally in package BIND and are:

PRINTPRED	(In LOGIC package) to print predicate terms
IS_VAR	Returns BOOLEAN on whether argument is a variable
IS_ATOM	Returns BOOLEAN on whether argument is atom (variable or constant)
RELEASE	Releases a bindings of specified depth
NEWDEPTH	Assigns a unique new depth to be used for new bindings
VALUE	Returns the ultimate value a variable is bound to
CAR	Like the eponymous LISP function, returns the first element of the list
NOOCCURS	Performs the occurs check in unification
UNIFY	Performs unification
ANSWER	Prints answer as a predicate with variables replaced by their bindings
EXPLAINIT	Explains deductions as to source rules and depths
USERVERIFIES	Procedure to query user (if allowable option) used to establish a fact only if there are no relevant rules.
GETRULE	Gets next relevant rule from index list
PROBOR	(In ANDOR) "or" confidence factors
PROBAND	(In ANDOR) "and" confidence factors
QUOTED	Returns BOOLEAN if predicate nonlogical (quoted)
EVAL_DEMON	Evaluates "demons" (nonlogical predicates)
ISBOUND	Returns BOOLEAN if variable is bound

These routines are largely self-explanatory in purpose and operation. Note that VALUE directly accesses the hash table for greatest efficiency. When verify is called, it tests to see if there are any more goals to satisfy. If not, it returns success to DIAGNOSE. If not, it pops the goal and attempts by resolution to achieve a contradiction. Thus, if the goal ~$g1$ is popped, it will call GETRULE to check the rule index for a relevant rule. Such a rule might be something like, if a and b then $g1$, which is ~a v ~b v $g1$ in clause form. The ~$g1$ and $g1$ terms resolve, and we are left with the resolvent ~a v ~b. These two terms are pushed on the goal stack in reverse order, so that ~a will be the first goal to be popped. Verify saves its current stack location and recursively calls itself to verify the subgoals. Upon failure, either because the confidence factor drops below the floor or because there are no relevant rules, verify returns indicating failure, to itself. The stack top is restored to its position before the failure ("backtracking"), and the next rule relevant to the goal is used to attempt a successful inference.

Other Data Structures

Rules are stored as a linked list of predicate terms, using the type PREDICATE defined in the STRNG package. Each term is a linked list of type PREDICATE records. Each such record has a pointer to the symbol in the binary tree of symbols, a pointer to the next record for the next symbol in the term, and an indexing value which will be used by the routines of Chapter 7.

The goals are kept on a "stack" of type GOALS. In addition to the pointer to the predicate term, the goal's depth (for standardizing apart), whether it is negated or not, the rule (if any) which gave rise to the goal as a subgoal (for explanation purposes), and a pointer to the next goal below on the stack, are saved. Bindings are stored in the hash table as a linked list for each hash value, with each record in the list of type BINDING. A pointer to the bound variable's symbol-tree entry is contained along with the depth (these together constitute the variable's tag), the rules which unified to create the binding (this information is retained for explanation purposes), the binding information, and a pointer to the next "bucket" in the linked list.

Depths and Contexts

The function NEWDEPTH generates the depth or context of a binding in order to standardize apart variables with the same names in different rules. The depth may be viewed as a suffix to the name which makes the variables tag unique. For maximum speed, the testing of whether a context or depth is valid or has been discarded should be $O(1)$, i.e., independent of the number of variables, rules, etc. The version of the code presented here achieves this by a static array CONTEXT of BOOLEAN values, CONTEXT(I) being true if that depth is currently active. Assigned depths are reused if they have generated no bindings to minimize the probability that we exhaust the number of contexts allowed by the array bounds. This may not be flexible enough in some applications. An alternative is to store the contexts which are alive on a linked list. A function ALIVE searches that list. Contexts are pushed onto the top of the list as generated and popped off the list while backtracking. (Such a version is to be found in Chapter 4.) Another approach, which may be used in conjunction with either the array or the linked-list methods, would be to "garbage collect" the contexts, either incrementally or when NEWDEPTH raised an exception on running out of contexts to assign.

Examples

The first example uses a query with the variable "who" and a set of facts and the grandfather rule. It is a self-explanatory example of an O-A-V system which could be used as a smart database. Try it with the cut (!) removed.

The second example illustrates the non-Horn clause power of the inference engine using an example due to Jerardi [31]. Both he and Butrick [32] have discussed a number of nonintuitive properties of PROLOG. Given a set of rules which according to propositional logic allow a clear deduction, PROLOG can easily give wrong answers or go into an infinite loop (which may terminate with a message such as "stack overflow," depending upon the system in use). There are a number of factors that lead to these difficulties. First, PROLOG's closed-world assumption means that if it cannot find a proof for something, it assumes it is false. It can miss a proof because the Horn clause formulation as typically implemented does not provide for contraposition. The statement $p \rightarrow q$ (if p then q) is logically equivalent to $\sim q \rightarrow \sim p$, because both can be written as $\sim p \lor q$ in clause form. But PROLOG will treat q as the "head" of the clause and will not attempt to treat $\sim p$ on an equal footing. Our inference engine is more flexible than this.

The reader can easily generate examples in which PROLOG will go into an infinite loop, while ours will not with the circularity check turned on (try the rule set if p then q, if q then p, p with the goal q). Of course, an infinite loop is possible in our system without the check. Our simple check prevents the simultaneous use of the same rule twice. For more sophisticated methods, see [33].

Jerardi gives the following five rules:

1. If it is raining or snowing, then it is precipitating.

2. If it is freezing, and it is precipitating, then it is snowing.

3. If it is not freezing, and it is precipitating, then it is raining.

4. It is snowing.

5. If it is raining, then it is not snowing.

Note the fourth rule is a fact. It should be possible on this basis to conclude that it is freezing from propositional logic. From fact 4, we conclude from rule 1 that it is precipitating. From rule 5, by contraposition, we can also conclude from fact 4 that it is not raining. Then using the contrapositive of rule 3, we may conclude that it is freezing or it is not precipitating. As we know the latter is false, we may conclude that it is freezing. Jerardi tested VMPROLOG with all five rules and just the first four. When he gave it the goal of "it is freezing" to establish, it said it was false, while the goal of not freezing was established as true! When he gave as goals precipitating or snowing, a stack overflow was the result. Note that stack overflow cannot be reliably interpreted as equivalent to false. These paradoxical results can be understood when the limitations of PROLOG as discussed above are considered.

Comparison with Other Backward-Chaining System Shells

Backward-chaining shells are typically used in diagnosis problems, because the number of goals may be limited. A typical example is the MYCIN [34] system, from which the EMYCIN shell is extracted. PROLOG [34] is another backward-chaining language. Like PROLOG, we use backward-chaining, depth-first search. We have additional flexibility in the occurs and the circularity check. PROLOG has somewhat more flexible input syntax rules. EMYCIN is a backward-chaining system in which confidence factors range from −1 (false) through 0 (unknown) to +1 (true). There is no pattern matching (unification), i.e., no variables, but there are a set of "contexts" so that facts are represented as O-A-V triplets for a set of contexts as the objects. A great deal of effort has gone into giving MYCIN a user-friendly interface with rules in a syntax close to English.

References

1. R. Lathrop, T. Webster, T. Smith, *Comm. ACM,* 30, 909 (1987).

2. W. Hodges, *Logic* (London: Penguin, 1977).

3. R. Kowalski, *Logic for Problem Solving* (Amsterdam/N.Y.: North-Holland/Elseiver, 1979).

4. J. H. Gallier, *Logic for Computer Science* (N.Y.: Harper & Row, 1986).

5. C-L. Chang and R. Lee, *Symbolic Logic and Mechanical Theorem Proving* (N.Y.: Academic Press, 1973).

6. R J. Brown III, *Dr. Dobb's Journal,* April 1986, p. 23.

7. E. Mendelson, *Introduction to Mathematical Logic* (N.Y.: D. Van Nostrand, 1964).

8. P. H. Winston and B. K. P. Horn, *LISP* (Reading, Mass.: Addison-Wesley, 1st ed., 1981, 2d ed., 1984).

9. R. O. Duda and John G. Gaschnig, *BYTE,* September 1981, p. 238.

10. D. Morgenson, *J. Pascal, Ada, & Modula-2,* January/February 1985, p. 29.

11. D. Kozen, *IBM J. Res. Develop.,* 24, 327(1981).

12. K. Schmucher, *Fuzzy Sets, Natural Language Computations, and Risk Analysis* (Rockville, Md.: Computer Science Press, 1985).

13. I. J. Good, I. *J. Math., Applics.* 2, 364(1966).

14. P. Rosenbloom, *The Elements of Mathematical Logic* (N.Y.: Dover, 1950).

15. C. I. Lewis and C. H. Langford, *Symbolic Logic* (N.Y.: Dover, 1st ed., 1932, 2d ed., 1959).

16. G. E. Hughes and M. J. Cresswell, *Modal Logic* (London: Methuen, 1968).

17. D. McDermott, *J. Assoc. Computing Machinery,* 29, p. 37 (1982).

18. E. Charniak and D. McDermott, *Introduction to Artificial Intelligence* (Reading, Mass.: Addison-Wesley, 1985).

19. A. Horn, *J. Symbolic Logic,* 16, p. 14 (1951).

20. J. A. Robinson, *J. ACM,* 12, 23 (1965).

21. N. Nilsson, *Problem Solving Methods in Artificial Intelligence* (N.Y.: McGraw-Hill, 1971).

22. M. A. Covington, D. Nute, Andre Vellino, *Prolog Programming in Depth* (Glenview, Ill.: Scott, Foresman, 1988).

23. S. Shapiro, *J. Symbolic Logic,* 50, 714 (1985).

24. V. Kumar and Y.-J. Lin, *J. Logic Programming,* 5, p. 195 (1988).

25. G. Booch, *Software Components with Ada* (Menlo Park, Calif.: Benjamin/Cummings, 1987).

26. E. Horowitz and S. Sahni, *Fundamentals of Data Structures* (Rockville, Md.: Computer Science Press, 1983).

27. K. Nakamura, in *Implementations of PROLOG* (J. A. Campbell, ed.) (Chichester:Ellis Horwood, 1984).

28. D. Shafer, *Artificial Intelligence Programming on the Macintosh* (Indianapolis, IN: H. W. Sams, 1986).

29. R. F. Stout and B. L. Warren, *Comm. ACM,* 29, p. 902 (1986).

30. A. Deliyanni and R. A. Kowalski, *Comm. ACM,* 22, 184 (1979).

31. T. W. Jerardi, *SIGPLAN Notices,* 22, April 1987, p. 63.

32. R. Butrick, *Dr. Dobbs Journal,* January 1987, p. 14, and July 1987, p. 30.

33. D. E. Smith, M. R, Genesereth, Matthew L. Ginsberg, *Artificial Intelligence,* 30, p. 343 (1986).

34. T. O'Shea and M. Eisenstadt, *Artificial Intelligence: Tools, Techniques, and Applications* (N.Y.: Harper & Row, 1984).

Program Listing and Test Problem Output

(Listing begins next page.)

-- Backward-Chaining Expert System Shell

```ada
with TEXT_IO; use  TEXT_IO;
with STRNG; use STRNG;
with LOGIC; use LOGIC;
with HASH;  use HASH;
with STACK; use STACK;
with READIN; use READIN;
with LIVE; use LIVE;
with BIND; use BIND;
with RULEIND; use RULEIND;
with CLAUSERD ;use CLAUSERD ;
with ANDOR; use ANDOR;
with MATH; use MATH;

procedure  BACK is

CUTFLAG  : constant  FLOAT := -1000.0;
-- a confidence factor of CUTFLAG indicates a cut.  use a value
-- that could not possibly be a confidence factor.
type  TRUTH is  (F,T,UNDEFINED);

subtype  RULERANGE is  INTEGER range  0..MAX_RULE_COUNT;
subtype  PTRANGE   is  INTEGER range  0..MAX_LENGTH_CLAUSE ;
subtype  GOALRANGE is  INTEGER range  0..MAX_TERM_COUNT;

package  INT_IO is  new  INTEGER_IO(NUM=>INTEGER);
package  FLT_IO is  new  FLOAT_IO(NUM=>FLOAT);
BIND: BINDPTR;
DUMP: BOOLEAN;
CUTAT:INTEGER;
GOAL_AT_CUT: GOALSPTR;

function  VERIFY( DEPTH: in  INTEGER ; PREVRUL: in  INTEGER)
               return  FLOAT is
NEWSTR,TGTSTRG: PHRASE;
NEWPRED,ANTECED,TGTPRED: PREDICPTR;
NEWPTR: SYMPTR;
```

```
RULEVALUE:TRUTH;
FOUND,NG1,NG2,NOMORE,PUSHTERM,UNIFIES:BOOLEAN;
HEADID: PTRANGE;
CURRULNUM: RULERANGE;
NEWSTRIND: PTRANGE;
NEWGOAL,CURRGOAL: GOALSPTR;
CURRDEPTH,TEMP_DEPTH,WORKINGDEPTH,PREVRULE: INTEGER;
TGTDEPTH,FDEPTH: INTEGER;
CURRBIND: BINDPTR;
RULINDEX: INDEXPTR;
INUSE,OLDINUSE: INPTR;
CONFIDENCE,CONFRULE,CONFIDE: FLOAT;

begin
PREVRULE:=PREVRUL;WORKINGDEPTH:=DEPTH;
-- previous rule=0 if input goal.
-- transfer to local variable so that on recursion, may be passed.
NEW_LINE;PUT(" VERIFY-PREVRULE=");INT_IO.PUT(PREVRULE);
<<DOIT>>
if GOALTOP=null then   --no remaining goals-success.
   ANSWER;
   if  EXPLAIN then
       EXPLAINIT;
   end  if ;
   return  1.0 ;
else  -- work on topmost goal
   CONFIDENCE:=0.0;
   POPGOAL(TGTPRED,TGTDEPTH,NG2,INUSE);
   if CUT(TGTPRED) then-- cut?
     CUTAT:= WORKINGDEPTH;--remember where cut is
     GOAL_AT_CUT:=GOALTOP;
     NEW_LINE;PUT(" CUT AT CONTEXT=");
     INT_IO.PUT(CUTAT);
     return  CUTFLAG;-- flag cut
   else
     NEW_LINE;PUT(" TO PROVE ");
     PRINTPRED(TGTPRED,TGTDEPTH);
     if NG2 then PUT(" NEGATED ");end if;
```

```
end  if ;
RULINDEX:=null;
OLDINUSE:=INUSE;
-- need FOUND value, HEADID
GETRULE(CURRULNUM,TGTPRED,RULINDEX,
 FOUND,HEADID,INUSE);
if FOUND then
   PUT(" FOUND");
else
   PUT(" not found");
end if;
if QUOTED(TGTPRED) then--non-logical term
   CONFIDENCE:=EVAL_DEMON(TGTPRED);
   return CONFIDENCE;
elsif (not  FOUND) then--no (more)relevant rules
   NEWSTRIND:=0;--query user
   CONFIDENCE:=
   USERVERIFIES(TGTPRED,TGTDEPTH,NG2,
   CURRULNUM,NEWSTRIND);
   if  CONFIDENCE<FLOOR then --failed
     return  CONFIDENCE;
   else --success-pursue further
     return  VERIFY(TGTDEPTH,-1);
   end  if ;
else  -- logical term to prove
   loop
     NEWSTRIND:=RULEINDX(CURRULNUM+1)-1;
     NG1:=RULES(HEADID).NEGATED;
     NEWPRED:=RULES(HEADID);
     CURRGOAL:=GOALTOP; CURRBIND:=BIND;
     OLDINUSE:=INUSE;
     if QUOTED(NEWPRED) then
       CONFIDENCE:= EVAL_DEMON(NEWPRED);
       return  CONFIDENCE;
     else
       TEMP_DEPTH:=NEWDEPTH(WORKINGDEPTH);
       NEW_LINE;PUT(" TO UNIFY");
       INT_IO.PUT(TEMP_DEPTH);
```

```
INT_IO.PUT(TGTDEPTH);
INT_IO.PUT(PREVRULE);
INT_IO.PUT(CURRULNUM);
UNIFIES:= (NG1 xor NG2) and then UNIFY
 (NEWPRED,TEMP_DEPTH,TGTPRED,
 TGTDEPTH,TEMP_DEPTH,CURRULNUM,PREVRULE);
if UNIFIES then
  NEW_LINE;PUT(" UNIFY SUCCESS");
  --rule might resolve
  CONFRULE:=1.0;
  NUMSTRRULES:=RULEINDX(CURRULNUM);
  loop --other terms goals
    if  NEWSTRIND< NUMSTRRULES
     then  exit ;
    end  if ;
    if NEWSTRIND/=HEADID then
      ANTECED:= RULES(NEWSTRIND);
      NEW_LINE;PUT(" PUSHED GOAL=");
      PRINTPRED(ANTECED,TEMP_DEPTH);
      PUSHTERM:=TRUE;
      if FACTOR and then
       (not(NG1 xor
       RULES(NEWSTRIND).NEGATED))
       then
        FDEPTH:=NEWDEPTH(FDEPTH);
        PUSHTERM:=
         (not UNIFY(ANTECED,
         TEMP_DEPTH,NEWPRED,
         TEMP_DEPTH,FDEPTH,
         CURRULNUM,CURRULNUM));
        RELEASE(FDEPTH);
        if not PUSHTERM then
          PUSHTERM:=
           (not UNIFY(ANTECED,
           TEMP_DEPTH,NEWPRED,
           TEMP_DEPTH,TEMP_DEPTH,
           CURRULNUM,CURRULNUM));
        end if;
```

```
        end if;
        if PUSHTERM then
          PUSHGOAL(ANTECED,
           TEMP_DEPTH,
           RULES(NEWSTRIND).NEGATED
           ,INUSE);
        else
          NEW_LINE;PUT(" FACTORED ");
          PRINTPRED(ANTECED,
           TEMP_DEPTH);
          PRINTPRED(NEWPRED,
           TEMP_DEPTH);
        end if;
      end if;
      NEWSTRIND:=NEWSTRIND-1;
    end loop ;
    CONFIDE:=VERIFY(TEMP_DEPTH,CURRULNUM);
    --solve new goals
    if CONFIDE=CUTFLAG then  --at cut
      NEW_LINE;PUT(" CUT RETURNED  CONTEXT");
      INT_IO.PUT(CUTAT);
      PUT(" TEMPORARY:");INT_IO.PUT(TEMP_DEPTH);
      PUT(" WORKING:");INT_IO.PUT(WORKINGDEPTH);
      WORKINGDEPTH:=CUTAT;
      GOALTOP:=GOAL_AT_CUT;
      goto  DOIT;
    elsif  CONFIDE>FLOOR     then --success-pursue
      CONFRULE:=
       PROBAND(CONFIDE,RULEPROB(CURRULNUM));
      if not EXHAUSTIVE then
        RELEASE(TEMP_DEPTH);
        GOALTOP:=CURRGOAL;
        return  CONFRULE;
      else
        CONFIDENCE:=
        PROBOR(CONFIDENCE,CONFRULE);
      end  if ;
    end  if ;
```

```
          NEW_LINE;PUT(" -ON TO NEXT  RULE");
        end  if  ;
        RELEASE(TEMP_DEPTH);
        GOALTOP:=CURRGOAL;
        INUSE:=OLDINUSE;
        GETRULE(CURRULNUM,
         TGTPRED,RULINDEX,FOUND,HEADID,INUSE);
        if not  FOUND then
          NEW_LINE;
          PUT(" NO MORE RELEVANT RULES FOUND");
          exit ;
        end  if ;
      end  if ;
    end  loop ;
  end  if ;
end  if ;
return  CONFIDENCE;
end  VERIFY;

-- overall control

procedure  DIAGNOSE is

GL: PREDICPTR;
HYPOTHESIS: PHRASE;
CONF: FLOAT;
COUNT: INTEGER;

begin

RULESINDEX;-- cross-index rules
DUMP:=TRUE;
for  KOUNT in  1..NUMGOALS loop -- index goals
  GL:=GOALPTR(KOUNT);
  GOALINDEX(GL,KOUNT,GOALPTR(KOUNT).NEGATED);
  DUMP:=FALSE;
end  loop ;
INTOP:=null;
```

```
GOALTOP:=null;
-- push goals onto goalstack
-- push in reverse order for PROLOG ordering- first goal on top of stack,
-- attempted first
for  COUNT in  1..NUMGOALS loop
   PUSHGOAL(GOALPTR(1+NUMGOALS-COUNT),0,
   GOALPTR(1+NUMGOALS-COUNT).NEGATED,INTOP);
end  loop ;
BIND:=null;
CONF:=VERIFY(0,0) ;-- can it be proved?
NEW_LINE;-- report final result
if CONF>FLOOR then
   PUT(" GOAL TRUE WITH CONFIDENCE="); FLT_IO.PUT(CONF);
else
   PUT(" GOAL FALSE- CONFIDENCE AS TRUE=");FLT_IO.PUT(CONF);
   PUT(" IS BELOW FLOOR ");FLT_IO.PUT(FLOOR);
end if;
end  DIAGNOSE;

begin
EXHAUSTIVE:=FALSE;
GETRULES;-- get input, options
DIAGNOSE;-- solve
end  BACK;
```

--Dynamic String Package. See text for generic version.

```
package STRNG is
  STRINGLENGTH : constant:=50;
  LONGPHRASE_LENGTH : constant:=250;
  HASHSIZE : constant :=256;


type LONGPHRASE is array (1..LONGPHRASE_LENGTH) of CHARACTER;
type PHRASE is array (1..STRINGLENGTH) of CHARACTER;

-- length of string:

function PHRASE_LENGTH( STRNG: in PHRASE) return INTEGER;

-- print

procedure PRINT (MSG: in LONGPHRASE) ;

procedure PRINT (MSG: in PHRASE);

-- copy portion of string to phrase.

procedure LONGPHRASE_TO_PHRASE( FROM : in LONGPHRASE ;
    TO:out PHRASE;START,STOP: in INTEGER);
-- convert

procedure STRING_TO_PHRASE( FROM: in STRING; TO: out PHRASE);

procedure STRING_TO_PHRASE( FROM: in STRING; TO: out PHRASE;
                LENGTH: in INTEGER);

procedure STRING_TO_PHRASE( FROM: in STRING; TO: out LONGPHRASE);

procedure STRING_TO_PHRASE( FROM: in STRING; TO: out LONGPHRASE;
                LENGTH: in INTEGER);

function PHRASE_TO_STRING (PHR : in PHRASE) return STRING;
```

-- COMPAREPHRASES. returns 0 if same, else +1 if X follows Y lexicographically
-- else –1. Functions "=","<",etc. may easily be built using COMPAREPHRASES

function COMPAREPHRASES(X,Y: PHRASE) return   INTEGER;

-- similar to BASIC LOCATE function. returns 0 if SOURCE
--   does not contain TARGET,
-- otherwise the index of the first character of TARGET in SOURCE

function FIND_PHRASE(TARGET,SOURCE: in PHRASE;
     TARGETLENGTH,SOURCELENGTH: in INTEGER) return INTEGER;

-- similar to above, but starts with FIRST_INDEX CHARACTER in SOURCE
--   useful to locate additional occurances of TARGET in SOURCE.

function FIND_PHRASE(TARGET,SOURCE: in PHRASE;
     TARGETLENGTH,SOURCELENGTH,
     FIRST_INDEX: in INTEGER) return INTEGER;

-- is target in source? uses FIND_PHRASE

function LOCATE(SOURCE,TARGET: in PHRASE;SOURCELENGTH: in INTEGER)
             return BOOLEAN;

-- CONCATENATE PHRASES

function "&"(A,B: PHRASE) return PHRASE ;

-- COPY PHRASE

procedure COPY_PHRASE(ORIGINAL: in PHRASE;DUPLICATE: out PHRASE);

-- generate a hash value (integer) given the (variable) name and an integer

function HASHKEY(NAME: in PHRASE; D: in INTEGER) return INTEGER;

end STRNG;

-- Dynamic String Package Body.

```ada
with  TEXT_IO; use  TEXT_IO;

package  body  STRNG is

package  INT_IO is  new  INTEGER_IO(NUM => INTEGER);

TERMINATOR: constant CHARACTER := '$';   -- change string terminator here

TEMPORARY: PHRASE;

function  PHRASE_LENGTH( STRNG : in  PHRASE) return  INTEGER is
LENGTH : INTEGER ;

begin
for LENGTH in  1..STRINGLENGTH loop
   if STRNG(LENGTH)= TERMINATOR then
     return  (LENGTH-1) ;
   end  if ;
end  loop ;
exception
   when CONSTRAINT_ERROR  =>
     return  (LENGTH-1);
end  PHRASE_LENGTH;

procedure  PRINT( MSG: in  LONGPHRASE) is

I: INTEGER;
CHAR: CHARACTER;

begin
for I in 1..LONGPHRASE_LENGTH loop
   CHAR:=MSG(I);
   if (CHAR=TERMINATOR) then  return ; end  if ;
   PUT(CHAR);
end  loop ;
exception
```

```
    when CONSTRAINT_ERROR=>
      return ;
 end  PRINT;

 procedure  PRINT( MSG: in  PHRASE) is

 I: INTEGER;
 CHAR: CHARACTER;

 begin
 for I in  1..STRINGLENGTH loop
   CHAR:=MSG(I);
   if (CHAR=TERMINATOR) then  return ; end  if ;
   PUT(CHAR);
 end  loop ;
 exception
   when CONSTRAINT_ERROR=>
      return ;
 end  PRINT;


 procedure  LONGPHRASE_TO_PHRASE( FROM : in  LONGPHRASE ;
   TO:out  PHRASE; START,STOP: in  INTEGER)  is
 K,TOCOPY:INTEGER;
 begin
 TOCOPY:= STOP+1-START;
 for K in  1..TOCOPY loop
    TO(K):=FROM(START-1+K);
 end  loop ;
 K:=TOCOPY+1;
 TO(K):=TERMINATOR;
 return ;
 exception
   when CONSTRAINT_ERROR =>
    NEW_LINE;
    PUT("CONSTRAINT ERROR in  LONGPHRASE_TO_PHRASE-FROM=");
    TO(STRINGLENGTH):=TERMINATOR;
    return ;
 end LONGPHRASE_TO_PHRASE;
```

```
procedure STRING_TO_PHRASE( FROM: in STRING; TO: out PHRASE;
                    LENGTH: in INTEGER) is
TOP,KOUNT: INTEGER;

begin
TOP:=LENGTH;
if TOP>=STRINGLENGTH then
  TOP:=STRINGLENGTH-1;
  PUT(" WARNING: STRING_TO_PHRASE Longer Than PHRASE,Truncated");
end if ;
for KOUNT in 1..TOP loop
  TO(KOUNT):=FROM(KOUNT);
end loop ;
TO(TOP+1):=TERMINATOR;
exception
  when CONSTRAINT_ERROR =>
    TOP:=LENGTH;
    if TOP>STRINGLENGTH then
      TOP:=STRINGLENGTH;
    end if ;
    TO(STRINGLENGTH):=TERMINATOR;
    return ;
end STRING_TO_PHRASE;

procedure STRING_TO_PHRASE( FROM: in STRING; TO: out LONGPHRASE;
                    LENGTH:in INTEGER) is

KOUNT,TOP: INTEGER;

begin
TOP:=LENGTH;
if TOP>LONGPHRASE_LENGTH-1 then
  TOP:=LONGPHRASE_LENGTH-1;
  PUT(" WARNING: STRING_TO_PHRASE STRING Too Long,Truncated");
end if ;
for KOUNT in 1..TOP loop
  TO(KOUNT):=FROM(KOUNT);
```

```
end  loop ;
TO(TOP+1):=TERMINATOR;
exception
  when  CONSTRAINT_ERROR =>
    TOP:=LENGTH+1;
    if TOP>LONGPHRASE_LENGTH then
      TOP:=LONGPHRASE_LENGTH;
    end  if ;
    TO(LONGPHRASE_LENGTH):=TERMINATOR;
    return ;
end  STRING_TO_PHRASE;

procedure STRING_TO_PHRASE(FROM: in STRING; TO:out LONGPHRASE) is

BOUND,TOP:INTEGER;

begin
BOUND:=LONGPHRASE_LENGTH-1;
TOP:=1;
loop
  if FROM(TOP)=TERMINATOR then  exit ; end  if ;
  TOP:=TOP+1;
  if TOP>LONGPHRASE_LENGTH then  exit ; end  if ;
end loop ;
STRING_TO_PHRASE(FROM,TO,TOP);
return ;
exception
  when  CONSTRAINT_ERROR =>
  STRING_TO_PHRASE(FROM,TO,LONGPHRASE_LENGTH-1);
  return ;
end  STRING_TO_PHRASE;

procedure  STRING_TO_PHRASE( FROM: in  STRING; TO: out  PHRASE ) is

BOUND,TOP:INTEGER;

begin
BOUND:=STRINGLENGTH-1;
```

```
TOP:=1;
loop
  if FROM(TOP)=TERMINATOR then  exit ; end  if ;
  TOP:=TOP+1;
  if TOP>BOUND then  exit ; end  if ;
end loop ;
STRING_TO_PHRASE(FROM,TO,TOP-1);
return ;
exception
  when CONSTRAINT_ERROR =>
    STRING_TO_PHRASE(FROM,TO,STRINGLENGTH-1);
    return ;
end  STRING_TO_PHRASE;

--copy PHRASE constant to STRING

function  PHRASE_TO_STRING( PHR: in  PHRASE) return  STRING is

ANS: STRING(1..STRINGLENGTH);        -- cannot have string length 0
CHR: CHARACTER;
INDEX,LENGTH: INTEGER;
begin
for INDEX in 1..STRINGLENGTH loop
  ANS(INDEX):=' ';
end loop;
LENGTH:=PHRASE_LENGTH(PHR);
if LENGTH<1 then return ANS; end if;
for INDEX in  1..LENGTH loop
  ANS(INDEX):= PHR(INDEX);
end loop ;
return  ANS;
end PHRASE_TO_STRING;

function  COMPAREPHRASES(X,Y: PHRASE) return   INTEGER is

KOUNT:INTEGER;
A,B: CHARACTER;
```

```
begin
for  KOUNT in  1..LONGPHRASE_LENGTH loop
  A:=X(KOUNT); B:=Y(KOUNT);
  if  A=TERMINATOR and  B=TERMINATOR then  return  0;
  elsif  A<B then  return  -1;
  elsif  A>B then  return  1;
  elsif  A=TERMINATOR then  return  -1;
  elsif  B=TERMINATOR then  return  1;
  end  if ;
end  loop ;
return  0;
exception
  when CONSTRAINT_ERROR =>
      return  0;
end  COMPAREPHRASES;


function FIND_PHRASE( TARGET,SOURCE: in PHRASE;
  TARGETLENGTH,SOURCELENGTH,FIRST_INDEX: in INTEGER)
            return INTEGER is

START,I,M,MTOP :INTEGER;

begin
MTOP:= SOURCELENGTH-TARGETLENGTH;
START:=FIRST_INDEX-1;--0 NORMALLY
for M in START..MTOP LOOP
  for I in 1..TARGETLENGTH loop
    if TARGET(I)/=SOURCE(I+M) then goto DIFF;end if;
  end loop;
  return(M+1);
  <<DIFF>> null;
end loop;
return (0);
end FIND_PHRASE;

function FIND_PHRASE( TARGET,SOURCE: in PHRASE;
  TARGETLENGTH,SOURCELENGTH: in INTEGER) return INTEGER is
```

```
begin
return FIND_PHRASE(TARGET,SOURCE,TARGETLENGTH,SOURCELENGTH,1);
end FIND_PHRASE;

function  CHAR_TO_INT (C:CHARACTER) return  INTEGER is
K:INTEGER;
begin
case C is
   when  'A'..'D'=> K:=1;
   when  'E'..'H'=> K:=2;
   when  'I'..'L'=> K:=3;
   when  'M'..'P'=> K:=4;
   when  'Q'..'S'=> K:=5;
   when  'T'..'W'=> K:=6;
   when  'Y'..'Z'=> K:=7;
   when  'a'..'d'=> K:=8;
   when  'e'..'h'=> K:=9;
   when  'i'..'l'=> K:=10;
   when  'm'..'p'=> K:=11;
   when  'q'..'s'=> K:=12;
   when  't'..'w'=> K:=13;
   when  'y'..'z'=> K:=14;
   when  'X' => K:=15;
   when  'x'=>  K:=15;
   when  others  => K:=0;
end  case ;
return  K;
end  CHAR_TO_INT;

function  HASHKEY( NAME: in  PHRASE; D: in  INTEGER) return  INTEGER is
L,J,K:INTEGER;
C: CHARACTER;
begin
J:=D mod  16;
C:=NAME(2);
K:=CHAR_TO_INT(C);
L:= (J*16+ K);
if L<1 or  else  L>HASHSIZE then
```

```
   L:=255;
end  if ;
return  L;
end  HASHKEY;

function LOCATE(SOURCE,TARGET: in PHRASE;SOURCELENGTH: in INTEGER
              return BOOLEAN is
TARGETLENGTH: INTEGER;
begin
--SOURCELENGTH:=PHRASE_LENGTH(SOURCE);
TARGETLENGTH:=PHRASE_LENGTH(TARGET);
return(FIND_PHRASE(TARGET,SOURCE,SOURCELENGTH,TARGETLENGTH)
         /= 0 );
end LOCATE;

function "&"(A,B: PHRASE) return PHRASE is

--   ******* CAVEAT ********
--   *** MODIFIES A    *****
LENGTHA,LENGTHB,INDEX: INTEGER;
begin
LENGTHA:=PHRASE_LENGTH(A);
LENGTHB:=PHRASE_LENGTH(B);
for INDEX in  1..LENGTHA loop
  TEMPORARY(INDEX):=A(INDEX);
end loop;
for INDEX in  1..LENGTHB loop
  TEMPORARY(INDEX+LENGTHA):=B(INDEX);
end loop;
TEMPORARY(LENGTHA+LENGTHB+1):='$';
return TEMPORARY;
exception
  when CONSTRAINT_ERROR =>
    NEW_LINE;PUT(" CONCATENATED PHRASE TOO LONG");
    return A;
end "&";

procedure COPY_PHRASE(ORIGINAL: in PHRASE;DUPLICATE: out PHRASE) is
```

```
INDEX,LENGTH: INTEGER;
begin
LENGTH:=PHRASE_LENGTH(ORIGINAL);
for INDEX in 1..LENGTH loop
  DUPLICATE(INDEX):=ORIGINAL(INDEX);
end loop;
end COPY_PHRASE;

end  STRNG;
```

-- Basic Data Structures and Procedures for Logical Clauses

```
with STRNG; use STRNG;
with TEXT_IO; use TEXT_IO;

package LOGIC is

MAX_LENGTH_CLAUSE : constant  :=250;
MAX_RULE_COUNT : constant  :=100;
MAX_TERM_COUNT : constant  :=10;   -- MAX # of And'ed goals or facts
type TRUTH is (F,T,UNDEFINED);   -- (former BACK, latter FWD syst)

subtype RULERANGE is INTEGER range 0..MAX_RULE_COUNT;
subtype PTRANGE  is INTEGER range 0..MAX_LENGTH_CLAUSE ;
subtype GOALRANGE is INTEGER range 0..MAX_TERM_COUNT;

package INT_IO is new INTEGER_IO(NUM=>INTEGER);
package FLT_IO is new FLOAT_IO(NUM=>FLOAT);


type INDEX;             --index to symbols
type INDEXPTR is access INDEX;

type SYMBOL;            --symbol table
type SYMPTR is access SYMBOL;
type SYMBOL is
  record           --binary search tree structure
    TOKEN: PHRASE;
    LEFT: SYMPTR;
    RIGHT: SYMPTR;
    ARITHMETIC,DEFINED: BOOLEAN;
    VALUE: FLOAT;
    INDX: INDEXPTR;   -- index for expert system shells
  end record ;

type PREDICATE;
type PREDICPTR is access PREDICATE;
type PREDICATE is
```

```
record
  ITEM: SYMPTR;
  NEXT : PREDICPTR;   -- linked-list
  INDX: INDEXPTR;        -- index for ATN
  NEGATED : BOOLEAN;
end  record ;

type STACK;
type STACKPTR is  access  STACK;
type STACK is
  record
  DATA: PREDICPTR;
  DEPTH: INTEGER;
  CONF: FLOAT;
  NEGATED: BOOLEAN;
  NEXT : STACKPTR;
end  record ;

type FACTLIST;             --facts. forward-chaining system
type FLISTPTR is  access  FACTLIST;
type FACTLIST is
  record
  DATA: PREDICPTR;
  DEPEND: FLISTPTR;
  CONF: FLOAT;
  NEGATED: BOOLEAN;
  USEDBY: FLISTPTR;
  NEXT : FLISTPTR;       --doubly-linked list
  PREV : FLISTPTR;       -- "     "     "
end  record ;

type INDEX is            --index
  record
  RULENUM: PTRANGE;
  NUMSTR: INTEGER;
  FACTPTR: FLISTPTR;
  NEXT: INDEXPTR;
end  record ;
```

ROOT: SYMPTR; --root of symbol table

procedure PRINTPRED(P: in PREDICPTR);

procedure PRINTPRED(P: in PREDICPTR; D: in INTEGER);

end LOGIC;

-- Package Body of Procedures for Use with Logical Clauses

package body LOGIC is

--print predicate term literally, with or without depth.
-- use ANSWER to print with variables instantiated.

```
procedure  PRINTPRED(P:in  PREDICPTR;D:in  INTEGER) is
PP:PREDICPTR;
begin
PP:=P;
loop
if  PP=null then  exit ;end  if ;
PUT(" ");PRINT(PP.ITEM.TOKEN);
PP:=PP.NEXT;
end  loop ;
PUT(" at  DEPTH=");INT_IO.PUT(D);
return ;
end  PRINTPRED;

procedure  PRINTPRED(P:in  PREDICPTR) is
PP:PREDICPTR;
begin
PP:=P;
loop
  if  PP=null then  exit ;end  if ;
  PUT(" ");PRINT(PP.ITEM.TOKEN);
  PP:=PP.NEXT;
end  loop ;
return ;
end  PRINTPRED;

begin
ROOT:=null;
end LOGIC;
```

```
-- Hash Table Processing Procedures
-- Bucket hashing. Key generated by HASHKEY in STRNG package
-- specifically designed for variable-binding data.

with STRNG; use STRNG;
with LOGIC; use LOGIC;

package HASH is

type  BINDING;
type  BINDPTR is  access  BINDING;
type  BINDING is
  record
    NAME: SYMPTR;
    DEPTH,CONTEXT: INTEGER;
    FATHER,MOTHER:INTEGER;
    IDENT: INTEGER;
    TEXT: PREDICPTR;
    NEXT : BINDPTR;        --next bucket
  end  record ;

HASHTABLE: array (1..HASHSIZE) of  BINDPTR;

-- locate symbol in table
procedure  LOCATE(SYMB:in  SYMPTR ;D:in  INTEGER;
              OP,OPREVIOUS: out  BINDPTR; OKEY: out  INTEGER;
              OFOUND: out  BOOLEAN) ;

-- install symbol and associated binding data
procedure  INSTALL(SYMB: in  SYMPTR;D: in  INTEGER;
        CONTXT,FATHER,MOTHER,IDENT: in  INTEGER;
        TEXT: in  PREDICPTR) ;

-- obtain binding information on symbol
PROCEDURE RECOVER(SYMB: in  out  SYMPTR; D: in  out  INTEGER;
        CONTEXT,FATHER,MOTHER,IDENT: out  INTEGER;
        TEXT: out  PREDICPTR) ;
end HASH;
```

-- Package Body Hash Binding Table

with STRNG; use STRNG;
with LOGIC; use LOGIC;
with LIVE; use LIVE;

package body HASH is

INDEX: INTEGER;

procedure LOCATE(SYMB:in SYMPTR ;D:in INTEGER;
          OP,OPREVIOUS: out BINDPTR; OKEY: out INTEGER;
          OFOUND: out BOOLEAN) is
FOUND: BOOLEAN;
P,PREVIOUS: BINDPTR;
KEY : INTEGER;

begin
FOUND:=FALSE;
PREVIOUS:=null;
KEY:=HASHKEY(SYMB.TOKEN,D);
P:=HASHTABLE(KEY);
loop
  if P=null then
    OFOUND:=FOUND;
    OKEY:=KEY;
    OPREVIOUS:=PREVIOUS;
    OP:=P;
    return ;
  elsif P.NAME=SYMB and then P.DEPTH=D then
    if ALIVE(P.CONTEXT) then
      FOUND:=TRUE;
      OFOUND:=FOUND;
      OKEY:=KEY;
      OPREVIOUS:=PREVIOUS;
      OP:=P;
      return ;
    else

```
       if PREVIOUS/=null then
          PREVIOUS.NEXT:=P.NEXT;
        end  if ;
      end  if ;
   else
      PREVIOUS:=P;
   end  if ;
   P:=P.NEXT;
end  loop ;
end  LOCATE;

procedure  INSTALL(SYMB: in  SYMPTR;D: in  INTEGER;
            CONTXT,FATHER,MOTHER,IDENT: in  INTEGER;
            TEXT: in  PREDICPTR) is
PREVIOUS,P:BINDPTR;
FOUND:BOOLEAN;
KEY:INTEGER;

begin
CONTUSED:=0;
if D/=0 then
   ACTIVATE_CONTEXT(D);
end  if ;
LOCATE  (SYMB,D,P,PREVIOUS,KEY,FOUND);
if not  FOUND then
   P:=NEW BINDING;
end if ;
   P.NAME:=SYMB;
   P.DEPTH:=D;
   P.CONTEXT:=CONTXT;
   P.FATHER:=FATHER;
   P.MOTHER:=MOTHER;
   P.IDENT:=IDENT;
   P.TEXT:=TEXT;
   P.NEXT:=null;
if PREVIOUS=null then
   HASHTABLE(KEY):=P;
else
```

```
    PREVIOUS.NEXT:=P;
end  if ;
return ;
end  INSTALL;

PROCEDURE RECOVER(SYMB: in  out  SYMPTR; D: in  out  INTEGER;
          CONTEXT,FATHER,MOTHER,IDENT: out  INTEGER;
          TEXT: out  PREDICPTR) is
FOUND:BOOLEAN;
P,PREV:BINDPTR;
KEY:INTEGER;
BEGIN
LOCATE(SYMB,D,P,PREV,KEY,FOUND);
if not  FOUND then
  SYMB:=null;
  return ;
else
  CONTEXT:=P.CONTEXT;
  FATHER:=P.FATHER;
  MOTHER:=P.MOTHER;
  D:=P.DEPTH;
  SYMB:=P.NAME;
  TEXT:=P.TEXT;
  IDENT:=P.IDENT;
end if ;
end RECOVER;

begin
for INDEX in 1..HASHSIZE loop
  HASHTABLE(INDEX):=null;
end loop;
end HASH;
```

-- POP and PUSH Routines for Stacks

```
with STRNG; use STRNG;
with LOGIC; use LOGIC;

package STACK is

type IN_USE;            -- rules in use for circularity ck.
type INPTR is access IN_USE;
type IN_USE is
  record
    RULE: INTEGER;
    NEXT: INPTR;
  end record;

type GOALS;             --goalstack
type GOALSPTR is access GOALS;
type GOALS is
  record
    DATA: PREDICPTR;
    DEPTH: INTEGER;
    NEGATED: BOOLEAN;
    USEDRULE:INPTR;
    NEXT: GOALSPTR;
  end record ;

TOPGOAL,LASTGOAL:PREDICPTR;
GOALTOP,GOALBTM: GOALSPTR;
INTOP: INPTR;

procedure PUSHGOAL (P:in PREDICPTR; DEPTH: in INTEGER;
      NEGATED: in BOOLEAN; USING: in INPTR) ;

procedure POPGOAL(P:out PREDICPTR ; D: out INTEGER;
      NEGATED: out BOOLEAN; USING: out INPTR) ;

procedure PUSHRULE (RULE:in INTEGER;INTOP: in out INPTR) ;
```

-- POPRULE not necessary

end STACK;

-- "Stack" Processing PUSH/POP

```
package body STACK is

procedure  PUSHGOAL (P:in  PREDICPTR; DEPTH: in  INTEGER;
      NEGATED: in BOOLEAN; USING: in INPTR) is

GLLS: GOALSPTR;
begin

GLLS:= new  GOALS;
GLLS.DATA:=P;
GLLS.DEPTH:=DEPTH;
GLLS.NEGATED:=NEGATED;
GLLS.USEDRULE:=USING;
GLLS.NEXT:=GOALTOP;
GOALTOP:=GLLS;
return ;
end  PUSHGOAL;


procedure  POPGOAL(P:out  PREDICPTR ; D: out  INTEGER;
      NEGATED: out BOOLEAN; USING: out INPTR) is

OLD: GOALSPTR;

begin
OLD:=GOALTOP;
P:=GOALTOP.DATA;
D:=GOALTOP.DEPTH;
NEGATED:=GOALTOP.NEGATED;
USING:=GOALTOP.USEDRULE;
GOALTOP:=GOALTOP.NEXT;
return ;
end  POPGOAL;

--note that we PUSH rules onto the in_use list.
-- the list can be searched for rules in use- access is not
```

-- limited to topmost item.

```
procedure  PUSHRULE (RULE:in  INTEGER;INTOP: in out INPTR) is

GLLS: INPTR;
begin

GLLS:= new  IN_USE;
GLLS.RULE:=RULE;
GLLS.NEXT:=INTOP;
INTOP:=GLLS;
return ;
end  PUSHRULE;

end STACK;
```

-- Procedures Which Deal with Bindings

with STRNG; use STRNG;
with LOGIC; use LOGIC;
with STACK; use STACK;

package BIND is

function   UNIFY(UIN:PREDICPTR; DUIN:INTEGER;
                 VIN:PREDICPTR; DVIN:INTEGER;
                 CONTEXT,FATHER,MOTHER: INTEGER) return BOOLEAN ;

procedure ANSWER ;

procedure EXPLAINIT ;

function   USERVERIFIES (TARGET: PREDICPTR; DD:INTEGER;
      NEG: in BOOLEAN;
      CURRULNUM: in RULERANGE; NEWSTRIND: PTRANGE)
              return FLOAT;

procedure GETRULE(RULOUT: out RULERANGE;
             TARGET: in PREDICPTR;
             INDEX:in out INDEXPTR;
             FOUND: out BOOLEAN;
             WHICH: out PTRANGE;
             RULESTK: in out INPTR)   ;

function QUOTED(P:PREDICPTR) return BOOLEAN ;

function CUT(P:PREDICPTR) return BOOLEAN ;

function BOUND (RULE: RULERANGE;
   PREDN: PTRANGE;DRULE: INTEGER) return PREDICPTR;

```
function  EVAL_DEMON(P:PREDICPTR) return  FLOAT ;

end BIND;
```

-- Package Body for Dealing with Variable Bindings

```
with STRNG; use STRNG;
with LOGIC; use LOGIC;
with HASH;  use HASH;
with READIN; use READIN;
with MATH; use MATH;
with TEXT_IO; use TEXT_IO;
with CLAUSERD; use CLAUSERD;
with LIVE; use LIVE;


package body BIND is

package INT_IO is new INTEGER_IO(NUM=>INTEGER);
package FLT_IO is new FLOAT_IO(NUM=>FLOAT);

-- is term a variable? variables begin with letters W, w or ?

function  IS_VAR(PREDIC: in  PREDICPTR ) return  BOOLEAN is
CH:CHARACTER;
TOKEN:PHRASE;
begin
TOKEN:= PREDIC.ITEM.TOKEN;
CH:=TOKEN(1);
if (CH='?' or  CH='W' or CH='w')
 and then PREDIC.NEXT=null then
   return TRUE;
else
   return FALSE;
end  if ;
end  IS_VAR;

-- is it an atom (variable or constant)?

function  IS_ATOM(U:in  PREDICPTR) return  BOOLEAN is

begin
if  U.NEXT=null then  return  TRUE;
```

```
else  return  FALSE;
end  if ;
end  IS_ATOM;

-- is the variable bound or free?

function  ISBOUND(VNAME:in  PREDICPTR; D: INTEGER) return  BOOLEAN is
PREVPTR,PTR: BINDPTR;
KEY:INTEGER;
FOUND: BOOLEAN;

begin
LOCATE(VNAME.ITEM,D,PTR,PREVPTR,KEY,FOUND);    -- lookup in hash table
if  not  FOUND then  return  FALSE;
else  return  ALIVE(PTR.CONTEXT);      -- is context active?
end  if ;            -- if dead, unbound
end  ISBOUND;

-- return binding of variable

procedure  VALUE(U:in  PREDICPTR;D: in  INTEGER;
          OV:out  PREDICPTR; ODPTH:out  INTEGER ) is

FOUND: BOOLEAN;
V:PREDICPTR;
P,PREV: BINDPTR;
KEY,DPTH:INTEGER;
DREK:SYMPTR;

begin
V:=U;DPTH:=D;
if U.ITEM.ARITHMETIC then
    -- its arithmetic variable, not logical
    -- might be present in logical predicate e.g. sizeof who value1
    -- depth irrelevant (global)
    ODPTH:=0;
    if U.ITEM.DEFINED then
       V:= new PREDICATE;
```

```
      DREK:=new SYMBOL;
      DREK.VALUE:=U.ITEM.VALUE;
      V.ITEM:=DREK;
      OV:=V;
    else
      OV:=null;
    end if;
  end if;
--
loop
  DREK:=V.ITEM;
  if not IS_VAR(V) then
    ODPTH:=DPTH;
    OV:=V;
    return ;
  else
    --if variable bound, its in binding hash table
    LOCATE(DREK,DPTH,P,PREV,KEY,FOUND);
    if not FOUND then  exit ;
    else
      DPTH:=P.IDENT;
      V:=P.TEXT ;
    end  if ;
  end  if ;
end  loop ;
OV:=V;
ODPTH:=DPTH;
return;
end  VALUE;


-- LISP CAR = head of list function

function  CAR( U : in  PREDICPTR) return  PREDICPTR is
P:PREDICPTR;
begin
P:= new  PREDICATE;
P.NEXT:=null;
P.ITEM:=U.ITEM;
```

```
return  P;
end  CAR;

-- do occurs check if option is specified

function  NOOCCURS(UIN:PREDICPTR;DUIN:INTEGER;
              VIN:PREDICPTR;DVIN:INTEGER) return  BOOLEAN is
U,V,W:PREDICPTR;
DU,DV,DW:INTEGER;
SYM: SYMPTR;

begin
if  NOOCCK then  return  TRUE; end  if ;
U:=UIN; V:=VIN; DU:=DUIN; DV:=DVIN;
<<DOIT>>
if V=null then  return  TRUE;end  if ;
  if IS_VAR(V) then
    if ISBOUND(V,DV) then
      VALUE (V,DV,W,DW);
      V:=W;
      DV:=DW;
    end  if ;
  end  if ;
    if IS_ATOM(V) then
      if  U.ITEM=V.ITEM and  DU=DV then  return  FALSE;
      else  return  TRUE;
      end  if ;
    else
      if NOOCCURS(U,DU,CAR(V),DV) then
        V:=V.NEXT;
        goto DOIT;
      else  return  FALSE;
      end  if ;
    end  if ;
end  NOOCCURS;
```

-- attempt unification of two predicate terms

```
function  UNIFY( UIN:PREDICPTR; DUIN:INTEGER;
              VIN:PREDICPTR; DVIN:INTEGER;
              CONTEXT,FATHER,MOTHER: INTEGER) return  BOOLEAN is
U,V,VALU:PREDICPTR;
DU,DV,DVALUE: INTEGER;
OPPOSITE: BOOLEAN;
begin
U:=UIN;
V:=VIN;
DU:=DUIN;
DV:=DVIN;
<<DOIT>>
if U=null and  V=null then
  return  TRUE;   --done
elsif  U=null or  V=null then
  return  FALSE;   -- one longer than other
end  if ;
if IS_VAR(U) then
  if not ISBOUND(U,DU) then --try to bind variable
    if NOOCCURS(U,DU,V,DV) then
      VALUE(V,DV,VALU,DVALUE);
      INSTALL(U.ITEM,DU,CONTEXT,FATHER,MOTHER
      ,DVALUE,VALU);
      return  TRUE;
    else
      return  FALSE;
    end  if ;
  else          --already bound-consistently?
    VALUE(U,DU,VALU,DVALUE);
    U:=VALU;
    DU:=DVALUE;
    goto  DOIT;
  end  if ;
elsif IS_VAR(V) then          -- try to bind U variable
  <<DOV>>
  if not ISBOUND (V,DV) then
    if NOOCCURS(V,DV,U,DU) then
      INSTALL(V.ITEM,DV,CONTEXT,FATHER,MOTHER,DU,U);
```

```
        return  TRUE;
      else
        return  FALSE;
      end  if ;
    else
      VALUE(V,DV,VALU,DVALUE);
      V:=VALU;
      DV:=DVALUE;
      if  IS_VAR(V) then  goto  DOV; end  if ;
    end  if ;
  elsif U.NEXT=null and  then  V.NEXT=null THEN
    if U.ITEM /= V.ITEM then
      return  FALSE;
    else
      return  TRUE;
    end  if ;
  end  if ;
  if UNIFY(CAR(U),DU,CAR(V),DV,CONTEXT,FATHER,MOTHER) then
-- try to unify first atom, recursively go atom by atom
    U:=U.NEXT;
    V:=V.NEXT;
    goto  DOIT;
  else
    return  FALSE;
  end  if ;
end  UNIFY;

-- print out an answer

procedure  ANSWER is
K,J:INTEGER;
P,Q,R:PREDICPTR;
S,T:SYMPTR;
begin
for K in  1..NUMGOALS loop
  P:=GOALPTR(K);
  loop
    Q:=CAR(P);
```

```
    if IS_VAR(Q) then
       VALUE(Q,0,R,J);
       NEW_LINE;PUT(" ANSWER: ");PRINT(R.ITEM.TOKEN);
       PUT(" is "); PRINT(Q.ITEM.TOKEN);
     end if ;
     P:=P.NEXT;
     if P=null then  exit ; end if ;
   end loop ;
 end loop ;
 end ANSWER;

-- explain answer- what variables were bound to what constants via
-- the resolution of which rules

procedure  EXPLAINIT is
I,J:INTEGER;B:BINDPTR;
begin
for I in  1..HASHSIZE loop
   B:=HASHTABLE(I);
   if B/=null then
     loop
       if B=null then  exit  ; end if ;
       J:=B.DEPTH;
       if J=0 or  else  ALIVE(J) then
         NEW_LINE;PUT("BOUND ");
         PRINT(B.NAME.TOKEN);PUT(" CONTEXT ");
         INT_IO.PUT(B.DEPTH);PUT(" TO ");
         PRINT(B.TEXT.ITEM.TOKEN);PUT(" CONTEXT ");
         INT_IO.PUT(B.IDENT);
         PUT(" RULES=");INT_IO.PUT(B.FATHER);
         INT_IO.PUT(B.MOTHER);
         PUT(" at ");INT_IO.PUT(B.CONTEXT);
       end if ;
       B:=B.NEXT;
     end  loop ;
   end  if ;
end loop ;
end EXPLAINIT;
```

```
-- query the user as to a fact
-- presently designed to do so only if no relevant rules
-- user can ask why and be told status of the rule being applied.

function  USERVERIFIES (TARGET: PREDICPTR; DD:INTEGER;
        NEG: in BOOLEAN;
        CURRULNUM: in RULERANGE; NEWSTRIND: PTRANGE)
              return  FLOAT is
CH:CHARACTER;
I,J:INTEGER;
ANTECEDENT: PHRASE;
CF: FLOAT;

begin
if CURRULNUM<1 or else NEWSTRIND<1  then
  return 0.0;
end if;
loop
  NEW_LINE;PUT(" is  IT TRUE THAT ");PRINTPRED(TARGET,DD);
  if NEG then
    PUT(" IS FALSE");
  end if;
  PUT("?");
  NEW_LINE;
  PUT(" ANSWER Y,N or  W for  EXPLANATION WHY THIS QUESTION");
  GET(CH);
  case  CH is
    when  'y'|'Y' =>
      if not EXHAUSTIVE then  return  1.0;
      else
        PUT(" ENTER CONFIDENCE FACTOR");
        FLT_IO.GET(CF);
        return  CF;
      end  if ;
    when  'n'|'N' =>
      return  0.0;
    when  'w'|'W' =>
```

```
        NEW_LINE;
        PUT(" TRYING TO use  RULE NUMBER ");
        INT_IO.PUT(CURRULNUM);
        I:=NEWSTRIND;
        loop
          I:=I-1;
          if I<RULEINDX(CURRULNUM)
            then  exit ;
          else
            NEW_LINE;
            PUT(" I KNOW THAT ");
            PRINTPRED(RULES(I),0);
          end  if ;
        end  loop ;
        I:=NEWSTRIND;
        loop
          ANTECEDENT:=RULES(I).ITEM.TOKEN;
          if I=RULEINDX(CURRULNUM+1)-1 then
            ANTECEDENT:=RULES(I).ITEM.TOKEN;
            NEW_LINE;PUT(" TO SHOW ");
            PRINTPRED(RULES(I),0);
            NEW_LINE;
            exit ;
          else
            NEW_LINE; PUT(" I NEED TO KNOW ");
            PRINTPRED(RULES(I),0);
          end  if ;
          I:=I+1;
        end  loop ;
      when others  =>
          PUT(" type  Y,N,OR W ");
    end  case ;
  end  loop ;
end  loop ;
end  USERVERIFIES;

-- find the next relevant rule

procedure  GETRULE(RULOUT: out  RULERANGE;
```

```
                TARGET: in  PREDICPTR;
                INDEX:in  out  INDEXPTR;
                FOUND: out  BOOLEAN;
                WHICH: out PTRANGE;
                RULESTK: in out INPTR)      is
-- on input:
--   TARGET: predicate term to resolve
--   INDEX : current state of index
--   RULESTK: rules in use
-- on output:
--   FOUND : true if usable rule found
--   RULOUT: rule number if one found
--   WHICH : the term of the rule on which to resolve
--   INDEX, RULESTK: suitably modified to reflect new rule in use


USING: INPTR;
RUL,LOOPRULE: RULERANGE;

begin
WHICH:=0;
RULOUT:=0;
FOUND:=TRUE;
if INDEX=null then
   INDEX:=TARGET.ITEM.INDX;
else
   INDEX:=INDEX.NEXT;
end  if ;
<<RETRY>>
if INDEX=null then
   FOUND:=FALSE;
   return ;
end  if ;
RUL:= INDEX.RULENUM;
WHICH:=INDEX.NUMSTR;
-- check for circularity
if NOLOOP then
   RULOUT:=RUL;
```

```
    return;
  end if;
  USING:=RULESTK;
  loop
    if USING=null then exit; end if;
    LOOPRULE:=USING.RULE;
    if LOOPRULE=RUL then
      NEW_LINE;
      PUT(" REJECTING LOOPING RULE# ");INT_IO.PUT(RUL);
      INDEX:=INDEX.NEXT;
      goto RETRY;
    end if;
    USING:=USING.NEXT;
  end loop;
  RULOUT:=RUL;
  PUSHRULE(RUL,RULESTK);
  return ;
  end  GETRULE;
```

-- is predicate non-logical?

```
function  QUOTED(P:PREDICPTR) return  BOOLEAN is
C:CHARACTER;
begin
C:=P.ITEM.TOKEN(1);
if  C="'" then  return  TRUE;
else  return  FALSE;
end  if ;
end  QUOTED;
```

-- is it cut?

```
function  CUT(P:PREDICPTR) return  BOOLEAN is
C:CHARACTER;
begin
C:=P.ITEM.TOKEN(1);
if  C='!' then  return  TRUE;
else  return  FALSE;
```

```
end  if ;
end  CUT;


-- produce a fact by binding variables in a rule

function  BOUND (RULE: RULERANGE;
   PREDN: PTRANGE;DRULE: INTEGER) return  PREDICPTR is
DUMMY,HEAD,DPTH: INTEGER;
P,HD,FIRSTP,RETV,PREVIOUS:PREDICPTR;
FIRSTC:CHARACTER;
FIRST: BOOLEAN;

begin
HEAD:=PREDN;
HD:=RULES(HEAD);
PREVIOUS:=null;
FIRST:=TRUE;
loop
   if HD=null and  then
     PREVIOUS = null then
      NEW_LINE;
      PUT(" WARNING-null PREDICATE HEAD");
      return  null ;
   end if ;
   P:=CAR(HD);
   VALUE(P,DRULE,RETV,DUMMY);
   P.ITEM:=RETV.ITEM;
   P.NEXT:=null;
   if FIRST then
      FIRSTP := P;
      FIRST := FALSE;
   end if ;
   if PREVIOUS/=null then
      PREVIOUS.NEXT := P;
   end if ;
   HD:=HD.NEXT;
   if HD=null
```

```
      then exit ;
    end if ;
    PREVIOUS:=P;
end loop ;
return FIRSTP;
end BOUND;


-- evaluate non-logical predicates
-- these may be "demons," i.e. have side effects
-- this version for backward shell

function EVAL_DEMON(P:PREDICPTR) return FLOAT is
C:CHARACTER;
begin
C:=P.ITEM.TOKEN(2);
if C='T' or C='t' then
   PUT(" demon ");PRINTPRED(P,0);PUT(" IS TRUE");
   return 1.0;
elsif C='F' or C='f' then
   PUT(" demon ");PRINTPRED(P,0);PUT(" IS FALSE");
return 0.0;
elsif C='#' then  return MATHD(P.NEXT);
else
   return 1.0;
end if ;
end EVAL_DEMON;



end BIND;
```

```
-- Package for Maintaining Contexts (Depths) of
-- Variable bindings

package LIVE is

function ALIVE ( DEPTH: in INTEGER) return BOOLEAN;

function NEWDEPTH (OLDDEPTH: in INTEGER) return INTEGER;

procedure RELEASE( DEPTH: in INTEGER) ;

procedure ACTIVATE_CONTEXT( DEPTH: in INTEGER) ;

GDEPTH: INTEGER;
CONTUSED: INTEGER;
end LIVE;
```

```
-- Package for Maintaining Contexts (Depths) of
-- Bindings.   Fast version using fixed array.

with TEXT_IO; use TEXT_IO;

package  body LIVE is

MAXDEPTH : constant :=100;

LIVING_CONTEXTS : array (1..MAXDEPTH) of BOOLEAN;
INDEX:INTEGER;

function ALIVE ( DEPTH: in INTEGER) return BOOLEAN is

begin
return  LIVING_CONTEXTS(DEPTH);
end ALIVE;

procedure  RELEASE(DEPTH: in INTEGER ) is
I:INTEGER;
begin
if  DEPTH=0 then
  NEW_LINE;
  PUT(" WARNING- ATTEMPT TO RESET GOAL DEPTH ");
  return ;
end  if ;
LIVING_CONTEXTS(DEPTH):=FALSE;
if DEPTH=CONTUSED and CONTUSED=GDEPTH then
  GDEPTH:=GDEPTH-1;
end if;
end  RELEASE;

procedure  ACTIVATE_CONTEXT(DEPTH: in INTEGER ) is
begin
LIVING_CONTEXTS(DEPTH):=TRUE;
end  ACTIVATE_CONTEXT;

-- generate a new depth for binding
```

```
function NEWDEPTH(OLDDEPTH: in INTEGER) return INTEGER IS
begin
GDEPTH:=GDEPTH+1;
LIVING_CONTEXTS(GDEPTH):=TRUE;
CONTUSED:=GDEPTH;
return GDEPTH;
end NEWDEPTH;

begin
for INDEX in 1..MAXDEPTH loop
  LIVING_CONTEXTS(INDEX):=FALSE;
end loop;
GDEPTH:=0;
end LIVE;
```

```
-- Package for Maintaining Contexts (Depths) of
-- Bindings.  Flexible linked-list version.

with TEXT_IO; use TEXT_IO;

package  body LIVE is

package INT_IO is new INTEGER_IO(NUM=>INTEGER);

type CONTEXTLIST_EL;
type CONTXTPTR is access CONTEXTLIST_EL;
type CONTEXTLIST_EL is
  record
  DEPTH: INTEGER;
  NEXT: CONTXTPTR;
  end record;

CONTTOP:CONTXTPTR;

procedure  PUSHCON(DEPTH: in  INTEGER)is

CONTEXT_LIST: CONTXTPTR;
begin
CONTEXT_LIST:= new CONTEXTLIST_EL;
CONTEXT_LIST.DEPTH:=DEPTH;
CONTEXT_LIST.NEXT:=CONTTOP;
CONTTOP:=CONTEXT_LIST;
NEW_LINE;PUT(" PUSHING CONTEXT ");INT_IO.PUT(DEPTH);
return ;
end  PUSHCON;

procedure POPCON( D: out  INTEGER;
      USING: out CONTXTPTR) is

OLD: CONTXTPTR;
begin
D:=-1;
USING:=null;
```

```
OLD:=CONTTOP;
if OLD=null then return;end if;
D:=CONTTOP.DEPTH;
USING:=CONTTOP;
CONTTOP:=CONTTOP.NEXT;
return ;
end  POPCON;

function ALIVE(DEPTH:in INTEGER) return BOOLEAN is
CONT:CONTXTPTR;
begin
CONT:=CONTTOP;
loop
  if CONT=null then
    return FALSE;
  end if;
  if CONT.DEPTH=DEPTH then
    return TRUE;
  end if;
  CONT:=CONT.NEXT;
end loop;
end ALIVE;

procedure  RELEASE(DEPTH: in INTEGER) IS
I:INTEGER;
TOPCON:CONTXTPTR;
begin
if  DEPTH=0 then
  NEW_LINE;
  PUT(" WARNING- ATTEMPT TO RESET GOAL DEPTH ");
  return ;
end  if ;
TOPCON:=CONTTOP;
loop
  if TOPCON=null then return; end if;
  I:=TOPCON.DEPTH;
  if (I/=DEPTH) then
    NEW_LINE;PUT(" attemp to release context ");
```

```
    INT_IO.PUT(DEPTH);PUT(" BEFORE ");INT_IO.PUT(I);
  else
    CONTTOP:=TOPCON.NEXT;
    NEW_LINE;PUT(" RELEASING CONTEXT ");
    INT_IO.PUT(DEPTH);PUT(" AND LATER");
    if CONTUSED=DEPTH and GDEPTH=DEPTH then
      GDEPTH:=GDEPTH-1;
    end if;
    return;
  end if;
  TOPCON:=TOPCON.NEXT;
end loop;
end RELEASE;

function NEWDEPTH(OLDDEPTH: in INTEGER) return INTEGER is
begin
GDEPTH:=GDEPTH+1;
PUSHCON(GDEPTH);
CONTUSED:=OLDDEPTH;
return GDEPTH;
end NEWDEPTH;

procedure ACTIVATE_CONTEXT( DEPTH: in INTEGER) is

begin
PUSHCON(DEPTH);
end ACTIVATE_CONTEXT;

begin
CONTTOP:=null;
GDEPTH:=0;
end LIVE;
```

-- Index Goals to Relevant Rules and Cross-Index Rules

with LOGIC; use LOGIC;

package RULEIND is

procedure RULESINDEX ;   --cross-index rules

procedure GOALINDEX(HYP: in PREDICPTR; GOALNUM: in INTEGER;
      NEGATED: in BOOLEAN) ; -- index goals
end RULEIND;

-- Index Goals to Relevant Rules and Cross-Index Rules

```
with STRNG; use STRNG;
with LOGIC; use LOGIC;
with READIN;use READIN;
with CLAUSERD; use CLAUSERD;
with TEXT_IO;use TEXT_IO;

package body RULEIND is

package INT_IO is new INTEGER_IO(NUM=>INTEGER);
package FLT_IO is new FLOAT_IO(NUM=>FLOAT);

-- index rule predicates to relevant predicates in other rules
-- as non-Horn clauses allowed, any predicate term can be a "head"

procedure  RULESINDEX is

HYPOTH,STRG: PHRASE;
HYP,HYPS: SYMPTR;
RULE,SOURCE:RULERANGE;
PREDICATE,HEAD,HEADTOP,HEADNUM:PTRANGE;
IND,OLD:INDEXPTR;
KOUNT:INTEGER;
NG1,NG2: BOOLEAN;

begin
for SOURCE in  1..NUMRULES loop      --loop over rules to index
   PREDICATE:=RULEINDX(SOURCE);
   HEADTOP:=RULEINDX(SOURCE+1)-1;
   if HEADTOP=PREDICATE then
     NEW_LINE;PUT(" RULE ");INT_IO.PUT(SOURCE);PUT(" is  A FACT");
   else
      for HEADNUM in PREDICATE..HEADTOP loop    --terms in rule
        NG1:=RULES(HEADNUM).NEGATED;
        HYPS:=RULES(HEADNUM).ITEM;
        if (HYPS.INDX=null) then
          STRG:=HYPS.TOKEN;
```

```
KOUNT:=0;
OLD:=null;
for RULE in  1..NUMRULES loop    --other rules
   for HEAD in         --terms in them
     RULEINDX(RULE)..(RULEINDX(RULE+1)-1) loop
      HYP:=RULES(HEAD).ITEM;
      NG2:=RULES(HEAD).NEGATED;
      HYPOTH:= HYP.TOKEN;
      if HYP=HYPS then
        if SOURCE=RULE and (NG2 xor NG2)
         then
          NEW_LINE;
          PUT(" POSSIBLE-SELF-REFERENCE RULE ");
          INT_IO.PUT(RULE);
        end  if ;
        IND:= new  INDEX;
        IND.RULENUM:=RULE;
        IND.NUMSTR:=HEAD;
        IND.NEXT:=null;
        if HYP.INDX=null then
          IND.NEXT:=null;
          HYP.INDX:=IND  ;
        else
           OLD.NEXT:=IND;
        end  if ;
        OLD:=IND;
        KOUNT:=KOUNT+1;
      end  if ;
    end loop;
   end loop ;
   NEW_LINE;PUT(" ANTECEDENT "); PRINT(STRG);
   PUT(" UNIFIES with  ");
   INT_IO.PUT(KOUNT);PUT(" RULES");
  end if ;
 end loop ;
end if ;
end  loop ;
end  RULESINDEX;
```

-- index an individual goal to relevant rules

```
procedure  GOALINDEX(HYP: in  PREDICPTR; GOALNUM: in  INTEGER;
      NEGATED: in BOOLEAN) is

HYPOTH: PHRASE;
RULE:RULERANGE;
HEADTOP,HEAD:RULERANGE;
SPTR1,SPTR2:SYMPTR;
IND,OLD:INDEXPTR;
KOUNT:INTEGER;
DREK:PREDICPTR;

begin
KOUNT:=0;
SPTR1:=HYP.ITEM;
OLD:=null;
if  SPTR1.INDX/=null then  return ;end  if ;
for RULE in  1..NUMRULES loop               --loop over rules
   HEADTOP:=  RULEINDX(RULE+1)-1;
   for HEAD in RULEINDX(RULE)..HEADTOP loop      -- over terms in rules
     SPTR2:=  RULES(HEAD).ITEM;
     if SPTR1=SPTR2 and (NEGATED xor RULES(HEAD).NEGATED) then
        IND:= new  INDEX;
        IND.RULENUM:=RULE;
        IND.NEXT:=  null ;
        IND.NUMSTR:=  HEAD;
        KOUNT:=KOUNT+1;
        if HYP.ITEM.INDX=null then
           HYP.ITEM.INDX:=IND  ;
        else
           OLD.NEXT:=IND;
        end  if ;
        OLD:=IND;
     end  if ;
   end loop;
end loop ;
```

```
NEW_LINE;PUT(" GOAL ");INT_IO.PUT(GOALNUM);
PUT(" with ");INT_IO.PUT(KOUNT);PUT(" APPLICABLE RULES");
if HYP.ITEM.INDX/=null then return ; end if ;
PUT_LINE(" PROBLEM- GOAL WITHOUT APPLICABLE RULES");
end GOALINDEX;

end RULEIND;
```

```
-- Confidence Factor Combination Rules

-- A variety of bodies are possible for Bayesin, MYCIN, fuzzy set models

package ANDOR is

function PROBAND(X,Y: in FLOAT) return FLOAT;

function PROBOR(X,Y: in FLOAT) return FLOAT;

end ANDOR;
```

```
-- Confidence/ Certainty Factor Combination Rules:
-- MYCIN-like model:    -1 <= factor <= 1

with TEXT_IO; use TEXT_IO;

package body ANDOR is

package FLT_IO is new FLOAT_IO(NUM=>FLOAT);

procedure BOUND(X: in FLOAT) is
MIN: constant FLOAT := -1.0;
MAX: constant FLOAT := 1.0;
begin
if X > MIN and then X < MAX then return; end if;
--warn but do not kill
NEW_LINE;PUT(" Confidence factor out of bounds");FLT_IO.PUT(X);
end BOUND;

function  PROBAND(X,Y: in FLOAT) return  FLOAT is
begin
BOUND(X);BOUND(Y);
return  X*Y;
end  PROBAND;

function MIN(X,Y: in FLOAT) return FLOAT is

begin
BOUND(X);BOUND(Y);
if X > Y then
  return Y;
else
  return X;
end if;
end MIN;

function  PROBOR(X,Y: in FLOAT) return  FLOAT is

begin
```

```
BOUND(X);BOUND(Y);
if X > 0.0 and then Y > 0.0 then
      return  X+Y–X*Y ;
elsif X < 0.0 and then Y < 0.0 then
      return   X+Y+X*Y ;
else
  return  (X+Y)/(1.0–MIN(X,Y));
end if;
end  PROBOR;

end ANDOR;
```

```
-- Confidence/ Certainty Factor Combination Rules:
-- Fuzzy set-theory model:    0 <= factor <= 1

with TEXT_IO; use TEXT_IO;
package body ANDOR is

package FLT_IO is new FLOAT_IO(NUM=>FLOAT);

procedure BOUND(X: in FLOAT) is
MIN: constant FLOAT := 0.0;
MAX: constant FLOAT := 1.0;
begin
if X > MIN and then X < MAX then return; end if;
--warn but do not kill
NEW_LINE;PUT(" Confidence factor out of bounds");FLT_IO.PUT(X);
end BOUND;

function MAX(X,Y: in FLOAT) return FLOAT is

begin
BOUND(X);BOUND(Y);
if X < Y then
  return Y;
else
  return X;
end if;
end MAX;

function MIN(X,Y: in FLOAT) return FLOAT is

begin
BOUND(X);BOUND(Y);
if X > Y then
  return Y;
else
  return X;
end if;
end MIN;
```

```
function  PROBAND(X,Y: in FLOAT) return  FLOAT is
begin
return  MIN(X,Y);
end  PROBAND;

function  PROBOR(X,Y: in FLOAT) return  FLOAT is

begin
return MAX(X,Y);
end  PROBOR;

end ANDOR;
```

```
-- Confidence Factor Combination Rules
-- Bayesian Probability

with TEXT_IO; use TEXT_IO;

package body ANDOR is

package FLT_IO is new FLOAT_IO(NUM=>FLOAT);

procedure BOUND(X: in FLOAT) is
MIN: constant FLOAT := 0.0;
MAX: constant FLOAT := 1.0;
begin
if X > MIN and then X < MAX then return; end if;
--warn but do not kill
NEW_LINE;PUT(" Confidence factor out of bounds");FLT_IO.PUT(X);
end BOUND;

function  PROBAND(X,Y: in FLOAT) return  FLOAT is
begin
BOUND(X);BOUND(Y);
return  X*Y;
end  PROBAND;

function  PROBOR(X,Y: in FLOAT) return  FLOAT is
begin
BOUND(X);BOUND(Y);
return    X+Y-X*Y ;
end  PROBOR;

end ANDOR;
```

```
-- Input Rules, Facts, and Goals
--for Backward-Chaining Expert System Shell

with STRNG; use STRNG;
with LOGIC; use LOGIC;
with CLAUSERD; use CLAUSERD;
package READIN is

GOALPTR: TERMARRAY ;                 --each goal
NUMGOALS: GOALRANGE;
NUMRULES: RULERANGE;
RULEPROB:array (1..MAX_RULE_COUNT) of  FLOAT;
NUMSTRRULES : RULERANGE;

-- user input:

FLOOR: FLOAT;              -- min TRUE conf.f.
EXHAUSTIVE,FACTOR,NOOCCK,EXPLAIN,NOLOOP,LOOPCK: BOOLEAN;-- opti
procedure  GETRULES  ;

end READIN;
```

-- Input Rules, Facts and Goals

```
with STRNG; use STRNG;
with LOGIC; use LOGIC;
with TEXT_IO; use TEXT_IO;
with CLAUSERD; use CLAUSERD;

package body READIN is
package INT_IO is new INTEGER_IO(NUM=>INTEGER);
package FLT_IO is new FLOAT_IO(NUM=>FLOAT);
```

-- principal input procedure

```
procedure  GETRULES is

RULEFILE: FILE_TYPE;
TXT: STRING(1..MAX_LENGTH_CLAUSE);
TEXT: LONGPHRASE;
KOUNT,LENGTHIS:INTEGER;
GOALS: PHRASE;
CHAR: CHARACTER;
NEGATED,ISNOT,ANTECED:BOOLEAN;

begin                --getrules body
--initialize
OPEN(RULEFILE,IN_FILE,"RULE5.DAT");
NUMGOALS:=0;
GET_LINE(RULEFILE, TXT,LENGTHIS);
STRING_TO_PHRASE(TXT,TEXT,LENGTHIS);
NEW_LINE;PUT(" EXPERT SYSTEM in  use  IS");NEW_LINE;PRINT(TEXT);

--query user for options
NEW_LINE;
PUT("DO YOU WANT EXHAUSTIVE SEARCH with  CONFIDENCE FACTORS?");
loop
  GET(CHAR);
  case CHAR is
   when  'y'|'Y'=>
```

```
      EXHAUSTIVE:=TRUE;
      exit ;
   when  'n'|'N'=>
      exit ;
   when  others  =>
      PUT(" type  Y or  N");NEW_LINE;
  end case ;
end loop ;
if EXHAUSTIVE then
  NEW_LINE;PUT(" ENTER FLOOR CONFIDENCE VALUE ");
  FLT_IO.GET(FLOOR);
end  if ;
NOOCCK:=TRUE;
NEW_LINE;PUT(" ENTER Y FOR OCCURS CHECK");
GET(CHAR);
if CHAR='Y' or CHAR='y' then
  NOOCCK:=FALSE;
end if;
EXPLAIN:=TRUE;
NOLOOP:=TRUE;
NEW_LINE;
PUT(" ENTER Y IF TEST TO PREVENT INFINITE LOOP OF RULES");
GET(CHAR);
if CHAR='Y' or CHAR='y' then
  NOLOOP:=FALSE;
end if;
FACTOR:=FALSE;
NEW_LINE;PUT(" ENTER Y TO PERFORM FACTORING ");
GET(CHAR);
if CHAR='Y' or CHAR='y' then
  FACTOR:=TRUE;
end if;
LOOPCK:= not NOLOOP;
NUMRULES:=1;
NUMSTRRULES:=1;
NEGATED:=FALSE;ISNOT:=FALSE;
ANTECED:=TRUE;
loop                  -- input goal(s)
```

```
GET__LINE(RULEFILE, TXT,LENGTHIS);
STRING_TO_PHRASE(TXT,TEXT,LENGTHIS);
if  LENGTHIS<1 then  exit ;
else
  READCLAUSE(TEXT,FALSE,GOALPTR,NUMRULES,
  NUMSTRRULES,NUMGOALS,
  NEGATED,ANTECED,ISNOT);
 end  if ;
end  loop ;
NEW__LINE;PUT(" NUMBER of  ANDED GOALS=");INT__IO.PUT(NUMGOALS);
NEGATED:=FALSE;ISNOT:=FALSE;
ANTECED:=TRUE;
loop                  -- input rules
  GET__LINE(RULEFILE,TXT,LENGTHIS);
  if  LENGTHIS<1 then  exit ; end  if ;
  STRING_TO_PHRASE(TXT,TEXT,LENGTHIS);
  READCLAUSE(TEXT,TRUE,GOALPTR,NUMRULES,
   NUMSTRRULES,NUMGOALS,
   NEGATED,ANTECED,ISNOT);
end  loop ;
if ANTECED then
  RULES(NUMSTRRULES-1).NEGATED:=
  not RULES(NUMSTRRULES-1).NEGATED;
end if;
RULEINDX(NUMRULES):=NUMSTRRULES;
NUMRULES:=NUMRULES-1;
CLOSE(RULEFILE);
-- more advanced program could input rule confidence factors individually
for KOUNT in  1..NUMRULES loop        --default conf. fact. rules
  RULEPROB(KOUNT):=0.90;
end  loop ;
end  GETRULES;

end READIN;
```

```
-- Utilities to Support Clause Input

with STRNG;use STRNG;
with LOGIC; use LOGIC;


package CLAUSERD is

type TERMARRAY is array (1..MAX_TERM_COUNT) of PREDICPTR;
type RULETERMS  is array (1..MAX_RULE_COUNT) of PREDICPTR;
-- USED FOR GOALS(BACKWARD) AND FACTS(FORWARD)

RULEINDX: array (1..MAX_RULE_COUNT) of  INTEGER;
--first term of each rule
RULES: array  (1..MAX_RULE_COUNT ) of  PREDICPTR;
--each predicate

procedure READCLAUSE(STRNG: in LONGPHRASE ; RULE: in BOOLEAN;
      TERM_PTR: in out TERMARRAY;
       NUMRULES,NUMSTRRULES, NUMTERM: in out INTEGER;
       NEGATED,ANTECED,ISNOT: in out BOOLEAN);

end CLAUSERD;
```

-- Utilities to Support the Input of Clauses

with STRNG; use STRNG;
with LOGIC; use LOGIC;

package body CLAUSERD is

NOTTOKEN,IFTOKEN,THENTOKEN,ELSETOKEN,ANDTOKEN,
        ORTOKEN: PHRASE;
P:INTEGER;

--locate symbol (token) in symbol table

procedure SEARCH(CURPTR: in out SYMPTR;
                PREVPTR: out SYMPTR;
                STRNG: in PHRASE;
                OFOUND: out BOOLEAN) is

COMP:INTEGER;
FOUND: BOOLEAN;

begin
FOUND:=FALSE;
loop   --traverse binary search tree
  PREVPTR:=CURPTR;
  COMP:=COMPAREPHRASES(STRNG,CURPTR.TOKEN);
  if COMP=0 then
    FOUND :=TRUE;
  elsif (COMP=-1) then
    CURPTR:=CURPTR.LEFT;
  else
    CURPTR:=CURPTR.RIGHT;
  end if ;
  if (FOUND or CURPTR=null) then exit;end if;
end loop;
OFOUND:=FOUND;
return ;

```
end  SEARCH;
```

--make a skeletal symbol table entry

```
procedure  MAKESYM(PTR:in out  SYMPTR; STRG: in  PHRASE) is
NEWPTR: SYMPTR;

begin
NEWPTR:= new  SYMBOL;
NEWPTR.TOKEN:=STRG;
NEWPTR.LEFT:=null;
NEWPTR.RIGHT:=null;
NEWPTR.INDX:=null;
NEWPTR.ARITHMETIC:=FALSE;
PTR:=NEWPTR;
end  MAKESYM;
```

-- input a rule,fact,or goal

```
procedure  READCLAUSE(STRNG: in  LONGPHRASE; RULE: in  BOOLEAN;
     TERM_PTR: in out TERMARRAY;
     NUMRULES,NUMSTRRULES,NUMTERM: in out INTEGER;
     NEGATED,ANTECED,ISNOT: in out BOOLEAN) is

I,OLDP,COMP,SIZE: INTEGER;
CHAR: CHARACTER;
PRED,LASTTOK: PHRASE;
FOUND,ISIF,ISTHEN,ISCONJ,ISPRE,ISPOST:BOOLEAN;
```

--make an individual predicate term
-- as a linked-list of tokens

```
procedure  MAKEPRED(OLDP:in  INTEGER;I:in  INTEGER) is

QUOTED:BOOLEAN;
POINTER,OLDPTR:PREDICPTR;
COUNTER,LOCALP:INTEGER;
C:CHARACTER;
```

```
CURPTR,PREVPTR: SYMPTR;

begin
QUOTED:=FALSE;          --always false-do lexical anal.
POINTER:= new  PREDICATE;
if RULE then       --rule
  RULES(NUMSTRRULES):=POINTER;
  POINTER.NEGATED:= NEGATED xor ANTECED;
else            --goal
  NUMTERM:=NUMTERM+1;
  POINTER.NEGATED:= not NEGATED;
  TERM_PTR(NUMTERM):=POINTER;
end  if ;
POINTER.NEXT:=null;
OLDPTR:=null;
LOCALP:=OLDP;
for COUNTER in  OLDP..(I) loop       --form symbols
   -- we could deliver quoted terms verbatim
   -- but it is simpler to do the lexical analysis here
   C:= STRNG(COUNTER);
   if ((C=' ' and  not  QUOTED)
     or  C=',') then
     LONGPHRASE_TO_PHRASE(STRNG,PRED,LOCALP,COUNTER-1);
     LOCALP:=COUNTER+1;
     if ROOT=null then
       MAKESYM(ROOT,PRED);
       CURPTR:=ROOT;
     else
       CURPTR:=ROOT;
       SEARCH(CURPTR,PREVPTR,PRED,FOUND);
       if not FOUND then
         MAKESYM(CURPTR,PRED);
         COMP:=COMPAREPHRASES(PREVPTR.TOKEN,PRED);
         if COMP=1 then
           PREVPTR.LEFT:=CURPTR;
         else  PREVPTR.RIGHT:=CURPTR;
         end  if ;
       end  if ;
```

```
  end  if ;
  if OLDPTR/=null then
    POINTER:= new  PREDICATE;
    POINTER.NEXT:=null;
    OLDPTR.NEXT:=POINTER;
  end  if ;
  POINTER.ITEM:=CURPTR;
  OLDPTR:=POINTER;
 end  if ;
end  loop ;
end  MAKEPRED;


-- is input symbol a terminator?

function ISTERM(INDEX,OFFSET: in INTEGER) return BOOLEAN is
ANSWER:BOOLEAN;
C: CHARACTER;
begin
if INDEX <= OFFSET then return FALSE; end if;
C:=STRNG(INDEX-OFFSET);
if C=',' or C=' ' then
  return TRUE;
else
  return FALSE;
end if;
end ISTERM;


begin              --loadrules body
P:=1;
I:=1;
loop
  CHAR:= STRNG(I);
  if  CHAR='$' then  exit ; end  if ;
  ISCONJ:=FALSE;
  ISPRE:=FALSE;
  ISPOST:=FALSE;
  SIZE:=1;
  if CHAR=' ' then
```

```
    if I=4 or else ISTERM(I,4) then
      LONGPHRASE_ TO_PHRASE(STRNG,LASTTOK,I-3,I-1);
      ISCONJ:=(COMPAREPHRASES(LASTTOK,ANDTOKEN)=0);
      ISPRE:= (COMPAREPHRASES(LASTTOK,NOTTOKEN)=0);
      if ISCONJ then SIZE:=5  ;end if;
    elsif I=3 or else ISTERM(I,3) then
      LONGPHRASE_ TO_PHRASE(STRNG,LASTTOK,I-2,I-1);
      ISCONJ:=(COMPAREPHRASES(LASTTOK,ORTOKEN)=0);
      ISPRE:= (COMPAREPHRASES(LASTTOK,IFTOKEN)=0);
      if ISCONJ then SIZE:=4  ;end if;
    elsif I=5 or else ISTERM(I,5) then
      LONGPHRASE_ TO_PHRASE(STRNG,LASTTOK,I-4,I-1);
      ISCONJ:=(COMPAREPHRASES(LASTTOK,ELSETOKEN)=0);
      ISPOST:= (COMPAREPHRASES(LASTTOK,THENTOKEN)=0);
      if ISPOST or ISCONJ then SIZE:=6  ;end if;
    end if;
  end if;
<<TERMI>>
if CHAR=',' or ISPRE or ISPOST or ISCONJ then
  LONGPHRASE_TO_PHRASE(STRNG,PRED,P,I-SIZE);
  OLDP:=P;
  if ISPOST then
    P:=I-SIZE+2;
  else
    P:=I+1;
  end if;
  ISIF:= (COMPAREPHRASES(PRED,IFTOKEN)=0);
  ISTHEN:=(COMPAREPHRASES(PRED,THENTOKEN)=0);
  if COMPAREPHRASES(PRED,NOTTOKEN)=0 then
      NEGATED:=TRUE; ISNOT:=TRUE;
  end  if ;
  if ISTHEN then
    ANTECED:=FALSE;
  end if;
  if ISIF then
    if ANTECED and (NUMRULES>1) then
      RULES(NUMSTRRULES-1).NEGATED:=
      not RULES(NUMSTRRULES-1).NEGATED;
```

```
          end if;
          RULEINDX(NUMRULES):=NUMSTRRULES;
          NUMRULES:=NUMRULES+1;
          ANTECED:=TRUE;
        end if ;
        if not (ISNOT or ISIF or ISTHEN) then
          MAKEPRED(OLDP,I+1-SIZE);
          if RULE then
            NUMSTRRULES:=NUMSTRRULES+1;
          end if ;
          NEGATED:=FALSE;
        end if ;
      end if ;
      ISNOT:=FALSE;
      if not ISPOST then
        I:=I+1;
        if I>MAX_LENGTH_CLAUSE then
          exit;
        end if;
      else
        ISPOST:=FALSE;
        ISCONJ:=FALSE;
        ISPRE:=FALSE;
        SIZE:=1;
        CHAR:=',';
        goto TERMI;
      end if;
    end loop ;
exception
      when  CONSTRAINT_ERROR =>   -- non-catastrophic if trouble
            return ;
end READCLAUSE;

procedure TOKEN_INIT is
begin
STRING_TO_PHRASE("if$",IFTOKEN);
STRING_TO_PHRASE("then$",THENTOKEN);
STRING_TO_PHRASE("not$",NOTTOKEN);
```

```
STRING_TO_PHRASE("or$",ORTOKEN);
STRING_TO_PHRASE("else$",ELSETOKEN);
STRING_TO_PHRASE("and$",ANDTOKEN);
end TOKEN_INIT;

begin
TOKEN_INIT;
end CLAUSERD;
```

var: who,?z?y ?x; with CUT ans:john,al
grandp dave who,

if,f ?x ?z,!,f ?z ?y,then,grandp ?x ?y,
if,then,f irving dave,
if,f dave lou,
if,f dave george,
if,f lou john,
if,f john mike,
if,f lou al,
if,f mike pete,
if,f dave mary,
if,f mary sue,

back

EXPERT SYSTEM in use IS
var: who,?z?y ?x; with CUT ans:john,al
DO YOU WANT EXHAUSTIVE SEARCH with CONFIDENCE FACTORS?

                                                                    y
ENTER FLOOR CONFIDENCE VALUE
                                        0.1

ENTER Y FOR OCCURS CHECKy
ENTER Y IF TEST TO PREVENT INFINITE LOOP OF RULES

                                                        y
ENTER Y TO PERFORM FACTORING
                                        y
NUMBER of ANDED GOALS=   1
ANTECEDENT f UNIFIES with   11 RULES
ANTECEDENT ! UNIFIES with   1 RULES
ANTECEDENT grandp UNIFIES with   1 RULES
RULE   2 is A FACT
RULE   3 is A FACT
RULE   4 is A FACT
RULE   5 is A FACT
RULE   6 is A FACT
RULE   7 is A FACT
RULE   8 is A FACT
RULE   9 is A FACT
RULE   10 is A FACT
VERIFY-PREVRULE=   0
TO PROVE grandp dave who at DEPTH=   0 NEGATED FOUND
TO UNIFY   1   0   0   1
UNIFY SUCCESS
PUSHED GOAL= f ?z ?y at DEPTH=   1
PUSHED GOAL= ! at DEPTH=   1
PUSHED GOAL= f ?x ?z at DEPTH=   1
VERIFY-PREVRULE=   1
TO PROVE f ?x ?z at DEPTH=   1 NEGATED
REJECTING LOOPING RULE#   1
REJECTING LOOPING RULE#   1 FOUND

```
TO UNIFY    2    1    1    2
TO UNIFY    2    1    1    3
UNIFY SUCCESS
VERIFY-PREVRULE=    3
CUT AT CONTEXT=    2
CUT RETURNED  CONTEXT    2 TEMPORARY:    2 WORKING:    1
TO PROVE  f ?z ?y at  DEPTH=    1 NEGATED
REJECTING LOOPING RULE#    1
REJECTING LOOPING RULE#        1 FOUND
TO UNIFY    3    1    1    2
TO UNIFY    3    1    1    3
TO UNIFY    3    1    1    4
TO UNIFY    3    1    1    5
UNIFY SUCCESS
VERIFY-PREVRULE=    5
ANSWER: john is  who
BOUND who CONTEXT    0 TO john CONTEXT    3 RULES=    5    1 at
BOUND ?y CONTEXT    1 TO who CONTEXT    0 RULES=    1    0 at    1
BOUND ?z CONTEXT    1 TO lou CONTEXT    2 RULES=    3    1 at    2
BOUND ?x CONTEXT    1 TO dave CONTEXT    0 RULES=    1    0 at    1
-ON TO NEXT  RULE
TO UNIFY    4    1    1    6
TO UNIFY    4    1    1    7
UNIFY SUCCESS
VERIFY-PREVRULE=    7
ANSWER: al is  who
BOUND who CONTEXT    0 TO al CONTEXT    4 RULES=    7    1 at    4
BOUND ?y CONTEXT    1 TO who CONTEXT    0 RULES=    1    0 at    1
BOUND ?z CONTEXT    1 TO lou CONTEXT    2 RULES=    3    1 at    2
BOUND ?x CONTEXT    1 TO dave CONTEXT    0 RULES=    1    0 at    1
-ON TO NEXT  RULE
TO UNIFY    5    1    1    8
TO UNIFY    5    1    1    9
TO UNIFY    5    1    1    10
NO MORE RELEVANT RULES FOUND
-ON TO NEXT  RULE
NO MORE RELEVANT RULES FOUND
GOAL TRUE WITH CONFIDENCE= 8.91000E-01
```

var: who,?z?y ?x;cannot omit if ,then optional. ans:john,al,sue
grandp dave who,

if,f ?x ?z,f ?z ?y,then,grandp ?x ?y,
if,then,f irving dave,
if,f dave lou,
if,f dave george,
if,f lou john,
if,f john mike,
if,f lou al,
if,f mike pete,
if,f dave mary,
if,f mary sue,

First example without cut operator (!).

Finds 3 solutions, total confidence .8831361 .

Jerardi test–NEW SYNTAX
freezing,

if raining then precip,
if snowing then precip,
if freezing and precip then snowing,
if not freezing,precip,raining,
if raining,then,not,snowing,
if snowing,

back

EXPERT SYSTEM in use IS
Jerardi test-NEW SYNTAX
DO YOU WANT EXHAUSTIVE SEARCH with CONFIDENCE FACTORS?y
ENTER FLOOR CONFIDENCE VALUE
                                    0.1

ENTER Y FOR OCCURS CHECKy
ENTER Y IF TEST TO PREVENT INFINITE LOOP OF RULES
                                                        y
ENTER Y TO PERFORM FACTORING
                                        y
NUMBER of ANDED GOALS=   1
ANTECEDENT raining UNIFIES with   3 RULES
ANTECEDENT precip UNIFIES with   4 RULES
ANTECEDENT snowing UNIFIES with   4 RULES
ANTECEDENT freezing UNIFIES with   2 RULES
RULE   6 is A FACT
VERIFY-PREVRULE=   0
TO PROVE freezing at DEPTH=   0 NEGATED FOUND
TO UNIFY   1   0   0   3
TO UNIFY   1   0   0   4
UNIFY SUCCESS
PUSHED GOAL= raining at DEPTH=   1
PUSHED GOAL= precip at DEPTH=   1
VERIFY-PREVRULE=   4
TO PROVE precip at DEPTH=   1 NEGATED FOUND
TO UNIFY   2   1   4   1
UNIFY SUCCESS
PUSHED GOAL= raining at DEPTH=   2
VERIFY-PREVRULE=   1
TO PROVE raining at DEPTH=   2 NEGATED
REJECTING LOOPING RULE#   1
REJECTING LOOPING RULE#   4 FOUND
TO UNIFY   3   2   1   5
NO MORE RELEVANT RULES FOUND
-ON TO NEXT RULE

TO UNIFY   3   1   4   2
UNIFY SUCCESS
PUSHED GOAL= snowing at DEPTH=   3
VERIFY-PREVRULE=   2
TO PROVE snowing at DEPTH=   3 NEGATED
REJECTING LOOPING RULE#   2
REJECTING LOOPING RULE#   3 FOUND
TO UNIFY   4   3   2   5
TO UNIFY   4   3   2   6
UNIFY SUCCESS
VERIFY-PREVRULE=   6
TO PROVE raining at DEPTH=   1 FOUND
TO UNIFY   5   1   6   1
UNIFY SUCCESS
PUSHED GOAL= precip at DEPTH=   5
VERIFY-PREVRULE=   1
TO PROVE precip at DEPTH=   5
REJECTING LOOPING RULE#   1 FOUND
TO UNIFY   6   5   1   2
REJECTING LOOPING RULE#   3
REJECTING LOOPING RULE#   4
NO MORE RELEVANT RULES FOUND
-ON TO NEXT RULE
REJECTING LOOPING RULE#   4
TO UNIFY   6   1   6   5
UNIFY SUCCESS
PUSHED GOAL= snowing at DEPTH=   6
VERIFY-PREVRULE=   5
TO PROVE snowing at DEPTH=   6 NEGATED FOUND
TO UNIFY   7   6   5   2
REJECTING LOOPING RULE#   3
REJECTING LOOPING RULE#   5
TO UNIFY   7   6   5   6
UNIFY SUCCESS
VERIFY-PREVRULE=   6
-ON TO NEXT RULE
NO MORE RELEVANT RULES FOUND
-ON TO NEXT RULE

NO MORE RELEVANT RULES FOUND
-ON TO NEXT RULE
NO MORE RELEVANT RULES FOUND
-ON TO NEXT RULE
REJECTING LOOPING RULE#   3
REJECTING LOOPING RULE#   4
NO MORE RELEVANT RULES FOUND
-ON TO NEXT RULE
NO MORE RELEVANT RULES FOUND
GOAL TRUE WITH CONFIDENCE= 5.90490E-01
C:\TEMP>

Chapter 4

Forward-Chaining Expert System Shell.
Arithmetic

Overview

A forward-chaining expert system is presented. Arithmetic predicates are considered, and a Reverse-Polish parser is presented for use with such predicates. The discussion of rule-based systems is concluded with discussions of nonmonotonic logic, metaknowledge, truth-maintenance systems, and hybrid forward-backward chaining.

Forward Chaining

Forward chaining is generally simpler than backward chaining. We still use the same unification subroutine, but now we start with facts and attempt to unify with rule predicate terms. This is facilitated by keeping facts and rules in distinct databases. Because facts do not generally have variables, we can usually simplify the unification procedure. However, certain universal facts might represent Herbrand sentences (e.g., a religious rule-based system might posit "father God $?x$" to represent "God is everyone's father").

Forward chaining, being "fact-driven," is most suitable when there are a large number of possible final goals or answers (making backward-chaining unattractive) or when a few key facts can quickly rule out many possible final states. It is used by the language OPS5 [1] which implements the XCON expert system. This system was developed at Carnegie-Mellon for Digital Research Corporation to configure VAX system computers. Forward chaining appears particularly suitable for "event-driven" systems in which an expert system, in real-time, must respond to a changing environment. Our approach is less like that of OPS5 and similar to that of [2], in that as soon as a new fact is established we attempt to use it to establish new facts and to take appropriate actions. For event-driven situations in particular, this should be a more appropriate design.

Some backward-chaining systems claim to be able to forward-chain. This is generally achieved through a very liberal definition of forward chaining. For example, EXSYS version 3.1, with the FORWARD option, examines rules in the order of occurrence in the rule base, instead of backward-chaining for each goal in order. In this process, the order of the rules is extremely critical—the "facts" need to precede the rules which use them. VP-EX-PERT uses a similarly loose definition of forward chaining in order to claim to support it.

Similarly, backward chaining may be simulated in OPS5 [1], although it is somewhat cumbersome to do so. Goals are hypothesized as true facts and effectively checked for consistency with other facts.

Arithmetic Predicates

We have postponed to this chapter a discussion of arithmetic predicates. These are probably necessary for any useful rule-based expert system, whatever the chaining employed, since much of the information about the real world is quantitative rather than merely TRUE or FALSE. The implementation of arithmetic predicates is identical for forward- and backward-chaining systems.

There are many ways of parsing arithmetic expressions. We have chosen to implement a form of bottom-up or operator precedence parsing which produces an intermediate, parenthesis-free representation of the expression commonly called postfix or Polish notation. This method is useful as it provides a partially interpreted form of the expression which could be stored as such in an interpreted rule base. The lexical analyzer of GETRULES/LOADRULES is made to serve double duty in parsing these expressions, so spaces are needed as delimiters between all symbols.

In Polish or postfix notation, the arithmetic expression is converted into a linked list. The arithmetic expression is scanned from left to right. Variables, constants, and function names are placed in the postfix string (linked list of symbols and operators) as they are encountered. Operators are placed in a push-down stack until a lower-weight operator is encountered. An open parenthesis is stacked, while a close parenthesis pops operators off the stack and onto the postfix string until a matching open parenthesis is popped. If the end of the expression is denoted by a symbol, say #, this symbol is treated as the lowest-weight operator possible, and pops the entire stack contents. Next in weight is the assignment operator := and then logical comparisons such as =, >, <, <=, and >=, next and of equal weight + and —, next * and /, then **, and, last, a function evaluation (a unary operator). Some care must be taken to distinguish the unary and binary minus signs and to represent them as different operators on the stack, or else convert the unary minus into a normal binary minus. The latter approach would replace (– *b*) by 0 – *b*. It is more efficient to treat it as a unary operator, as we will do. It will be represented as the "@" character in the infix string. The unary minus will be recognized as it will be preceded by an open parenthesis, the assignment operator, or one of the comparison operators. All other minus signs (except in constants) being taken as a binary subtraction operator.

The postfix expression is evaluated left to right as follows. Operators are assumed to be of known arity, and operate on the appropriate number of values to their immediate left. The result of such a calculation is given a dummy name and replaces those operands and the operator, with scanning continuing. It is not necessary to store that temporary result in a storage register unless *n* subsequent operands are encountered in the scan of the postfix string followed by an operator of arity *n* or less. This scheme for the evaluation of postfix expressions is simply performed with a stack.

We define an exponentiation operation, ∧, similar to the notation of PASCAL. Unlike the Ada ** operator, it raises numbers to a type FLOAT power. We use a "trick" to have the function package MFUNCT do the calculation, but return the value NOTFUNCT during the conversion of infix to postfix so that ∧ is treated with the syntax appropriate to an operator.

Consider the example illustrated by the test driver, namely *Y* := *ABC* * (–*BA* + *ABC*∧*D*). The variable *Y* is immediately written to the postfix output string. The assignment operator is pushed onto the stack. The variable ABC is now written to the output list. The operator * is of greater weight that :=, so it is pushed onto the stack after it. The open parenthesis is placed directly onto the stack. The minus sign is detected as a unary minus, since it was preceded by the open parenthesis, so @ is stacked. The variable BA is written to the output. The addition operator + forces out the @, which is of greater weight, and is then pushed onto the stack, as no operator is heavier than the open parenthesis. The variable ABC is written to the output string. The exponentiation operator enters the stack as it is heavier than the addition operator +. Then D is written directly to the postfix string. The close parenthesis forces out the @ and + and then removes the matching open parenthesis from the stack. The output string now is

Y ABC BA @ABC D∧ +

while the stack is

*

:=

The end of expression "operation," of lower weight than any operator, forces out the * and then the :=. Thus, the postfix expression is

Y ABC BA @ABC D ^+ * :=

The postfix expression is evaluated from left to right. The first operator to be encountered, @, takes one argument (the definition of unary). The result is placed on the top of the accumulator stack. The result, in effect, is

Y ABC (–BA) ABC D ^ + * :=

Here, (– BA) denotes a pointer to the accumulator stack which contains the numerical value —BA. The next operator encountered, ^, causes the result of (ABC^D) to be pushed on the accumulator stack. The postfix expression is now, in effect,

Y ABC (– BA) (ABC ^ D) + * :=

Now the + is applied to the preceding operands, giving in effect:

Y ABC ((– BA) + ABC ^ D) * :=

Continuing the scan from where it had left off, the * operator is applied to the preceding two operands, giving effectively:

Y ABC*(– BA + ABC^D) :=

Finally, the assignment operator := is recognized and the computed value is assigned to the variable Y.

The sample program MDRIVE executes this example and two examples using functions. The function PUT is used to output the results of the calculation just discussed. This demonstrates the ability of the arithmetic package to retain variable values between predicate evaluations. Functions must be written in the form FUNCTIONAME (ARG1 ; ARG2 ; ...). It is permissible to have no arguments. In the current version of the program, ten is the maximum argument count; this may easily be changed. The MFUNCT package body must be altered to recognize any new functions which you desire to use. The start of the argument list is recorded in the postfix string by the & operator. This permits functions to have a variable number of arguments. Examples are the functions MIN and MAX, which return the minimum and maximum values, respectively, of a list of arguments. The binary function ATAN2 is used to illustrate a more complex function call. Note that, due to the use of a stack, it is simplest to present the function arguments to the function via the ARGVALUE array in reverse order.

Special-Action Predicates

Special predicates are available for asserting or retracting facts. The predicate "ASSERT ... causes the fact ... to be placed on the fact list. This differs from what normally happens when a fact is a consequent of a rule which is satisfied in that normally, an attempt is immediately made to apply the fact to the creation of other facts. Instead, "ASSERT f george mike would cause the fact f george mike to be indexed against the other facts and rules, and then be pushed to the top of the fact list, set the dependency list of this fact to the facts on the dependency stack, and set the used-by information of the facts on the dependency stack to indicate they had be used to support the fact. The processing of this fact would then cease. If the consequent had omitted the symbol "ASSERT after all this had been done the rules to this fact would be tested to see if any were now enabled to fire.

There are three predicates for "killing" facts: "DENY, "RETRACT, and "CANCEL. The first merely removes the indicated fact. The second removes all facts which are direct descendants of this fact. The last does a full search to cancel any fact which is dependent on this fact for its support. In the last two operations, the dependent facts are removed only if the specified fact is part of the sole support of the dependent fact. If there is an alternate chain of reasoning which supports the dependent fact, the dependent fact is not removed. Instead, its confidence is reduced according to Bayesian rules discussed in the previous chapter. The program keeps track of the number of facts retracted. Facts can be canceled, in effect, by reducing their confidence factor to 0.0 instead of actually removing them from the fact list. This has the virtue that any pointers to that fact will not give erroneous references, which would happen unless we removed references by the rule predicate term index lists to the canceled fact.

The used-by lists of other facts which had supported the dependent fact are not altered. Thus, on the final summary output a rule might say it was used to conclude a fact which had been removed. This was chosen as the most informative approach. If it is not desired, it would be easy to remove such information. For each removed fact, loop over the facts in its dependency list. For each of these facts, loop over the items in its used-by list and remove the one which points to the deleted fact. The code for doing this would be quite similar to the code for removing facts from the fact list.

The "DENY predicate is similar in effect to the REMOVE action in OPS5.

Nonmonotonic Logic

It is often assumed in the construction of an inference engine that once something is determined to be a true fact, it remains so. This is often an undesirable restriction. For example, it might be desirable to ask a what-if question, i.e., tentatively assert a fact, within the context of a forward-chaining system. For a backward-chaining system, of course, that type of question can often be resolved by making the fact a goal. The classic example is a default, e.g., assuming something is a fact (birds can fly in the classic example) unless this is contradicted later. Because rules and facts are generally not known with absolute certainty, the ability to retract a fact which has been guessed is often useful. Another possible example would be a real-time expert system which has to deal with a constantly changing environment. Various assumptions may have to be retracted as new information is received. The ability for "true" facts to be "falsified" is generally termed nonmonotonic reasoning. A number of expert systems support the ability to reason with a number of assumptions, often simultaneously. These different set of assumptions are called *worlds* or *views*.

The predicates for retracting facts listed above provide a flexible mechanism for nonmonotonic reasoning. The **"CANCEL** predicate, which will retract not only the fact itself but all the facts which it has lead to, is probably the most useful operator in this regard.

Heuristics, Metaknowledge

Exhaustive search methods, such as the depth-first search of the backward-chaining inference engine of Chapter 3 or the forward-chaining methods of this chapter, are complete in the sense discussed in Chapter 3, but can be quite slow. The reason is that they often spend inordinate amounts of time examining reasoning chains that are either unlikely or impossible. For this reason, it is quite desirable to have a smarter search procedure, which will examine the most promising rules first. These are not necessarily the rules most likely to succeed in establishing a fact, if that fact is itself of little value in determining what we are really after. Similarly, in a backward-chaining system, a tautological rule is of no value—what is needed is a rule which distinguishes between possibilities, and will help us eliminate a number of other rules as irrelevant. Smarter searches are generally called *heuristic*. The term heuristic generally refers to a method which is not guaranteed to give an exact answer. Thus, many (but not all) heuristic methods sacrifice completeness so as to get a good answer (most of the time) rapidly rather than the best answer after a lot of effort.

Heuristic methods can be strong or weak (in the sense of the definitions of these terms in Chapter 1). A weak heuristic makes little or no use of information about the specific problem domain. Instead, it might be a rule such as "when selecting which rule to attempt to use next from the potentially applicable rules, choose the rule with the fewest antecedent terms." A great many criteria could be imagined for the optimal order of rule choice. Typical schemes for weak rule selection compute a measure of the discriminating power of the rules, e.g., the maximum a posteriori probability that a goal is true given that the rule fires and given the known facts or established subgoals is compared to the average probability, and the rule which maximizes this difference is used.

Strong heuristics require more information than the rules and their confidence factors. This additional data is "metaknowledge," i.e., knowledge about knowledge. Rules might be given a numerical value, and we would then use the strongest rule. Search procedures such as the alpha-beta search (see Chapter 1), used principally in exploring possible moves in competitive games, need an inexpensively computed function to give them an estimate of the most likely ways to proceed. Such functions in chess estimate material advantage, area controlled, etc., to provide an educated guess. Similar information might be provided for rules, perhaps "learned" from previous runs of the expert system (see below). The value of a rule should be dynamic for maximum flexibility, rather than a static value which cannot change during the solution of the specific problem. There is an obvious tradeoff in the effort expended by the evaluator function—in that a more effective evaluator is probably more complicated and costly than a simpler one, which will generally give poorer guesses.

It is possible to enhance and hybridize the basic forward- and backward-chaining strategies, in order to attempt to gain the advantages of each. Backward-chaining systems tend to be unfocused and ask many questions whose answers are not really useful. It is therefore desirable to obtain a few facts to limit the scope of a search. Generally, this involves specifying whether a rule is allowed to act forward, or backward, or both, whether the rule is active (permitted to be applied), along with predicate terms whose "side effects" are to activate or deactivate rules (or groups of rules). A typical strategy for a diagnostic expert system might be something like:

1. Activate only a small set of rules whose answers will establish facts which will narrow down the diagnosis to certain categories. For example, if the diagnostic system is to fix a car which won't start, initially backward-chain on rules to query the user and establish if the problem is in the electrical or fuel systems.

2. Forward-chain from these facts to activate the appropriate rules to query and diagnose for the appropriate subset of relevant rules. Thus, we might have established in step 1 that the electrical system was probably faulty.

3. Loop back to 1, i.e., backward-chain using the active rules.

This iteration can continue until convergence, that is, until either no more rules fire or until we have arrived at a fact being established which is the diagnosis we desired. Such facts can be in a list (see below) of acceptable final diagnoses. At step 2, we can either choose to switch to backward chaining as soon as a potentially useful rule (or group) has been activated or let the second stage continue to establish whatever facts it can.

Comparison with OPS5

The OPS5 language has a somewhat different philosophy [1]. Rather than try to use facts instantly as they are deduced, a "conflict set" of "instantiations" or bindings of rules capable of firing is built up. Then a strategy, either one called LEX or a slightly different method named MEA, is used to choose one instantiation to employ. Because nonmonotonic reasoning is possible, the order of rule firing matters. The strategy controls this sequence of rule firings. The bindings or instantiations are kept in what is called working memory, while the rules are said to be in production memory. OPS5 compiles the rules using the RETE method [3] discussed next. It provides predicates for asserting, removing, and modifying the facts or bindings in working memory but not for tracking down dependent facts and removing or altering these.

Compiling Rules: RETE

For maximum speed, OPS5 uses the RETE method [1,3] for compiling the rules. The basic idea is to develop a network of rules to be traced given certain facts. Suppose we have two rules of the form

>   if a and b then d
>   if a and c then e

The key idea is to use the fact that both rules need fact a to fire. A network is created with the antecedent facts a, b, and d at one end:

When working memory is set to reflect that a has been established, this information is propagated along the network, in effect "priming" nodes c and e. This is said to improve efficiency, in that the validity of a is not tested separately by the two rules.

The RETE method trades memory for speed. It has been argued that this is not necessarily an attractive trade [4], particularly in real-time embedded

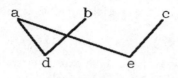

systems. Furthermore, changes to working memory must propagate through the network, which can be costly.

Various other methods can be used if the rules are to be compiled. For example, the hash table and standardizing apart are unnecessary if the variables can be assigned unique names. Rules can often be factored, i.e.,

> if a and b and c then d
> if a and b and e then f

could be converted to the set

> if a and b then intermediate
> if intermediate and c then d
> if intermediate and e then f

(with appropriate treatment of variables if necessary). This would prevent unnecessary backtracking.

The approach of OPS5, the nature of the RETE algorithm, and the MEA and LEX strategies are probably conditioned by its major application, the development of the XCON (formerly called R-1) expert system for configuring DEC VAX systems. The approach we have discussed as an alternative is perhaps more suited to an embedded application where we want appropriate action as soon as possible, rather than after all alternatives have been explored. As noted in the previous chapter, there is no ideal or perfect inference engine. This holds for forward-chaining systems as well.

Truth-Maintenance Systems

If nonmonotonic logic is employed, it is possible for contractions to arise. This usually occurs because of assumptions (defaults) which are inconsistent among the views or worlds.

A truth-maintenance system [5,6] is a system which is used in conjunction with an inference engine to detect such inconsistencies, report their existence to the inference engine, and often to suggest means of resolving the problem. This aid is of most value when a large fraction of the potential solution set must be considered [6], e.g., when multiple solutions are possible and/or an exhaustive list of possible solutions is needed.

Learning

There are a variety of ways in which an expert system can improve itself. Learning, of course, requires an ability to make alterations and remember these changes.

The simplest learning would be to alter the confidence factors or values of rules. A common model for this is the "economic" model [7]. Rules are given a bank account and must buy facts to satisfy themselves. They bid against each other. As it is undesirable to have a rule which may momentarily be richer than others to shut those rules out, or to bankrupt itself on one problem, it is desirable to have various rules to constrain the bidding, such a maximum bids and a stochastic element in the selection of the winning bid. Rules are then rewarded if they contribute to a successful goal or solution by having the "money" passed back down the chain (bucket-brigade method [7]), each rule paying off the rules which supported it. The poorest rules are periodically culled from the rule base.

How might new rules be developed? One approach mirrors Darwinian selection [7]. Rules "mate" with one another to produce new rules as their progeny, with the richer rules producing fewer child rules. A "genetic" model forms new rules by randomly exchanging predicate terms, as genes are randomly exchanged between chromosomes to cause mutations.

The Program

Data Structures

In the backward-chaining system, facts were merely a special case of rules, namely those rules without antecedent terms. In addition to the data structures representing the rules, a stack of goals (the original goal along with subgoals generated by the rules) and a stack of rules "in use" was kept. In the forward-chaining system, the representation of rules is identical to that of the backward-chaining system. Facts must be maintained in a separate list, however. Because of the forward-chaining or fact-driven architecture, a rule without antecedents would simply never fire (unless, of course, the system were designed so that all such rules were to fire initially and put themselves on the fact list). The fact list of the forward-chaining system plays a similar role to the goal stack of the backward-chaining or goal-driven system. Also analogous to the in-use stack is a dependency stack of facts which are currently in use for the current rule. This information is attached to the new fact actually deduced, both for later diagnostic purposes and for use when a fact is to be retracted.

A doubly-linked list (Fig. 4.1) is used to store the known facts. This additional complexity compared to the backward-chaining system is necessary to permit easy retraction of facts. The role of the various pointers (access types) in each record is illustrated by the figure. Each fact lists those facts which rely on its validity for their deduction via a linked list pointed to by the .USEDBY field. The elements in this list are linked via the .NEXT field. The .DEPEND field lists those facts upon which the given fact depends for its deduction. Again, subsequent elements which are also necessary are linked via the .NEXT field. Such a chain represents the anded antecedents of a rule. The .USEDBY field of each of these records contains a pointer to that used fact on the fact stack, in addition to the .DATA field containing a pointer to the symbolic expression of the fact. If the fact has been obtained by a number of lines of argument, then the .DEPEND field of the first dependent fact of each anded chain points to the next chain of facts. The .DEPEND fields then form a chain of or-ed chains of reasoning, any one of which is sufficient to obtain the given fact on the fact list. This is again used in retraction, since if one line of reasoning is canceled, the fact may be supported by another independent line of reasoning and should not be canceled.

Figure 4.2 illustrates the dependency stack. This is a true stack and is much simpler than the fact list. The .NEXT pointer is used to access the element below the present one in the stack. The .DEPEND field is used to point to the fact itself in the fact list. This information is used upon retraction. As

FACTSTACK

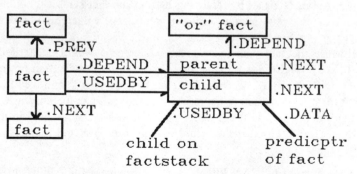

Fig. 4.1 The fact list.

antecedents are successfully unified with facts, the fact information is pushed onto the dependency stack. If a successful conclusion is reached, the information in the dependency stack is used to construct the dependency information of that fact.

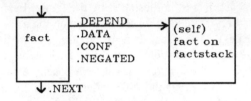

Fig. 4.2 The dependency stack.

Program Code

The program uses the STRNG package for dynamic strings and the code of GETRULES, LOADRULES, etc., for the input of rules. The code for the dynamic hash table for storing bindings, etc., is essentially unchanged from the backward-chaining system. We have also kept much of the inference engine the same, although some changes are possible (see "enhancements" below). For a discussion of these routines, see Chapter 3.

The first five "new" procedures are associated with canceling facts.

ASSERTP—calls ASSERT to assert a fact without that fact being used immediately to establish other facts.

DEINDEX—retracts a fact by removing it from the fact stack (in addition to or as an alternative to merely setting its confidence value equal to zero). It is necessary to first remove it from the index list of rules which could potentially use the fact. Otherwise invalid references would occur if the removed FACTSTACK record is accessed after garbage collection has occurred. DEINDEX removes references to the fact before it is removed from the list. It must be done before list removal because this is the only way to ensure that the pointers in the record (specifically the .DATA field in this case) are still valid, i.e., that the record has not been affected by any garbage collection.

SSEARCH—is used by CANCEL to search recursively for "child" or dependent facts to be canceled, to determine if there are alternative logic chains supporting the fact. The variable SCOUNT is returned with the value 0 if this is not the case, and the child should be canceled.

CANCEL—removes the dependent facts, if any. It finds them, and if they have no supporting chains of reasoning independent of the given retracted fact, cancels them. If COMPLETE is true, i.e., all generations of dependent facts are to be canceled, CANCEL recursively calls itself to do this. Note that the children are deleted before the parent, to avoid the potential for invalid pointers due to garbage collection as discussed under DEINDEX.

RETRACT—cancels (as does DENY) the parent fact and invokes CANCEL to retract the appropriate children. Figure 4.3 illustrates how information is passed from RETRACT to CANCEL to SSEARCH. RETRACT passes to CANCEL the USEDBY list of the canceled parent. CANCEL in turn passes to SSEARCH the USEDBY "pointer" (access type) which actually contains an access type or pointer to the user fact on the fact list.

INDEXHD, CHKGOAL are modified to index the predicate terms of rules and facts one at a time. INDEXHD loops through the predicate terms of the rules and adds the new fact to the head of the index list of those terms which might make use of the fact. This ensures that the latest facts will

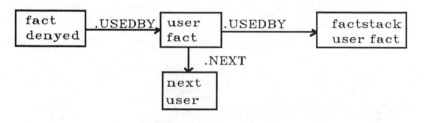

Fig. 4.3 Data flow between RETRACT, CANCEL, and SSEARCH.

have priority in use. CHKGOAL indexes the fact to rules which it might be used by.

ASSERT, VERIFY are a recursively coupled pair of procedures which establish and make use of facts. When assert is given a fact, it first checks to see if this fact is actually a special predicate term (e.g., one with side effects), such as a mathematical term, and invokes the appropriate procedure if so. If not, it first establishes if the fact is already known ("stale"). If so, the new supporting chain of evidence is added to those already known, and then processing of the stale fact ceases. Otherwise, the fact is pushed onto the fact list and CHKGOAL and INDEXHD are called to make the fact useful. This entails letting the rules know about it and letting it know about relevant rules. The dependency list of the fact is printed and attached to the fact on the fact stack. If TRYIT is false, the procedure returns. This will be the case for the first fact sent in by DIAGNOSE and if ASSERT is called by ASSERTP. Otherwise, the fact is added to the dependency stack as it is used with the indexed predicates in an attempt to fire rules. VERIFY is called with each such rule and attempts to unify all the antecedent predicates with facts. If so, it calls ASSERT with those facts, in an attempt to fire other rules and establish new facts.

Examples

We illustrate the behavior of the forward-chaining shell with two examples. The first is a forward-chaining version of the Jerardi problem (see Chapter 3). The other is a forward-chaining version of the "relatives" problem. Because the rule requires at least two facts to fire, the first fact is asserted with TRYIT set equal to false.

References

1. L. Brownston, R. Farrell, E. Kent, N. Martin, *Programming Expert Systems in OPS5* (Reading, Mass.: Addison-Wesley, 1985).

2. H. Shrobe and D. Barstow, *AI Programming,* Ninth Int. Joint Confr. on AI Tutorial Program, 1985.

3. C. L. Forgy, *Artificial Intelligence,* 19, p. 17 (1982).

4. E. Nuutila, J. Kuusela, M. Tamminen, J. Veilahti, J. Arkko, N. Bouteldja, *SIGPLAN Notices,* 22, 23 (September 1987).

5. J. Doyle, *Artificial Intelligence,* 12, 231 (1979).

6. J. de Kleer, *Artificial Intelligence,* 28, 127 (1986).

7. J. Holland, talk to ARTI, Albuquerque, Apr. 7, 1986.

Program Listing and Test Problems

-- Forward-Chaining Expert System Shell

```
with TEXT_IO; use  TEXT_IO;
with  STRNG; use STRNG;
with LOGIC; use LOGIC;
--with HASH; use HASH;
--with BIND; use BIND;
--with ANDOR; use ANDOR;
with FWDREAD; use FWDREAD;
--with CLAUSERD; use CLAUSERD;
--with FWDINDEX; use FWDINDEX;
with NONMON; use NONMON;
--with FWDSTK; use FWDSTK;
--with LIVE; use LIVE;
--with MATH; use MATH;
with ASSRT;use ASSRT;

procedure  FWD is

package  INT_IO is  new  INTEGER_IO(NUM => INTEGER);
package  FLT_IO is  new  FLOAT_IO(NUM=> FLOAT);

procedure  DIAGNOSE is

GL: PREDICPTR;
HYPOTHESIS: PHRASE;
CONF: FLOAT;
COUNT: INTEGER;
TRYIT: BOOLEAN;
USER,FCT: FLISTPTR;

begin
DUMP:=TRUE;
GOALTOP:=null;BIND:=null;
FACTKT:=0;TOTFACT:=0;
CONF:=0.9;
TRYIT:=FALSE;
for COUNT in  1..NUMTERM loop
```

```
    if COUNT>1 then
      TRYIT := TRUE;
    end if ;
    DEP:=null;
    -- CLAUSERD inverts truth value as if goal
    ASSERT(FACT_PTR(COUNT),(not FACT_PTR(COUNT).NEGATED)
    ,CONF,TRYIT);
end  loop ;
FACTNEW:=FACTKT-NUMTERM;
TOTFACT:=TOTFACT-NUMTERM;
TOTFACT:=TOTFACT-FACTNEW;
new_LINE;INT_IO.PUT(FACTKT);PUT(" FACTS of  WHICH ");
INT_IO.PUT(FACTNEW);PUT(" ARE DISCOVERIES.");
NEW_LINE;PUT("RETRACTED ");INT_IO.PUT(TOTFACT);PUT(" FACTS");
FCT:=FACTTOP;
loop
    if FCT=null  then
      exit;
    end if ;
    NEW_LINE;PUT(" FACT ");
    PRINTFACT(FCT.DATA,FCT.NEGATED);
    FLT_IO.PUT(FCT.CONF);
    USER:=FCT.USEDBY;
    loop
      if USER=null then
        exit;
      end if ;
      NEW_LINE;PUT(" ..USED TO ESTABLISH ");
      PRINTFACT(USER.DATA,USER.NEGATED);
      USER:=USER.NEXT;
    end loop;
    FCT:=FCT.NEXT;
end loop;
end  DIAGNOSE;

begin
EXHAUSTIVE := FALSE;
FACTTOP := null;
```

```
FACTBTM := null;
INTOP := null;
GETRULES;
DIAGNOSE;
end FWD;
```

```
-- Assert/Verify Mutually Recursive routines
-- for Forward-Chaining Expert System Shell

with TEXT_IO; use TEXT_IO;
with STRNG; use STRNG;
with LOGIC; use LOGIC;
with HASH; use HASH;
with BIND; use BIND;
with ANDOR; use ANDOR;
with FWDREAD; use FWDREAD;
with CLAUSERD; use CLAUSERD;
with FWDINDEX; use FWDINDEX;
with NONMON; use NONMON;
with FWDSTK; use FWDSTK;
with LIVE; use LIVE;
with MATH; use MATH;

package ASSRT is

type IN_USE;
type INPTR is access IN_USE;
type IN_USE is
    record
      RULE: INTEGER;
      NEXT: INPTR;
    end record;

TOPGOAL,LASTGOAL:PREDICPTR;
GOALTOP,GOALBTM: STACKPTR;
FACTBTM,DEP: FLISTPTR;
BIND: BINDPTR;
INTOP:INPTR;
DUMP: BOOLEAN;
TOTFACT,FACTNEW: INTEGER;

procedure ASSERT(FACT: in PREDICPTR; NG0:in BOOLEAN;
  CONF: in FLOAT; TRYIT: in BOOLEAN) ;
end ASSRT;
```

```
begin
STRING_TO_PHRASE("""ASSERT$",ATOKEN);
STRING_TO_PHRASE("""DENY$",DTOKEN);
STRING_TO_PHRASE("""RETRACT$",RTOKEN);
STRING_TO_PHRASE("""CANCEL$",CTOKEN);
end ASSRT;
```

```
-- Assert/Verify Mutually Recursive Routines
-- Forward-Chaining Expert System Shell

with TEXT_IO; use  TEXT_IO;
with  STRNG; use STRNG;
with LOGIC; use LOGIC;
with HASH; use HASH;
with BIND; use BIND;
with ANDOR; use ANDOR;
with FWDREAD; use FWDREAD;
with CLAUSERD; use CLAUSERD;
with FWDINDEX; use FWDINDEX;
with NONMON; use NONMON;
with FWDSTK; use FWDSTK;
with LIVE; use LIVE;
with MATH; use MATH;


package body ASSRT is


package  INT_IO is  new  INTEGER_IO(NUM => INTEGER);
package  FLT_IO is  new  FLOAT_IO(NUM=> FLOAT);


ATOKEN,CTOKEN,DTOKEN,RTOKEN: PHRASE;


function DEPEND_LIST(DEP: in FLISTPTR) return FLISTPTR is
--Copy dependency list for new fact
NEW_DEP,DEP_LIST,PREV_ENTRY: FLISTPTR;
begin
PREV_ENTRY:=null;
DEP_LIST:=null;
NEW_DEP:=DEP;
loop
  if NEW_DEP= null then exit; end if;
  DEP_LIST:= new FACTLIST;
  DEP_LIST.DEPEND:=null;
  DEP_LIST.DATA:=NEW_DEP.DATA;
  DEP_LIST.NEGATED:=NEW_DEP.NEGATED;
  DEP_LIST.CONF:=NEW_DEP.CONF;
```

```
       DEP_LIST.USEDBY:=null;
       DEP_LIST.NEXT:=PREV_ENTRY;
       PREV_ENTRY:=DEP_LIST;
       NEW_DEP:=NEW_DEP.NEXT;
    end loop;
    return DEP_LIST;
    end DEPEND_LIST;


    procedure ASSERT(FACT: in  PREDICPTR; NG0:in  BOOLEAN;
       CONF: in  FLOAT;
                        TRYIT: in  BOOLEAN) is
    DRK,OLDDRK,DREK,USED,WORKTOP: FLISTPTR;
    FCT: PREDICPTR;
    HEADN,RULEDEPTH,NUMSTR,RULNUM,NUMPRED: INTEGER;--DUMMY
    IND:INDEXPTR;
    CONFIDE,CONFOLD: FLOAT;
    STALE,NG3,NG4,SPECIAL: BOOLEAN;

    function ASSERTP(P: in PREDICPTR) return FLOAT is
       Q:PREDICPTR;


    begin
    Q:=P.NEXT;
    NEW_LINE;PUT(" ASSERTING-");PRINTPRED(Q,0);
    ASSERT(Q,FALSE,1.0,FALSE);
    return 1.0;
    end ASSERTP;


    function  EVAL_DEMON(P:PREDICPTR) return  FLOAT is
    C:CHARACTER;
    PH:PHRASE;
    begin
    PH:=P.ITEM.TOKEN;
    C:=PH(2);
    if C='T' or  C='t' then
       return  1.0;
    elsif  C = 'F' or  C = 'f' then
       return  0.0;
```

```
elsif COMPAREPHRASES(PH,ATOKEN)=0 then
  return ASSERTP(P);
elsif COMPAREPHRASES(PH,DTOKEN)=0 then
  return RETRACT(P,FALSE,FALSE);
elsif COMPAREPHRASES(PH,RTOKEN)=0 then
  return RETRACT(P,FALSE,TRUE);
elsif COMPAREPHRASES(PH,CTOKEN)=0 then
  return RETRACT(P,TRUE,TRUE);
else
  return 1.0;
end if ;
end EVAL_DEMON;


procedure VERIFY( DEPTH: in INTEGER ; RULENUM: in  RULERANGE;
  NUMSTRR: in INTEGER; NEG: in BOOLEAN;
                CONFACT: in FLOAT ) is

INSTFACT,NEWPRED,ANTECED,TGTPRED: PREDICPTR;
TGTDEPTH: INTEGER;
LDEP: FLISTPTR;
NG1,NG2,UNIFIES:BOOLEAN;
TDEPTH: INTEGER;
RULINDEX,WORK: INDEXPTR;
CONFIDENCE,CONFIDE: FLOAT;

begin
TDEPTH:=NEWDEPTH(0); CONFIDENCE:=CONFACT;LDEP:=DEP;
NG1:=NEG;
<<DOIT>>
if GOALTOP=null then
  NEW_LINE;PUT(" GOALTOP=null SUCCESS in  VERIFY");
  INSTFACT := BOUND(RULENUM,NUMSTRR,DEPTH);
  NEWPRED:= RULES(NUMSTRR);
  if QUOTED(NEWPRED ) then
    CONFIDENCE:=EVAL_DEMON(NEWPRED);
  else
    NEW_LINE;PRINTPRED(INSTFACT,DEPTH);
    if NEG then PUT(" FALSE ");end if ;
```

```
      PUT(" with CONFIDENCE=");FLT_IO.PUT(CONFIDENCE);
      NEW_LINE;PUT(" VIA RULE=");INT_IO.PUT(RULENUM);
      DEP:=LDEP;
      EXPLAINIT;
      ASSERT(INSTFACT,NEG,CONFIDENCE,TRUE);
   end if;
else
   POP(TGTPRED,TGTDEPTH,CONFIDE,NG2,GOALTOP);
   if QUOTED(TGTPRED) then
      CONFIDENCE := PROBAND(CONFIDENCE,EVAL_DEMON(TGTPRED));
   else
     WORK := TGTPRED.ITEM.INDX;
     loop
        if WORK=null then
          exit ;
        end if ;
        if WORK.FACTPTR/=null then
          NEWPRED := WORK.FACTPTR.DATA;
          NG1 := WORK.FACTPTR.NEGATED;
          UNIFIES := FALSE;
          if NG1 xor NG2 then
             UNIFIES := UNIFY(NEWPRED,0,TGTPRED,
             TGTDEPTH,TDEPTH,RULENUM,0);
          end if ;
          if UNIFIES then
             CONFIDENCE := PROBAND(CONFIDENCE,FPREVIOUS.CONF);
             if CONFIDENCE>FLOOR then
                PUSH(NEWPRED,WORK.FACTPTR,null,
          FPREVIOUS.CONF,NG1,LDEP);
                goto DOIT;
             end if ;
          end if ;
          CONFIDENCE:=CONFACT;
          LDEP:=DEP;
          RELEASE(TDEPTH);
          TDEPTH:=NEWDEPTH(0);
        end if ;
        WORK:=WORK.NEXT;
```

```
    end  loop ;
  end  if ;
end  if ;
if ALIVE(TDEPTH) then
  RELEASE(TDEPTH);
end if ;
return ;
end  VERIFY;


begin
CONFIDE:=CONF;
NG3:=NG0;
SPECIAL:=QUOTED(FACT);
if SPECIAL then
  CONFIDE := EVAL_DEMON(FACT);
  if CONFIDE=0.0 then
    return ;
  end if ;
end  if ;
WORKTOP:=FACTTOP;
STALE:=FALSE;
loop--has fact already been established?
  if WORKTOP=null then
    exit ;
  end if ;
  POP(FCT,DREK,DRK,CONFOLD,NG4,WORKTOP);
  STALE:=UNIFY(FCT,0,FACT,0,0,0,0) ;
  if STALE then
    NEW_LINE;
    PUT(" STALE FACT");
    --return;--for debug
      FPREVIOUS.CONF := PROBOR(CONFOLD,CONFIDE);
    loop
      if FPREVIOUS.DEPEND=null then
      FPREVIOUS.DEPEND := DEPEND_LIST(DEP);
        exit;
      end if ;
```

```
        FPREVIOUS:=FPREVIOUS.DEPEND;
      end loop ;
      return ;
    end if;
  end  loop ;
  if not  SPECIAL or  not  TRYIT  then
    PUSH(FACT,DEPEND_LIST(DEP),null,CONFIDE,NG3,FACTTOP);
    FACTKT := FACTKT+1;
    TOTFACT :=TOTFACT+1;
    NEW_LINE;
    PUT(" LISTED DEPENDENCIES: ");
    DREK := DEP;
    loop
      if DREK=null then
        exit ;
      end if ;
      NEW_LINE;PRINTFACT(DREK.DATA,DREK.NEGATED);
      DREK:=DREK.NEXT;
    end  loop ;
    NEW_LINE;PUT(" end of DEPENDENCY LIST");
    FACTINDEX(FACTTOP);
    RULE_FACT_INDEX(FACTTOP);
  end  if ;
  DREK:=FACTTOP;
  loop
    if DREK= null then exit; end if;
    NEW_LINE; PUT(" FACT=");PRINTPRED(DREK.DATA);
    if DREK.PREV/=null then
      PUT(" PARENT=");PRINTPRED(DREK.PREV.DATA);
    end if;
    if DREK.NEXT/=null then
      PUT(" CHILD=");PRINTPRED(DREK.NEXT.DATA);
    end if;
    DREK:=DREK.NEXT;
  end loop;
  DREK := DEP;
  loop
    if DREK=null then
```

```
  exit;
end if ;
DRK:=DREK.DEPEND;
NEW__LINE;PUT(" used fact is ");PRINTFACT(DRK.DATA,DRK.NEGATED);
USED:= new FACTLIST;
USED.NEXT:=null;
USED.DATA:=FACT;
USED.NEGATED:=NG3;
USED.CONF:=CONFIDE;
USED.USEDBY:=FACTTOP;
USED.DEPEND:=null;
if DRK.USEDBY=null then
  DRK.USEDBY := USED;
else
  DRK := DRK.USEDBY;
  loop
    if DRK.NEXT=null then
      exit;
    end if ;
    DRK:=DRK.NEXT;
  end loop;
  DRK.NEXT:=USED;
end if;
  DREK:=DREK.NEXT;
end loop;
if not TRYIT then
  return ;
end if ;
--Now attempt to use fact to prove other facts
PUSH(FACT,FACTTOP,null,CONFIDE,NG3,DEP);
if SPECIAL then
  return ;
end if ;
IND:=FACT.ITEM.INDX;
loop
  if IND=null then
    POP(FCT,DREK,DRK,CONFIDE,NG4,DEP);
    return ;
```

```
  end if ;
  if IND.FACTPTR=null then
    NUMSTR := IND.NUMSTR;
    RULNUM := IND.RULENUM;
    FCT := RULES(NUMSTR);
    NG4 := RULES(NUMSTR).NEGATED;
    for HEADN in  RULEINDX(RULNUM)..RULEINDX(RULNUM+1)-1
      loop
      if HEADN /=NUMSTR then
        RULEDEPTH := NEWDEPTH(0);
        if (NG3 xor NG4) and then
         UNIFY(FACT,0,FCT,RULEDEPTH,RULEDEPTH,RULNUM,0)
        then
          NUMPRED := RULEINDX(RULNUM+1) -1;
          loop
            if NUMPRED<RULEINDX(RULNUM) then
              exit ;
            end if ;
            if (NUMPRED/=NUMSTR) and (NUMPRED/=HEADN)
              then
              PUSH(RULES(NUMPRED),RULEDEPTH,
              1.0,RULES(NUMPRED).NEGATED,GOALTOP);
            end  if ;
            NUMPRED:=NUMPRED-1;
          end loop ;
          VERIFY(RULEDEPTH,RULNUM,HEADN,
           RULES(HEADN).NEGATED,CONFIDE);
        else
         RELEASE(RULEDEPTH);
          exit;
        end if ;
        RELEASE(RULEDEPTH);
      end if;
    end loop;
  end  if ;
  IND:=IND.NEXT;
end  loop ;
end  ASSERT;
```

```
begin
STRING_TO_PHRASE("""ASSERT$",ATOKEN);
STRING_TO_PHRASE("""DENY$",DTOKEN);
STRING_TO_PHRASE("""RETRACT$",RTOKEN);
STRING_TO_PHRASE("""CANCEL$",CTOKEN);
end ASSRT;
```

-- Additional PUSH/POPs for Forward-Chaining Shell

```
with STRNG; use STRNG;
with LOGIC; use LOGIC;

package  FWDSTK is


PREVIOUS: STACKPTR;          --globals(top of stacks)
FPREVIOUS: FLISTPTR;

procedure  PUSH (P:in  PREDICPTR;D:in  INTEGER; CONF: in  FLOAT;
    NEG: in BOOLEAN;
                        S: in  out  STACKPTR);
procedure  POP(P:out  PREDICPTR ; D: out  INTEGER; C: out  FLOAT;
    NEG: out BOOLEAN;
                        S:in  out  STACKPTR) ;

procedure  PUSH (P:in  PREDICPTR;D,U: in  FLISTPTR; CONF: in  FLOAT;
    NEG:in BOOLEAN;
                        S: in  out  FLISTPTR);

procedure  POP(P:out  PREDICPTR; D,U: out  FLISTPTR; C: out  FLOAT;
    NEG: out BOOLEAN;
                        S:in  out  FLISTPTR);

end FWDSTK;
```

-- Additional PUSH/POPs for Forward-Chaining Shell

```
with STRNG; use STRNG;
with LOGIC; use LOGIC;

package body FWDSTK is

procedure  PUSH (P:in  PREDICPTR;D:in  INTEGER; CONF: in  FLOAT;
    NEG: in BOOLEAN;S: in  out  STACKPTR) is

GLLS: STACKPTR;
begin
GLLS:= new  STACK;
GLLS.DATA:=P;
GLLS.DEPTH:=D;
GLLS.CONF:=CONF;
GLLS.NEGATED:=NEG;
GLLS.NEXT:=S;
S:=GLLS;
return ;
end  PUSH;

procedure  POP(P:out  PREDICPTR ; D: out  INTEGER; C: out  FLOAT;
    NEG: out BOOLEAN;S:in  out  STACKPTR) is

begin
P:=S.DATA;
D:=S.DEPTH;
NEG:=S.NEGATED;
C:=S.CONF;
PREVIOUS:=S;
S:=S.NEXT;
return ;
end  POP;

procedure  PUSH (P:in  PREDICPTR;D,U: in  FLISTPTR; CONF: in  FLOAT;
    NEG:in BOOLEAN;S: in  out  FLISTPTR) is
```

```
GLLS: FLISTPTR;
begin
GLLS:= new  FACTLIST;
GLLS.DATA:=P;
GLLS.DEPEND:=D;
GLLS.CONF:=CONF;
GLLS.NEGATED:=NEG;
GLLS.USEDBY:=U;
GLLS.NEXT:=S;
if S/=null then
  S.PREV:=GLLS;
end if;
S:=GLLS;
GLLS.PREV:=null;
return ;
end  PUSH;

procedure  POP(P:out  PREDICPTR; D,U: out  FLISTPTR; C: out  FLOAT;
   NEG: out BOOLEAN;S:in  out  FLISTPTR) is

begin
P:=S.DATA;
D:=S.DEPEND;
U:=S.USEDBY;
NEG:=S.NEGATED;
C:=S.CONF;
FPREVIOUS:=S;
S:=S.NEXT;
return ;
end POP;

end FWDSTK;
```

-- Index Facts to Rules and Vice Versa
-- for Forward-Chaining shell

with LOGIC; use LOGIC;
with STRNG;use STRNG;

package FWDINDEX is

procedure RULE_FACT_INDEX(FAT: in FLISTPTR);

procedure FACTINDEX(HYP: in FLISTPTR);

end FWDINDEX;

```
-- Index Rules to Facts and Vice Versa
-- for Forward-Chaining Shell

with STRNG; use STRNG;
with LOGIC; use LOGIC;
with FWDREAD; use FWDREAD;
with CLAUSERD; use CLAUSERD;
with TEXT_IO; use TEXT_IO;

package body FWDINDEX is

package INT_IO is new INTEGER_IO(NUM=>INTEGER);

procedure  RULE_FACT_INDEX(FAT: in  FLISTPTR) is

HYPOTH,STRG: PHRASE;
FCT,HYP: SYMPTR;
FACT: PREDICPTR;
HEADTOP,HEADNUM,RULE,SOURCE,PREDICATE:RULERANGE;
HEAD:PTRANGE;
IND,OLD:INDEXPTR;
KOUNT:INTEGER;
NG1,NG2:BOOLEAN;

begin
FACT:=FAT.DATA;
NG2:= FAT.NEGATED;
FCT:=FACT.ITEM;
HYPOTH:=FCT.TOKEN;
KOUNT:=0;
for SOURCE in  1..NUMRULES loop
   PREDICATE:=RULEINDX(SOURCE);
   HEADTOP:=RULEINDX(SOURCE+1)-1;
   if HEADTOP=PREDICATE then
     NEW_LINE;
     PUT(" RULE ");
     INT_IO.PUT(SOURCE);
     PUT(" is  A FACT");
```

```
PUT(" IT WILL not  BE INDEXED TO OTHER RULES");
else
  for HEADNUM in PREDICATE..HEADTOP loop
    NG1 := RULES(HEADNUM).NEGATED;
    HYP := RULES(HEADNUM).ITEM;
    STRG := HYP.TOKEN;
    if FCT=HYP and (NG1 xor NG2)
      then
      if HYP.INDX/=null
        then
        IND := HYP.INDX;
        loop
          if IND=null then
            exit ;
          end if ;
          if  IND.FACTPTR/=null then
            if  IND.FACTPTR=FAT then
              goto  SKIP;
            end if ;
          else
            null ;
          end  if ;
          IND := IND.NEXT;
        end  loop ;
      end  if ;
      IND := new  INDEX;
      IND.FACTPTR:=FAT;
      IND.NUMSTR:=0; IND.RULENUM:=0;
      IND.NEXT:=null;
      if HYP.INDX=null then
        HYP.INDX := IND;
      else
        OLD := HYP.INDX;
        HYP.INDX := IND;
        IND.NEXT := OLD;
      end if ;
      <<SKIP>>KOUNT:=KOUNT+1;
    end  if ;
```

```
      end loop ;
    end if ;
  end loop ;
  new_LINE;INT_IO.PUT(KOUNT);PUT(" PREDICATES UNIFY with  FACT");
  return ;
  end  RULE_FACT_INDEX;

procedure  FACTINDEX(HYP: in  FLISTPTR) is

HYPOTH: PHRASE;
FCT,SYMBOL:SYMPTR;
RULE:RULERANGE;
TAIL,NUMSTR,HEAD:RULERANGE;
STRG: PHRASE;
IND,OLD:INDEXPTR;
KOUNT:INTEGER;
DREK:PREDICPTR;
NG2:BOOLEAN;

begin
DREK:=HYP.DATA;
NG2:= HYP.NEGATED;
FCT:=DREK.ITEM;
OLD:=null;
KOUNT:=0;
for RULE in  1..NUMRULES loop
   HEAD:= RULEINDX(RULE+1)-1;
   TAIL:= RULEINDX(RULE);
   for NUMSTR in  TAIL..HEAD loop
     SYMBOL:= RULES(NUMSTR).ITEM;
     STRG:=SYMBOL.TOKEN;
     if SYMBOL=FCT and ( RULES(NUMSTR).NEGATED xor NG2)
        then
        if FCT.INDX/=null
          then
          IND := FCT.INDX;
          loop
             if IND=null then
```

```
            exit ;
          end if ;
          if IND.FACTPTR=null then
            if RULE=IND.RULENUM and NUMSTR=IND.NUMSTR
              then
              goto SKIP;
            end if ;
          end  if ;
          IND := IND.NEXT;
        end loop ;
      end if ;
      IND:= new  INDEX;
      IND.RULENUM:=RULE;
      IND.NUMSTR:=NUMSTR;
      IND.FACTPTR:=null ;
      IND.NEXT:=  null  ;
      if FCT.INDX=null then
        FCT.INDX := IND  ;
      else
        OLD := FCT.INDX;
        FCT.INDX := IND;
        IND.NEXT := OLD;
      end if ;
      <<SKIP>>KOUNT:=KOUNT+1;
    end  if ;
  end  loop ;
end  loop ;
NEW_LINE;PUT(" FACT UNIFIES with ");
INT_IO.PUT(KOUNT);PUT(" PREDICATES");
end  FACTINDEX;

end FWDINDEX;
```

```
-- Utilities for Non-Monotonic Reasoning
-- Retracting Facts for Forward-Chaining Shell

with STRNG; use STRNG;
with LOGIC; use LOGIC;

package NONMON is

procedure CANCEL(S: in FLISTPTR;COMPLETE: in BOOLEAN);

function RETRACT(P:in PREDICPTR; COMPLETE,FOLLOW: in BOOLEAN)
          return FLOAT;

FACTTOP: FLISTPTR;
FACTKT: INTEGER;

end NONMON;
```

-- Utilities for Non-Monotonic Reasoning

```
with STRNG; use STRNG;
with LOGIC; use LOGIC;
with BIND; use BIND;
with TEXT_IO; use TEXT_IO;

package body NONMON is

procedure SSEARCH(TARGET: in FLISTPTR;SCOUNT: in out INTEGER;
              PARENT: in FLISTPTR) is

CHAIN,NODE:FLISTPTR;
LCOUNT:INTEGER;

begin
if PARENT= null  then
   return;
end if ;
NODE:=PARENT.DEPEND;
if NODE=null  then
   return;
end if ;
CHAIN:=NODE.DEPEND;
if CHAIN/= null then
   LCOUNT := 1;
   SSEARCH(TARGET,LCOUNT,CHAIN);
   SCOUNT := SCOUNT+LCOUNT;
end if ;
if NODE.USEDBY=TARGET then
   PARENT.DEPEND := null;
   SCOUNT := 0;
   return;
end if ;
CHAIN:=NODE.NEXT;
LCOUNT:=SCOUNT;
SSEARCH(TARGET,LCOUNT,CHAIN);
SCOUNT:=LCOUNT;
```

```
return;
end SSEARCH;

procedure CANCEL(S: in FLISTPTR;COMPLETE: in BOOLEAN) is

Q:PREDICPTR;
USER,TRACK,PARENT,CHILD:FLISTPTR;
SCOUNT:INTEGER;
RFCON:FLOAT;
ORDERS:BOOLEAN;

begin
NEW_LINE;PUT(" ENTER CANCEL WITH ");PRINTPRED(S.DATA,-2);
if COMPLETE then PUT(" COMPLETE");end if;
if S=null then return; end if;
TRACK:=S.USEDBY;
if TRACK=null then return;end if;
RFCON:=S.CONF;
if S=TRACK then
NEW_LINE;PUT(" AUTO-USAGE ");PRINTPRED(S.DATA);
return;
end if;
loop
  NEW_LINE;PUT(" ENTER LOOP WITH TRACK=");
  if TRACK /= null then PRINTPRED(TRACK.DATA);end if;
  PRINTPRED(S.DATA);
  if TRACK/=null then
    USER:=TRACK.USEDBY;
    if COMPLETE then
      ORDERS:= USER.USEDBY /= null ;
      CANCEL(USER,ORDERS);
      NEW_LINE;
      PUT(" RETURN FROM CANCEL IN CANCEL");
    end if ;
    SCOUNT := 0;
    SSEARCH(S,SCOUNT,TRACK);
    if SCOUNT=0 then
      USER.CONF := 0.0;
```

```
   PARENT:=USER.PREV;
   CHILD:= USER.NEXT;
   NEW_LINE;PUT(" FACTTOP=");
   PRINTPRED(FACTTOP.DATA);
   if PARENT /= null then
     PUT(" PARENT(PREV) ");
     PRINTPRED(PARENT.DATA);
     PARENT.NEXT := CHILD;
   else
     FACTTOP:=CHILD;
     NEW_LINE;PUT(" CANCELING LATEST FACT");
   end if;
   if CHILD /= null then
     PUT(" CHILD ");
     PRINTPRED(CHILD.DATA);
     CHILD.PREV := PARENT;
   end if;
   FACTKT := FACTKT-1;
   NEW_LINE;
   PUT("CANCELING ");
   PRINTPRED(USER.DATA);
else
   USER.CONF :=
   (USER.CONF-RFCON)/(1.0-RFCON);
end if ;
USER:=FACTTOP;
loop
   if USER= null then exit; end if;
   NEW_LINE; PUT(" FACT=");PRINTPRED(USER.DATA);
   if USER.PREV/=null then
     PUT(" PARENT=");
     PRINTPRED(USER.PREV.DATA);
   end if;
   if USER.NEXT/=null then
     PUT(" CHILD=");
     PRINTPRED(USER.NEXT.DATA);
   end if;
   USER:=USER.NEXT;
```

```
      end loop;
      TRACK:=TRACK.NEXT;
   else
        return;
   end if;
 end loop;
 end CANCEL;

function RETRACT(P:in PREDICPTR; COMPLETE,FOLLOW: in BOOLEAN)
            return FLOAT is
F:PREDICPTR;
Q:PREDICPTR;
OLDSUP,S,SOLD:FLISTPTR;

begin
Q:=P.NEXT;
S:=FACTTOP;
SOLD:=null;
if S=null then
   return 0.0;
end if;
loop
  F:=S.DATA;
  if UNIFY(F,0,Q,0,0,0,0)  then
    if FOLLOW then
        CANCEL(S,COMPLETE);
    end if;
    S.CONF:=0.0;
    SOLD:=S.PREV;
    if SOLD /=null then
      NEW_LINE;PUT(" PARENT ");
      PRINTPRED(SOLD.DATA);
      SOLD.NEXT := S.NEXT;
    else
      FACTTOP := FACTTOP.NEXT;
      NEW_LINE;
      PUT(" RETRACTING MOST RECENT FACT");
    end  if ;
```

```
    if S.NEXT /= null then
       NEW_LINE;PUT(" CHILD ");
       PRINTPRED(S.NEXT.DATA);
       S.NEXT.PREV:=SOLD;
    end if;
    NEW_LINE;PUT(" RETRACTING ");
    PRINTPRED(Q);
    PRINTPRED(S.DATA);
    FACTKT:=FACTKT-1;
    S:=FACTTOP;
    loop
       if S= null then exit; end if;
       NEW_LINE; PUT(" FACT=");PRINTPRED(S.DATA);
       if S.PREV/=null then
          PUT(" PARENT=");PRINTPRED(S.PREV.DATA);
       end if;
       if S.NEXT/=null then
          PUT(" CHILD=");PRINTPRED(S.NEXT.DATA);
       end if;
       S:=S.NEXT;
    end loop;
    return 1.0;
  end if;
  SOLD:=S;
  S:=S.NEXT;
end loop;
return 0.0;
end RETRACT;

end NONMON;
```

```
-- Input for Forward-Chaining System

with STRNG;use STRNG;
with LOGIC; use LOGIC;
with CLAUSERD; use CLAUSERD;

package FWDREAD is

FACT_PTR: TERMARRAY ;              --each fact
NUMTERM: GOALRANGE;
NUMRULES: RULERANGE;
RULEPROB:array (1..MAX_RULE_COUNT) of FLOAT;
NUMSTRRULES : RULERANGE;

-- user input:

FLOOR: FLOAT;
-- minimum TRUE confidence factor
EXHAUSTIVE,FACTOR,NOOCCK,EXPLAIN,NOLOOP,LOOPCK: BOOLEAN;
-- user-specified options

procedure PRINTFACT(FACT: PREDICPTR; NEGATED:BOOLEAN);

procedure  GETRULES  ;

end FWDREAD;
```

```
-- Input for Forward-Chaining System

with STRNG; use STRNG;
with LOGIC; use LOGIC;
with CLAUSERD; use CLAUSERD;
with TEXT_IO;use  TEXT_IO;

package body FWDREAD is

--package INT_IO is new INTEGER_IO(NUM=>INTEGER);


procedure PRINTFACT(FACT:PREDICPTR;NEGATED: BOOLEAN) is
begin
if NEGATED then PUT(" not "); end if;
PRINTPRED(FACT);
end PRINTFACT;


procedure  GETRULES is
RULEFILE: FILE_type;
TXT: STRING(1..LONGPHRASE_LENGTH);
TEXT: LONGPHRASE;
KOUNT,LENGTHIS:INTEGER;
GOALS: PHRASE;
CHAR: CHARACTER;
NEGATED,ISNOT,ANTECED:BOOLEAN;

begin
OPEN(RULEFILE,in_FILE,"RULE.FWD");
GET_LINE(RULEFILE, TXT,LENGTHIS);
STRING_TO_PHRASE(TXT,TEXT,LENGTHIS);
new_LINE;PUT(" EXPERT SYSTEM in  use  is");new_LINE;PRINT(TEXT);
new_LINE;
PUT(" do YOU WANT EXHAUSTIVE SEARCH with  CONFIDENCE FACTORS?")
loop
  GET(CHAR);
  case CHAR is
```

```
    when 'Y'|'y'=>
      EXHAUSTIVE:=TRUE;
      exit ;
    when 'N'|'n'=>
      exit ;
    when others =>
      PUT(" type Y or N");new_LINE;
    end case ;
end loop ;
if EXHAUSTIVE then
  new_LINE;PUT(" ENTER FLOOR CONFIDENCE VALUE ");
  FLT_IO.GET(FLOOR);
end if ;
NOOCCK:=TRUE;
new_LINE;PUT(" do YOU WANT OCCURS CHECK in UNIFICATION?");
loop
  GET(CHAR);
  case CHAR is
    when 'Y'|'y'=>
      NOOCCK:=FALSE;
      exit ;
    when 'N'|'n'=>
       exit ;
    when others =>
      PUT(" type Y or N");new_LINE;
    end case ;
end loop ;
EXPLAIN:=TRUE;
NOLOOP:=TRUE;
LOOPCK:= not NOLOOP;
NUMRULES:=1;
NUMSTRRULES:=1;
NUMTERM:=0;
NEGATED:=FALSE;
ISNOT:=FALSE;
ANTECED:=TRUE;
--GET FACTS
loop
```

```
    GET_LINE(RULEFILE, TXT,LENGTHIS);
    if LENGTHIS<1 then
       exit ;
    else
       STRING_TO_PHRASE(TXT,TEXT,LENGTHIS);
       READCLAUSE(TEXT,FALSE,
        FACT_PTR,
        NUMRULES,NUMSTRRULES, NUMTERM,
        NEGATED,ANTECED,ISNOT);
    end if ;
end loop ;
new_LINE;PUT(" NUMBER of  FACTS = "); INT_IO.PUT(NUMTERM);
NEGATED := FALSE;
ISNOT := FALSE;
ANTECED := TRUE;
--NOW READ RULES
NEW_LINE;PUT(" NUMSTRRULES=");INT_IO.PUT(NUMSTRRULES);
loop
    GET_LINE(RULEFILE,TXT,LENGTHIS);
    --NEW_LINE;INT_IO.PUT(LENGTHIS);
    if LENGTHIS<1 then
       exit ;
    end if ;
    STRING_TO_PHRASE(TXT,TEXT,LENGTHIS);
    --PRINT(TEXT);
    READCLAUSE(TEXT,TRUE,FACT_PTR,NUMRULES,NUMSTRRULES,
    NUMTERM,NEGATED,ANTECED,ISNOT);
end loop ;
NEW_LINE;PUT(" NUMSTRRULES=");INT_IO.PUT(NUMSTRRULES);
if ANTECED then
    PUT(" ANTECED");
    RULES(NUMSTRRULES-1).NEGATED
     := not RULES(NUMSTRRULES-1).NEGATED;
end if;
RULEINDX(NUMRULES):=NUMSTRRULES;
NUMRULES:=NUMRULES-1;
CLOSE(RULEFILE);
for KOUNT in  1..NUMRULES loop
```

```
  RULEPROB(KOUNT):=0.9;
end  loop ;
end  GETRULES;

end FWDREAD;
```

Jerardi test-fwd.
dummy,
snowing,

if,raining,then,precip,
if,snowing,then,precip,
if,freezing,precip,then,snowing,
if,not,freezing,precip,raining,
if,raining,then,not,snowing,

            fwd

EXPERT SYSTEM in use is
Jerardi test-fwd.
do YOU WANT EXHAUSTIVE SEARCH with CONFIDENCE FACTORS?

                                                              y

ENTER FLOOR CONFIDENCE VALUE
                           0.1

do YOU WANT OCCURS CHECK in UNIFICATION?y
NUMBER of FACTS =   2
NUMSTRRULES=   1
NUMSTRRULES=   13
LISTED DEPENDENCIES:
end of DEPENDENCY LIST
FACT UNIFIES with   0 PREDICATES
   0 PREDICATES UNIFY with FACT
FACT= dummy
LISTED DEPENDENCIES:
end of DEPENDENCY LIST
FACT UNIFIES with   2 PREDICATES
   2 PREDICATES UNIFY with FACT
FACT= snowing CHILD= dummy
FACT= dummy PARENT= snowing
GOALTOP=null SUCCESS in VERIFY
raining at DEPTH=   1 FALSE with CONFIDENCE= 9.00000E-01
VIA RULE=   5
LISTED DEPENDENCIES:
snowing
end of DEPENDENCY LIST
FACT UNIFIES with   1 PREDICATES
   1 PREDICATES UNIFY with FACT
FACT= raining CHILD= snowing
FACT= snowing PARENT= raining CHILD= dummy
FACT= dummy PARENT= snowing
used fact is snowing
GOALTOP=null SUCCESS in VERIFY
precip at DEPTH=   5 with CONFIDENCE= 9.00000E-01

VIA RULE=   2
LISTED DEPENDENCIES:
snowing
end of DEPENDENCY LIST
FACT UNIFIES with   2 PREDICATES
   2 PREDICATES UNIFY with FACT
FACT= precip CHILD= raining
FACT= raining PARENT= precip CHILD= snowing
FACT= snowing PARENT= raining CHILD= dummy
FACT= dummy PARENT= snowing
used fact is snowing
GOALTOP=null SUCCESS in VERIFY
freezing at DEPTH=   7 with CONFIDENCE= 8.10000E-01
VIA RULE=   4
LISTED DEPENDENCIES:
not raining
precip
snowing
end of DEPENDENCY LIST
FACT UNIFIES with   1 PREDICATES
   1 PREDICATES UNIFY with FACT
FACT= freezing CHILD= precip
FACT= precip PARENT= freezing CHILD= raining
FACT= raining PARENT= precip CHILD= snowing
FACT= snowing PARENT= raining CHILD= dummy
FACT= dummy PARENT= snowing
used fact is not raining
used fact is precip
used fact is snowing
GOALTOP=null SUCCESS in VERIFY
snowing at DEPTH=   10 with CONFIDENCE= 7.29000E-01
VIA RULE=   3
STALE FACT
GOALTOP=null SUCCESS in VERIFY
snowing at DEPTH=   13 with CONFIDENCE= 8.10000E-01
VIA RULE=   3
STALE FACT
   5 FACTS of WHICH   3 ARE DISCOVERIES.

```
RETRACTED        0 FACTS
 FACT  freezing 8.10000E-01
 FACT  precip 9.00000E-01
 ..USED TO ESTABLISH  freezing
 FACT  not  raining 9.00000E-01
 ..USED TO ESTABLISH  freezing
 FACT  snowing 9.94851E-01
 ..USED TO ESTABLISH  not  raining
 ..USED TO ESTABLISH  precip
 ..USED TO ESTABLISH  freezing
 FACT  dummy 9.00000E-01
C:\TEMP>
```

```
-- Mathematical Predicate Evaluation
-- See Package Body for discussion of capabilities

with STRNG; use STRNG;
with LOGIC; use LOGIC;

package  MATH is

function  MATHD(PRED : in  PREDICPTR) return  FLOAT;

end  MATH;
```

```
-- Evaluate Mathematical Predicates.
-- These can compare expressions and set variables.
-- These variables are globally defined
-- and are remembered between formulae and rules.
-- They may therefore be used as global "registers."

with  TEXT_IO;use  TEXT_IO;
with STRNG; use STRNG;
with LOGIC; use LOGIC;
with MFUNCT; use MFUNCT;

package  body  MATH is

type  ACCUM;                --stack accumulator
type  ACCUMPTR is  access  ACCUM;
type  ACCUM is
      record
      VALUE: FLOAT;
      next : ACCUMPTR;
      end  record ;

type  POSTFX;               -- linked-list for postfix expression
type  POSTFXPTR is  access  POSTFX;
type  POSTFX is
      record
      DATA:SYMPTR;
      next :POSTFXPTR;
      end  record ;

type OPERATION is
(VARNAME,CONSTNT,FUNCTIONNAME,HEADFUNCTION,ADD,SUBTRACT,
SIGNFLIP,MULTIPLY,DIVIDE,EXPON,ASSIGN,EQUALS,LT,GT,
LTE,GTE,ENDEXPRS,OPENPAREN,CLOSEPAREN,ARGSEPARATOR);

function  MATHD( PRED: in  PREDICPTR) return  FLOAT is

LAST: POSTFXPTR;
TOPSTACK,POLISH,POSTF: POSTFXPTR;
```

```
TERMINATOR,ACCUMFLAG: SYMPTR;
ZERO,TSYMB,UNARYMINUS,FUNCTIONHEAD: SYMPTR;
FPHRASE,UMPHRASE,TPHRASE,ZEROP,ACCUMP: PHRASE;
FIRST: BOOLEAN;
VSTACK: SYMPTR;
ACCUMULATOR:ACCUMPTR;
VAR:SYMPTR;
ANS:FLOAT;

package FLT_IO is new FLOAT_IO(NUM=> FLOAT);
package INT_IO is new INTEGER_IO(NUM=> INTEGER);

procedure PRINTPRED( P: in POSTFXPTR) is
PP:POSTFXPTR;
begin
PP:=P;
while PP/=null loop
  PUT(" ");PRINT(PP.DATA.TOKEN);
  PP:=PP.NEXT;
end loop ;
end PRINTPRED;

function WEIGHT( OPCODE: in OPERATION) return INTEGER is

begin
if OPCODE=ASSIGN then return 0 ;
elsif OPCODE in EQUALS..GTE then return 1;
elsif OPCODE in ADD..SUBTRACT then return 2 ;
elsif OPCODE in MULTIPLY..DIVIDE then return 3 ;
elsif OPCODE=SIGNFLIP then return 4 ;
elsif OPCODE=EXPON then return 5 ;
elsif OPCODE=ENDEXPRS then return -1 ;
elsif OPCODE=FUNCTIONNAME then return 6 ;
elsif OPCODE=OPENPAREN then return 0 ;--immaterial
elsif OPCODE=CLOSEPAREN then return 0 ;
elsif OPCODE=ARGSEPARATOR then return 0 ;
elsif OPCODE=HEADFUNCTION then return 0 ;
else return -1;  -- error?
```

```
end   if ;
end   WEIGHT;

-- input a constant. string converted to float in INFIX

function  CONST(TOKEN: in  PHRASE) return  OPERATION is
LOC:INTEGER;
DIGTS:BOOLEAN;
CHR:CHARACTER;
begin
LOC:=1;
DIGTS:=FALSE;
loop
   CHR:=TOKEN(LOC);
   case CHR is
     when '0'|'1'|'2'|'3'|'4'|'5'|'6'|'7'|'8'|'9' =>
       DIGTS:=TRUE;
     when  '.'|'-'|'+'|'_'|'#' =>
       null ;
     when  'E'|'e'|'D'|'d'=>
       if not  DIGTS then
         return  VARNAME;
       end  if ;
     when ' '|'$' =>
       if DIGTS then
         return CONSTNT;
       else
         return VARNAME;
       end if;
     when others  =>
       return  VARNAME;
   end case ;
   LOC:=LOC+1;
end  loop ;
exception
   when CONSTRAINT_ERROR =>
     if DIGTS then
       PUT(" CE -2");
```

```
      return  CONSTNT;
    else
      PUT(" CE -1 ");
      return  VARNAME;
    end  if ;
end  CONST;
```

-- identify operators

```
function  OPERATOR(TOKENP: in  SYMPTR) return  OPERATION is

LENGTH: INTEGER;
TOKEN: SYMPTR;
TOKENS: PHRASE;
CH2,CHR: CHARACTER;
ANSWER: OPERATION;

begin
TOKEN:=TOKENP;
TOKENS:=TOKEN.TOKEN;
LENGTH:=PHRASE_LENGTH(TOKENS);
if FUNCT(TOKEN)/= NOTFUNCT then
  return  FUNCTIONNAME;
end  if ;
if LENGTH>2 then
  return  CONST(TOKENS);
end  if ;
CHR:=TOKENS(1);
if LENGTH=2 then
  CH2:=TOKENS(2);
  if CHR=':' then
    if CH2='=' then
      ANSWER:=ASSIGN;
    else
      PUT(" MATH- UNKNOWN OP ");PRINT(TOKENS);
    end  if ;
  elsif  CHR='<' and  CH2='=' then
    ANSWER:=LTE;
```

```
    elsif  CHR='>'  and  CH2='=' then
      ANSWER:=GTE;
    else
      return  CONST(TOKENS);
    end  if ;
elsif LENGTH=1 then
  case CHR is
    when  '='  => ANSWER:=EQUALS;
    when  '<'  => ANSWER:=LT;
    when  '>'  => ANSWER:=GT;
    when  '+'  => ANSWER:=ADD;
    when  '-'  => ANSWER:=SUBTRACT;
    when  '*'  => ANSWER:=MULTIPLY;
    when  '/'  => ANSWER:=DIVIDE;
    when  '^'  => ANSWER:=EXPON;
    when  '('  => ANSWER:=OPENPAREN;
    when  ')'  => ANSWER:=CLOSEPAREN;
    when  '#'  => ANSWER:=ENDEXPRS;
    -- 14 is function opcode
    when  ';'  => ANSWER:=ARGSEPARATOR;
    when  '&'  => ANSWER:=HEADFUNCTION;
    when  '@'  =>  ANSWER:=SIGNFLIP; -- unary minus
    when  others  =>
      ANSWER:=CONST(TOKENS);
  end case ;
else
  PUT(" ERROR in  MATH-STRING LENGTH<1");
  ANSWER:= VARNAME;
end  if ;
return  ANSWER;
end  OPERATOR;

-- stack processing for infix to postfix conversion

procedure  POP( TOKEN: out  SYMPTR) is

begin
TOKEN:=TOPSTACK.DATA;
```

```
TOPSTACK:=TOPSTACK.NEXT;
return ;
end  POP;

procedure  PUSH( TOKEN: in  SYMPTR) is

NEWTOK: POSTFXPTR;

begin
NEWTOK:= new  POSTFX;
NEWTOK.DATA:=TOKEN;
NEWTOK.NEXT:=TOPSTACK;
TOPSTACK:=NEWTOK;
return ;
end  PUSH;

-- accumulator stack processing

procedure  POP( TOKEN: out  FLOAT) is

begin
TOKEN:=ACCUMULATOR.VALUE;
ACCUMULATOR:=ACCUMULATOR.NEXT;
return ;
end  POP;

procedure  PUSH( TOKEN: in  FLOAT) is

NEWTOK: ACCUMPTR;

begin
NEWTOK:= new  ACCUM;
NEWTOK.VALUE:=TOKEN;
NEWTOK.NEXT:=ACCUMULATOR;
ACCUMULATOR:=NEWTOK;
return ;
end  PUSH;
```

-- weight of operator at top of stack

```
procedure WTS(ANSWER:out INTEGER) is
begin
if TOPSTACK=null then
  ANSWER:=-100;
  return ;
end if ;
ANSWER:= WEIGHT(OPERATOR(TOPSTACK.DATA));
return ;
end WTS;
```

--write to postfix string

```
procedure WRITE(TOKEN: in SYMPTR) is

LATEST:POSTFXPTR;

begin
LATEST:= new POSTFX;
LATEST.DATA:= TOKEN;
LATEST.NEXT:=null;
if FIRST then
  FIRST:=FALSE;
  POLISH:=LATEST;
  LAST:=LATEST;
  return ;
end if ;
LAST.NEXT:=LATEST;
LAST:=LATEST;
return ;
end WRITE;
```

--look up variable in search tree

```
procedure SEARCHV( TOK : in SYMPTR; RESULT: out INTEGER;
            ATTACHPT: out SYMPTR ) is
- RESULT is 0 if found else -1 if new name to be inserted as
```

```
-- left child of ATTACHPT or +1 if right child
NEWPHR,OLDPHR:PHRASE;
VARS:SYMPTR;
LRESULT: INTEGER;
begin
if ROOT=null then
  RESULT:= -10;
  ATTACHPT:=ROOT;
  return ;
end if ;
ATTACHPT:=null;
NEWPHR:=TOK.TOKEN;
VARS:=ROOT;
loop
  OLDPHR:=VARS.TOKEN;
  LRESULT:=COMPAREPHRASES(NEWPHR,OLDPHR);
  ATTACHPT:=VARS;
  if LRESULT=0 then
    RESULT:=LRESULT;
    return ;
  end if ;
  if LRESULT=-1 then
    VARS:=VARS.LEFT;
  else
    VARS:=VARS.RIGHT;
  end if ;
  if VARS=null then
    RESULT:=LRESULT;
    return ;
  end if ;
end loop ;
end SEARCHV;

-- enter variable into table (if not already in table)

procedure  ENTER ( TOK : in  SYMPTR; OFOUND :out BOOLEAN) is

ATTACHPT: SYMPTR;
```

```
RESULT: INTEGER;
FOUND: BOOLEAN;
begin
SEARCHV(TOK,RESULT,ATTACHPT);
FOUND := (RESULT=0);
OFOUND:=FOUND;
if FOUND then return ; end if ;
VAR:= new SYMBOL;--NOT FOUND
VAR.TOKEN:=TOK.TOKEN;
VAR.ARITHMETIC:=TRUE;
VAR.DEFINED:=FALSE;
VAR.RIGHT:=null;
VAR.LEFT:=null;
if RESULT=-10 then
  ROOT:=VAR;
elsif RESULT=-1 then
  ATTACHPT.LEFT:=VAR;
else
  ATTACHPT.RIGHT:=VAR;
end if ;
return ;
end ENTER;

-- INFIX to POSTFIX

procedure INFIX is

PREDIC: PREDICPTR;
STACK: POSTFXPTR;
TOKEN,OTOKEN:SYMPTR;
NWEIGHT,SWEIGHT: INTEGER;
FOUND,UNARY: BOOLEAN;
CVALUE:FLOAT;
LAST:POSITIVE;
OPCODE: OPERATION;
BEGIN
PREDIC:=PRED;
UNARY:=TRUE;
```

```
while PREDIC/=null loop
  TOKEN:=PREDIC.ITEM;
  OPCODE:=OPERATOR(TOKEN);
  if UNARY and  OPCODE=SUBTRACT then        -- unary minus
    --WRITE( ZERO);   -- CONVERT TO BINARY -
    --alternatively
    TOKEN:=UNARYMINUS;
    OPCODE:=SIGNFLIP;
  elsif  UNARY and  OPCODE=ADD then        --ignore unary plus
    goto  SKIP;
  end  if ;
  UNARY:=TRUE;        --default
  if OPCODE = VARNAME then
    WRITE(TOKEN);
    ENTER(TOKEN,FOUND);--variable
    UNARY:=FALSE;
   elsif  OPCODE = FUNCTIONNAME then
    PUSH(TOKEN);      --function
    WRITE(FUNCTIONHEAD);   --can have adjustable arity
    UNARY:=FALSE;
  elsif  OPCODE= CONSTNT then        --constant
    WRITE(TOKEN);
    FLT_IO.GET(PHRASE_TO_STRING(TOKEN.TOKEN),CVALUE,LAST);
    --PUT(" CONSTANT =");FLT_IO.PUT(CVALUE);
    ENTER(TOKEN,FOUND);
    if not FOUND then
      VAR.DEFINED:=TRUE;
      VAR.VALUE:=CVALUE;
    end if;
    UNARY:=FALSE;
  elsif  OPCODE=CLOSEPAREN then
    UNARY:=FALSE;
    loop        -- find matching ( and remove it
      POP(OTOKEN);
      OPCODE:=OPERATOR(OTOKEN);
      if  OPCODE=OPENPAREN then  exit ; end  if ;
      WRITE(OTOKEN);
    end  loop ;
```

```
  elsif  OPCODE=OPENPAREN then        -- PUSH  immediately
    PUSH(TOKEN);
    UNARY:=TRUE;
  elsif  OPCODE=ARGSEPARATOR then      -- POP to (but do not remove)
    loop
      POP(OTOKEN);
      OPCODE:=OPERATOR(OTOKEN);
      if OPCODE=OPENPAREN then
        PUSH(OTOKEN);--push back (
        exit ;
      end  if ;
      WRITE(OTOKEN);
    end  loop ;
    UNARY:=TRUE;
  else            --other operator,e.g. logical
    loop
      NWEIGHT:=WEIGHT(OPCODE);
      WTS(SWEIGHT);
      if  NWEIGHT>SWEIGHT then  exit ; end  if ;
      POP(OTOKEN);
      WRITE(OTOKEN);
    end  loop ;
    PUSH(TOKEN);       --restore last token
  end  if ;
<<SKIP>>
PREDIC:=PREDIC.NEXT;
end  loop ;
loop
  if  TOPSTACK=null then  exit ; end  if ;
  POP(TOKEN) ;
  if  TOKEN=null then  exit ; end  if ;
  WRITE(TOKEN);
end  loop ;
WRITE( TERMINATOR);
return ;
end  INFIX;

-- read postfix list
```

```
procedure  READ(TOKEN: out  SYMPTR) is

begin
TOKEN:=POLISH.DATA;
POLISH:=POLISH.NEXT;
return ;
end READ;

-- get value for variable. query user if necessary
procedure GETFLT( NUMVALUE: out FLOAT) is
begin
FLT_IO.GET(NUMVALUE);
--
exception
  when DATA_ERROR =>
    NEW_LINE;
    PUT(" DATA ERROR- ENTER FLOAT VALUE SUCH AS 1.0");
    NEW_LINE;
    PUT(" MUST HAVE DIGITS ON BOTH SIDES OF .");
    FLT_IO.GET(NUMVALUE);
    return;
end GETFLT;

-- numerical value of variable returned

function  VALUE( X: in  SYMPTR) return  FLOAT is

RESULT: INTEGER;
VALPTR: SYMPTR;
NUMVALUE: FLOAT;

begin
if X=ACCUMFLAG then
  POP(NUMVALUE);
  return  NUMVALUE;
elsif  X=ZERO then
  return  0.0;
```

```
end  if ;
SEARCHV(X,RESULT,VALPTR);
if VALPTR.DEFINED then
   return  VALPTR.VALUE;
end  if ;
-- if not yet assigned value, query user
NEW_LINE;
PUT(" ENTER FLOATING PT. VALUE for  SYMBOL");
PRINT(X.TOKEN);
GETFLT(NUMVALUE);
VALPTR.VALUE:=NUMVALUE;
VALPTR.DEFINED:=TRUE;
return  NUMVALUE;
end VALUE;

-- evaluate postfix expression

procedure  POSTFIX(ANS: out  FLOAT) is

TOKEN,TOP,NEXT,ARGUMENT:SYMPTR;
FUNCTARG: ARGS;
ARGVALUE: ARGVALS;
TPARG,NEXTARG: SYMPTR;
IGNORE,ARGCOUNT: INTEGER;
OPCODE: OPERATION;
A,B,C:FLOAT;

-- pop off two values from accumulator stack for binary operators

procedure  BINARY(X,Y:out  FLOAT) is

TOP,NEXT:SYMPTR;
TP,NT: SYMPTR;

begin
POP(TOP);
Y:=VALUE(TOP);
POP(NEXT);
```

```
X:=VALUE(NEXT);
return ;
end  BINARY;

procedure  UNARY(X:out  FLOAT) is

TOP:SYMPTR;
TP,NT: SYMPTR;

begin
POP(TOP);
X:=VALUE(TOP);
return ;
end  UNARY;

-- temporarily stack accumulator value

procedure  TEMPSTACK(X: in  FLOAT) is
begin
PUSH(X);
PUSH(ACCUMFLAG);
end  TEMPSTACK;


begin             --body of postfix
ANS:=1.0; --default
FIRST:=TRUE;
TOPSTACK:=null;
READ(TOKEN);
while  TOKEN/=null and  TOKEN/=TERMINATOR loop
OPCODE:=OPERATOR(TOKEN);
case OPCODE is
  when ASSIGN =>
    POP(TOP);
    B:=VALUE(TOP);
    POP(NEXT);
    SEARCHV(NEXT,IGNORE,TPARG);
    if IGNORE/=0 then
```

```
    NEW_LINE;
    PUT(" BAD LHS in  ASSIGNMENT");
  end  if ;
  TPARG.VALUE:=B;
  TPARG.DEFINED:=TRUE;
  NEW_LINE;PUT(" ASSIGNING");FLT_IO.PUT(B);PUT(" TO ");
  PRINT(NEXT.TOKEN);
  return ;
when  EQUALS =>
  BINARY(A,B);
  if A=B then  return ;
  else
    ANS:=0.0;
    return ;
  end  if ;
when   LT =>
  BINARY(A,B);
  if A<B then  return ;
  else
    ANS:=0.0;
    return ;
  end  if ;
when   GT =>
  BINARY(A,B);
  if A>B then  return ;
  else
    ANS:=0.0;
    return ;
  end  if ;
when LTE =>
  BINARY(A,B);
  if  A<=B then  return ;
  else
    ANS:=0.0;
    return ;
  end  if ;
when GTE =>
  BINARY(A,B);
```

```
  if  A>=B then  return ;
  else
    ANS:=0.0;
    return ;
  end  if ;
when   ADD =>
  BINARY(A,B);
  C:=A+B;
  TEMPSTACK(C);
when  SUBTRACT =>
  BINARY(A,B);
  C:=A-B;
  TEMPSTACK(C);
when MULTIPLY =>
  BINARY(A,B);
  C:=A*B;
  TEMPSTACK(C);
when DIVIDE =>
  BINARY(A,B);
  C:=A/B;
  TEMPSTACK(C);
when EXPON =>
  --BINARY(A,B);
  --C:=A**INTEGER(B);   -- ADA only allows integer powers
  POP(ARGUMENT);
  ARGVALUE(1):=VALUE(ARGUMENT);
  FUNCTARG(1):=ARGUMENT;
  POP(ARGUMENT);
  ARGVALUE(2):=VALUE(ARGUMENT);
  FUNCTARG(1):=ARGUMENT;
  C:=FUNCTV(TOKEN,FUNCTARG,ARGVALUE,2);
  TEMPSTACK(C);
when  FUNCTIONNAME =>
  ARGCOUNT:=1;
  loop           -- pop until &
    POP(ARGUMENT);     -- must be at least 1 argumt
    if OPERATOR(ARGUMENT)=HEADFUNCTION then exit; end if;
    ARGVALUE(ARGCOUNT):= VALUE(ARGUMENT);
```

```
      FUNCTARG(ARGCOUNT):=ARGUMENT;
      ARGCOUNT:=ARGCOUNT+1;
    end  loop ;
    ARGCOUNT:=ARGCOUNT-1;-- & was last POP
    TEMPSTACK(FUNCTV(TOKEN,FUNCTARG,ARGVALUE,ARGCOUNT));
  when SIGNFLIP =>
    UNARY(A);          -- UNARY MINUS
    TEMPSTACK(-A);
  when others  =>        -- HEADFUNCTION,VARNAME,CONSTNT
    PUSH(TOKEN);
end case ;
READ(TOKEN);
end  loop ;
return ;
end POSTFIX;


begin            --initialize and convert infix to postfix

STRING_TO_PHRASE("#$",TPHRASE);
TERMINATOR:= new  SYMBOL;
TERMINATOR.TOKEN:=TPHRASE;
STRING_TO_PHRASE("0.0$",ZEROP);  -- for converting unary minus to binary
ZERO:=new SYMBOL;
ZERO.TOKEN:=ZEROP;
STRING_TO_PHRASE("&$",FPHRASE);  -- remembers head of function
FUNCTIONHEAD:= new SYMBOL;
FUNCTIONHEAD.TOKEN:=FPHRASE;
STRING_TO_PHRASE("@$",UMPHRASE); -- unary minus
UNARYMINUS:= new SYMBOL;
UNARYMINUS.TOKEN:=UMPHRASE;
FIRST:=TRUE;         -- no postfix string yet
TOPSTACK:=null;          -- initially empty operator stack
INFIX;
-- output  postfix (polish notation) expression
POSTF:=POLISH;
NEW_LINE;PUT(" POSTFIX EXPRESSION IS:");NEW_LINE;
loop
  if POSTF=null then exit; end if;
```

```
  PUT(" ");PRINT(POSTF.DATA.TOKEN);
  POSTF:=POSTF.NEXT;
end loop;
NEW_LINE;
--
STRING_TO_PHRASE("!#--&",ACCUMP);
--evaluate postfix after initialization
ACCUMFLAG:=new SYMBOL;
ACCUMFLAG.TOKEN:=ACCUMP;
ACCUMULATOR:=null;
POSTFIX(ANS);
return  ANS ;
end MATHD;
end  MATH;
```

```
-- Library of Mathematical Functions for Use by Math
-- They can have a variable number of arguments
-- up to MAXARGS (presently 10).
-- All arguments must be type FLOAT.
-- Note that the arguments are sent in "PASCAL" order,
-- i.e., the last argument is sent first.

with STRNG; use STRNG;
with LOGIC; use LOGIC;

package MFUNCT is

MAXARGS: constant := 10 ;   -- maximum number of function arguments
NOTFUNCT: constant := -1;   -- flag FUNCT returns if symbol not function

type ARGS is array (1..MAXARGS) of SYMPTR;
type ARGVALS is array(1..MAXARGS) of FLOAT;

function  FUNCT( TOK : in  SYMPTR) return  INTEGER ;

function FUNCTV(FUNAME: in SYMPTR; TOKV: in ARGS;
   ARGVALU: in ARGVALS; ARGCOUNT: in INTEGER) return FLOAT ;

end MFUNCT;
```

-- Math Function Library (Body)

-- It is assumed that the reader will expand this package
-- to suit his needs.

```
with STRNG; use STRNG;
with LOGIC; use LOGIC;
with TEXT_IO; use TEXT_IO;
--with SMATHLIB; use SMATHLIB;
--with FLOATOPS; use FLOATOPS;
with MATH87; use MATH87;

package body MFUNCT is

package FLT_IO is new FLOAT_IO(NUM=>FLOAT);
INIT: BOOLEAN :=TRUE;       -- initialize mfunct

POWSYM,PUTSYM,GETSYM,MINSYM,MAXSYM,SINSYM,
      ARCTAN2SYM: PHRASE;
FUNCTID: INTEGER;

function  FUNCT( TOK : in  SYMPTR) return  INTEGER is
begin
if INIT then
  INIT:=FALSE;
  STRING_TO_PHRASE("PUT",PUTSYM,3);
  STRING_TO_PHRASE("GET",GETSYM,3);
  STRING_TO_PHRASE("SIN",SINSYM,3);
  STRING_TO_PHRASE("MIN",MINSYM,3);
  STRING_TO_PHRASE("MAX",MAXSYM,3);
  STRING_TO_PHRASE("ARCTAN2",ARCTAN2SYM,7);
  STRING_TO_PHRASE("^",POWSYM,1);
  NEW_LINE;PUT(" END INITIALIZATION FUNCT");
end if;
if COMPAREPHRASES(TOK.TOKEN , PUTSYM) = 0 then
  FUNCTID:=1;
  return 1;
elsif COMPAREPHRASES(TOK.TOKEN , GETSYM) = 0 then
```

```
  FUNCTID:=2;
  return 1;
elsif COMPAREPHRASES(TOK.TOKEN , SINSYM) = 0 then
  FUNCTID:=10;
  return 1;
elsif COMPAREPHRASES(TOK.TOKEN , ARCTAN2SYM) = 0 then
  FUNCTID:=11;
  return 1;
elsif COMPAREPHRASES(TOK.TOKEN , MINSYM) = 0 then
  FUNCTID:=3;
  return 1;
elsif COMPAREPHRASES(TOK.TOKEN , MAXSYM) = 0 then
  FUNCTID:=4;
  return 1;
elsif COMPAREPHRASES(TOK.TOKEN , POWSYM) = 0 then
  FUNCTID:=5;
  return NOTFUNCT;
-- DO NOT TREAT AS RECOGNIZED FUNCTION, BUT AS OPERATOR
else
  return  NOTFUNCT;
end if;
end  FUNCT;

function FUNCTV(FUNAME: in SYMPTR; TOKV: in ARGS;
  ARGVALU: in ARGVALS; ARGCOUNT: in INTEGER) return FLOAT is

INDEX:INTEGER;
FNAME:PHRASE;
ANSWER,OTHER: FLOAT;
begin
FNAME:=FUNAME.TOKEN;
case FUNCTID is
  when  1=>
    NEW_LINE;PRINT(TOKV(1).TOKEN);PUT("=");
    FLT_IO.PUT(ARGVALU(1));
    return ARGVALU(1);
  when  2=>
    --use GET when variable already defined
```

```
--and you wish to change its value
  NEW_LINE;PUT(" ENTER FLOAT VALUE FOR ");PRINT(TOKV(1).TOKEN);
  FLT_IO.GET(ANSWER);
  RETURN ANSWER;
when  3=>
  if  ARGCOUNT <2 then
    PUT(" LESS THAN TWO ARGUMENTS TO MIN");
    return 0.0;
  end if;
  ANSWER:=ARGVALU(1);
  FOR INDEX in 2..ARGCOUNT loop
    OTHER:=ARGVALU(INDEX);
    if ANSWER > OTHER then
      ANSWER:=OTHER;
    end if;
  end loop;
  return ANSWER;
when  4=>
  if ARGCOUNT <2 then
    PUT(" LESS THAN TWO ARGUMENTS TO MAX");
    return 0.0;
  end if;
  ANSWER:=ARGVALU(1);
  FOR INDEX in 2..ARGCOUNT loop
    OTHER:=ARGVALU(INDEX);
    if ANSWER < OTHER then
      ANSWER:=OTHER;
    end if;
  end loop;
  return ANSWER;
when 5      =>
  return EXP(ARGVALU(1)*LOG(ARGVALU(2)) );
when 10     =>
  return SIN(ARGVALU(1));
when 11     =>
  -- notice the reverse ordering of arguments
  return ARCTAN2(ARGVALU(2),ARGVALU(1));
when others =>
```

```
      NEW_LINE; PUT(" UNKNOWN FUNCTION CHECK MFUNCT PACKAGE");
      PRINT(FNAME);
      return 0.0;
end case;
exception
  when  NUMERIC_ERROR =>
    NEW_LINE;PUT(" Numeric error in functv");
    if FUNCTID=5 then
      PUT(" evaluating power");
    else
      PUT(" evaluating "); PRINT(FNAME);
    end if;
    for INDEX in 1..ARGCOUNT loop
      NEW_LINE;PRINT(TOKV(INDEX).TOKEN);
      PUT(" = ");FLT_IO.PUT(ARGVALU(INDEX));
    end loop;
    return 0.0;
  when  CONSTRAINT_ERROR  =>
    NEW_LINE;PUT(" Constraint error in functv");
    if FUNCTID=5 then
      PUT(" evaluating power");
    else
      PUT(" evaluating "); PRINT(FNAME);
    end if;
    for INDEX in 1..ARGCOUNT loop
      NEW_LINE;PRINT(TOKV(INDEX).TOKEN);
      PUT(" = ");FLT_IO.PUT(ARGVALU(INDEX));
    end loop;
    return 0.0;
end FUNCTV;

end MFUNCT;
```

```
-- Test Driver for Math and Mfunct packages

with TEXT_IO; use  TEXT_IO;
with STRNG; use  STRNG;
with LOGIC;use LOGIC;
with  MATH; use  MATH;


procedure  MDRIVE is

-- generic INSTANTIATIONS for  NUMERIC I/O
package  INT_IO is  new  INTEGER_IO(NUM => INTEGER);
package  FLT_IO is  new  FLOAT_IO(NUM=> FLOAT);


ANS: FLOAT;
EXPR,OTERM,TERM:PREDICPTR;
P:PHRASE;
S:SYMPTR;
BEGIN-- Y= ABC *(-BA+ABC^D)
TERM:=new PREDICATE;
S:=new SYMBOL;
STRING_TO_PHRASE(")",P,1);
S.TOKEN:=P;
TERM.ITEM:=S;
TERM.NEXT:=null;
OTERM:=TERM;
TERM:=new PREDICATE;
S:=new SYMBOL;
STRING_TO_PHRASE("D",P,1);
S.TOKEN:=P;
TERM.ITEM:=S;
TERM.NEXT:=OTERM;
OTERM:=TERM;
TERM:=new PREDICATE;
S:=new SYMBOL;
STRING_TO_PHRASE("^",P,1);
S.TOKEN:=P;
TERM.ITEM:=S;
TERM.NEXT:=OTERM;
```

```
OTERM:=TERM;
TERM:=new PREDICATE;
S:=new SYMBOL;
STRING_TO_PHRASE("ABC",P,3);
S.TOKEN:=P;
TERM.ITEM:=S;
TERM.NEXT:=OTERM;
OTERM:=TERM;
TERM:=new PREDICATE;
S:=new SYMBOL;
STRING_TO_PHRASE("+",P,1);
S.TOKEN:=P;
TERM.ITEM:=S;
TERM.NEXT:=OTERM;
OTERM:=TERM;
TERM:=new PREDICATE;
S:=new SYMBOL;
STRING_TO_PHRASE("BA",P,2);
S.TOKEN:=P;
TERM.ITEM:=S;
TERM.NEXT:=OTERM;
OTERM:=TERM;
TERM:= new PREDICATE;
S:= new SYMBOL;
STRING_TO_PHRASE("-",P,1);
S.TOKEN:=P;
TERM.ITEM:=S;
TERM.NEXT:=OTERM;
OTERM:=TERM;
TERM:=new PREDICATE;
S:=new SYMBOL;
STRING_TO_PHRASE("(",P,1);
S.TOKEN:=P;
TERM.ITEM:=S;
TERM.NEXT:=OTERM;
OTERM:=TERM;
TERM:=new PREDICATE;
S:=new SYMBOL;
```

```
STRING_TO_PHRASE("*",P,1);
S.TOKEN:=P;
TERM.ITEM:=S;
TERM.NEXT:=OTERM;
OTERM:=TERM;
TERM:=new PREDICATE;
S:=new SYMBOL;
STRING_TO_PHRASE("ABC",P,3);
S.TOKEN:=P;
TERM.ITEM:=S;
TERM.NEXT:=OTERM;
OTERM:=TERM;
TERM:=new PREDICATE;
S:=new SYMBOL;
STRING_TO_PHRASE(":=",P,2);
S.TOKEN:=P;
TERM.ITEM:=S;
TERM.NEXT:=OTERM;
OTERM:=TERM;
TERM:=new PREDICATE;
S:=new SYMBOL;
STRING_TO_PHRASE("Y",P,1);
S.TOKEN:=P;
TERM.ITEM:=S;
TERM.NEXT:=OTERM;
EXPR:=TERM;
--
NEW_LINE; PRINTPRED(EXPR);
ANS:=MATHD(EXPR);
NEW_LINE;PUT(" MATHD=");FLT_IO.PUT(ANS);

TERM:=new PREDICATE;
S:=new SYMBOL;
STRING_TO_PHRASE(")",P,1);
S.TOKEN:=P;
TERM.ITEM:=S;
TERM.NEXT:=null;
OTERM:=TERM;
```

```
TERM:=new PREDICATE;
S:=new SYMBOL;
STRING_TO_PHRASE("Y",P,1);
S.TOKEN:=P;
TERM.ITEM:=S;
TERM.NEXT:=OTERM;
OTERM:=TERM;

TERM:=new PREDICATE;
S:=new SYMBOL;
STRING_TO_PHRASE("(",P,1);
S.TOKEN:=P;
TERM.ITEM:=S;
TERM.NEXT:=OTERM;
OTERM:=TERM;

TERM:=new PREDICATE;
S:=new SYMBOL;
STRING_TO_PHRASE("PUT",P,3);
S.TOKEN:=P;
TERM.ITEM:=S;
TERM.NEXT:=OTERM;
OTERM:=TERM;
EXPR:=TERM;
NEW_LINE; PRINTPRED(EXPR);
ANS:=MATHD(EXPR);
NEW_LINE;PUT(" MATHD=");FLT_IO.PUT(ANS);

TERM:=new PREDICATE;
S:=new SYMBOL;
STRING_TO_PHRASE(")",P,1);
S.TOKEN:=P;
TERM.ITEM:=S;
TERM.NEXT:=null;
OTERM:=TERM;

TERM:=new PREDICATE;
```

```
S:=new SYMBOL;
STRING_TO_PHRASE("3.0",P,3);
S.TOKEN:=P;
TERM.ITEM:=S;
TERM.NEXT:=OTERM;
OTERM:=TERM;

TERM:=new PREDICATE;
S:=new SYMBOL;
STRING_TO_PHRASE(";",P,1);
S.TOKEN:=P;
TERM.ITEM:=S;
TERM.NEXT:=OTERM;
OTERM:=TERM;

TERM:=new PREDICATE;
S:=new SYMBOL;
STRING_TO_PHRASE("1.0",P,3);
S.TOKEN:=P;
TERM.ITEM:=S;
TERM.NEXT:=OTERM;
OTERM:=TERM;

TERM:=new PREDICATE;
S:=new SYMBOL;
STRING_TO_PHRASE("(",P,1);
S.TOKEN:=P;
TERM.ITEM:=S;
TERM.NEXT:=OTERM;
OTERM:=TERM;

TERM:=new PREDICATE;
S:=new SYMBOL;
STRING_TO_PHRASE("ARCTAN2",P,7);
S.TOKEN:=P;
TERM.ITEM:=S;
TERM.NEXT:=OTERM;
OTERM:=TERM;
```

```
EXPR:=TERM;

TERM:=new PREDICATE;
S:=new SYMBOL;
STRING_TO_PHRASE(":=",P,2);
S.TOKEN:=P;
TERM.ITEM:=S;
TERM.NEXT:=OTERM;
OTERM:=TERM;
EXPR:=TERM;

TERM:=new PREDICATE;
S:=new SYMBOL;
STRING_TO_PHRASE("Y",P,1);
S.TOKEN:=P;
TERM.ITEM:=S;
TERM.NEXT:=OTERM;
OTERM:=TERM;
EXPR:=TERM;
NEW_LINE; PRINTPRED(EXPR);
ANS:=MATHD(EXPR);
NEW_LINE;PUT(" MATHD=");FLT_IO.PUT(ANS);

-- TEST OF MAX
TERM:=new PREDICATE;
S:=new SYMBOL;
STRING_TO_PHRASE(")",P,1);
S.TOKEN:=P;
TERM.ITEM:=S;
TERM.NEXT:=null;
OTERM:=TERM;

TERM:=new PREDICATE;
S:=new SYMBOL;
STRING_TO_PHRASE("3.0",P,3);
S.TOKEN:=P;
TERM.ITEM:=S;
TERM.NEXT:=OTERM;
```

```
OTERM:=TERM;

TERM:=new PREDICATE;
S:=new SYMBOL;
STRING_TO_PHRASE(";",P,1);
S.TOKEN:=P;
TERM.ITEM:=S;
TERM.NEXT:=OTERM;
OTERM:=TERM;

TERM:=new PREDICATE;
S:=new SYMBOL;
STRING_TO_PHRASE("1.0",P,3);
S.TOKEN:=P;
TERM.ITEM:=S;
TERM.NEXT:=OTERM;
OTERM:=TERM;

TERM:=new PREDICATE;
S:=new SYMBOL;
STRING_TO_PHRASE("(",P,1);
S.TOKEN:=P;
TERM.ITEM:=S;
TERM.NEXT:=OTERM;
OTERM:=TERM;

TERM:=new PREDICATE;
S:=new SYMBOL;
STRING_TO_PHRASE("MAX",P,3);
S.TOKEN:=P;
TERM.ITEM:=S;
TERM.NEXT:=OTERM;
OTERM:=TERM;
EXPR:=TERM;

TERM:=new PREDICATE;
S:=new SYMBOL;
STRING_TO_PHRASE(":=",P,2);
```

```
S.TOKEN:=P;
TERM.ITEM:=S;
TERM.NEXT:=OTERM;
OTERM:=TERM;
EXPR:=TERM;

TERM:=new PREDICATE;
S:=new SYMBOL;
STRING_TO_PHRASE("Y",P,1);
S.TOKEN:=P;
TERM.ITEM:=S;
TERM.NEXT:=OTERM;
OTERM:=TERM;
EXPR:=TERM;
NEW_LINE; PRINTPRED(EXPR);
ANS:=MATHD(EXPR);
NEW_LINE;PUT(" MATHD=");FLT_IO.PUT(ANS);
-- END MAX TEST

end  MDRIVE;
```

mdrive

Y := ABC * (– BA + ABC ^ D)
END INITIALIZATION FUNCT
POSTFIX EXPRESSION IS:
Y ABC BA @ ABC D ^ + * := #

ENTER FLOATING PT. VALUE for SYMBOLBA –1.0

ENTER FLOATING PT. VALUE for SYMBOLD 0.5

ENTER FLOATING PT. VALUE for SYMBOLABC 16.0

ASSIGNING 8.00000E+01 TO Y
MATHD= 1.00000E+00
PUT (Y)
POSTFIX EXPRESSION IS:
& Y PUT #

Y= 8.00000E+01
MATHD= 1.00000E+00
Y := ARCTAN2 (1.0 ; 3.0)
POSTFIX EXPRESSION IS:
Y & 1.0 3.0 ARCTAN2 := #

ASSIGNING 3.21751E–01 TO Y
MATHD= 1.00000E+00
Y := MAX (1.0 ; 3.0)
POSTFIX EXPRESSION IS:
Y & 1.0 3.0 MAX := #

ASSIGNING 3.00000E+00 TO Y
MATHD= 1.00000E+00
C:\TEMP>

Chapter 5

Frames

Overview

In this chapter we discuss the concept and implementation of frames, a user-friendly, hierarchical form of database. By hierarchical we mean that various classes and subclasses of objects may be defined. The hierarchical nature of frames enables "inheritance," in which default information can be defined for the various classes of objects. We present an in-core implementation which includes the ability to save and recover data from permanent storage.

The Ada code in this chapter does a good deal of file input/output, including exception handling, which might be of interest to Ada newcomers.

The Frame Concept

Database systems are typically classed as hierarchical, network, or relational. The relational model is currently in vogue. A relational database appears to the user as a collection of tables, or relations. This in no way constrains how the data is actually stored or manipulated. For efficient searching, it is typical to maintain index files and to store the data in a tree structure (often a B+ tree), all of which is transparent to the user.

In the hierarchical model, the data appears to the user to be a hierarchy (ordered set) of trees [1]. Each tree data element is called a segment. Each data record is a hierarchy of segments. Such models must be more closely tailored to the data to be represented, but generally repay that effort in greater efficiency. The user of a relational database generally has an easier time of specifying an arbitrary query. The hierarchical model, particularly employing the frames concept, permits a number of enhancements, such as inheritance, which enable the queries natural to the hierarchy to be handled with great efficiency in speed and storage.

The network model is similar to the hierarchical model, except that a child is allowed to have more than one parent. In other words, the tree structure is replaced by a directed acyclic graph structure. This is usually implemented by separately maintaining the data records and the set of links between segments. These links can be pointers (access types in Ada terminology) if the database is in core. By contrast, the relational model eschews links, using instead *key* values to access corresponding items in other tables.

Table 5.1 translates conventional database terminology to the terminology customary for frames. The hierarchy of records containing fields with attributes is mirrored in the structure of Frames, which contain slots composed of facets.

Table 5.1

Corresponding Terms

Database	Frames
Record	Frame
Field, Segment	Slot
Attribute	Facet

Frames augment the conventional database with a number of features. The number of facets per slot is flexible, while databases typically are created with a fairly rigid record specification (for the sake of storage efficiency). The hierarchical construction permits the inheritance of data. Suppose we have a database of the animal kingdom. We would set up a hierarchy, perhaps along the lines of the Linnaean classification of animals. Thus, humans would be in order primates of class *Mammalia* of phylum *Cordata* of the kingdom of animals (more recent classification schemes draw distinctions between Protistia and Eukaryotes rather than plants and animals). Using the inheritance feature, the properties of the animals would all be inherited by default (unless overridden) by all animals—the properties of primates by all primates, etc. A single frame for all primates, containing the default primate properties, is all that is needed to accomplish this for the primates. For example, the "bird" frame could specify that birds can fly. All birds would be facets of the slot "examples" of the bird frame. For penguins or kiwis, we would include a slot/facet entry specifying that they don't fly. For all other birds, the appropriate query for flying ability would not be found in the frame for that particular bird. The inheritance mechanism would cause the search to progress through the hierarchy to find that birds do fly (in general).

The flexibility of inheritance is enhanced by the use of the "isa" slot. Inheritance can then take place from any of the classes listed as facets of this slot. Thus, penguins might list in their "isa" slot bird, fish-eater, Antarctic-dweller, etc. They could inherit values then of a number of specified classes. In this way, frames approximate a network database because an individual may contain a number of facets in its "isa" slot and thereby inherit from a number of parents.

Another enhancement to conventional databases is the "demon." This is a facet entry which is a function call to return the appropriate value rather than a value itself. One trivial example might be an "age" slot in an employee database, which would call a function with the employee's date of birth. That function would read the system clock and compute the employee's present age. This example is trivial since if the database contains the date of birth, the "age" slot demon would be identical for all entries, and could therefore be implemented far more efficiently simply by computing the age from the date of birth without such a slot. A common demon is the "if-needed" [2,3] entry. This default produces a request for data entry when the requisite data cannot otherwise be found. *Active values* are closely related to demons. They trigger actions whenever they change.

Demons are far more natural in LISP than in Ada for two reasons. First, LISP is generally interpreted, so the information passed by the function call can be encoded in the frame no differently from any other data item. In a compiled implementation, all such call linkages would have to be resolved beforehand. Such a database would not be flexible in that adding a demon would be a major undertaking. Second, the strong typing in Ada would prevent such calls from being easily handled. The Ada compiler wants to know at compilation time that the arguments in the function call are all correctly typed. There is no aesthetic way to circumvent this. For these reasons, demons have not been implemented in this frames database package.

Frames and Rules

Frames can be useful in providing a hierarchical database of rules, as illustrated by the KNOBS [3] and KEE [4] systems. The idea is to store each rule as a frame member, with slots for the predicates, confidence factors, conditions for the activation of the rules, etc. The inheritance feature is useful in providing economy in the use of defaults in a dynamic sense—we need not select or deactivate each rule individually but can deal with them as groups. This is also useful in the user interface, as the knowledge engineer can deal with groups of rules, examine the class for similar rules, etc. Typical user interfaces in such systems can print trees of rules to aid in the editing of the rule set.

The inference engine must of course have the appropriate "hooks" into the frame's data structure but otherwise can be quite independent of the frame's structure. However, the frame structure provides us with additional flexibility if we care to make use of it. For example, a predicate term of the form

    father ?x ?y

is treated by the shells of Chapters 3 and 4 as requiring bindings to be created and stored in a table. In a frame-based system, ?x and ?y could be subfacets of the facet representing this predicate term (the slot of terms would have a facet for each term). They would be empty if unbound. Multiple bindings might be possible as alternatives. Or, anticipating the idea of the next chapter on *unification grammars,* variables could be vectors, represented by frames or lists, with unification succeeding only if each element in the vector could be unified or matched. The frame could then be a useful means for storing a dictionary or other grammatical information, both syntactical and semantic.

The Program

Functions
The database supports the following commands:

Q   Quit session.
C   Create a database.
R   Recall database (read from permanent storage).
E   Enter new member (frame).
A   Add data (slot/facet) to an existing member.
L   List all members.
M   List the slots of a member.
D   Delete data of a member.
K   Delete member.
I   Inquire for values of a specified member's specified slot if no value is specified or for members matching a given slot/facet value.
G   Global search for members that satisfy condition.

Note that the I operation makes use of the inheritance of values through "isa" slot entries. It is beyond the scope of this book to produce a relational database interface.

Representation in Core
In conventional LISP implementations, the a-list is maintained as a linked list. This is, of course, simple to implement with the usual LISP cell of two

pointers, the first to the current symbol and the second to the next cell. In the present Ada implementation, we have used binary trees to make the search more efficient in time. Of course, the differences will be small if the number of slots/frame, or facets/slot, etc., are small. No effort is made to ensure that the binary trees are balanced, and a pathological input sequence could result in a binary tree that has in fact degenerated to a linear linked list. Such trees can be balanced "off-line," for example by simply traversing them and building an AVL tree [6] from nodes as they are encountered. The identical situation was, of course, encountered in the two previous chapters. Similarly, if the database were part of an embedded, real-time system, the tree could be converted to an optimal binary search tree if the frequency of searches for the various elements were known [7].

In a database too large to reside in core, all that would be necessary to do would be to change the in-core binary trees into something like B-trees residing on a mass storage device. Again, programs for B-tree manipulation are well known [6] so we omit the details here. They are trees which maintain their height balance automatically and are quite well-suited for databases with disk storage in which the number of file accesses and modifications are to be minimized.

Representation out of Core

The conversion from the frames tree to the list form for permanent storage is fairly straightforward. Procedure SAVE performs this function. SAVE contains the file input/output processing and exception handling. The real work is done by procedure PROCESSN. This does a preorder traversal of the frames tree. A preorder traversal processes a node, then the left and right children in that order, and may be done by a recursive procedure of the form

```
PREORDER(NODE)

if NODE=null then return; end if;

--process node

...

PREORDER(NODE.LEFTCHILD);
PREORDER(NODE.RIGHTCHILD);
return;
end;
```

Alternatively, a push-down stack may be used to simulate the recursion. Similarly, the slots (and facets thereof) are treated as encountered by recursive calls to PROCESSN. Each such call is characterized by an integer depth, which is written to the output file to enable the subsequent read to determine whether the data constitutes a frame, slot, facet, etc. The frames will all have the lowest depth, the slots the next depth, etc. RESTORE proceeds from that list to rebuild the frame's database tree as well as the symbol table. A push-down stack is used to enable us to return to a given depth after information of a greater depth is encountered. The same effect could of course be done with recursion, but the push-down stack in this case seemed more straightforward. The Ada novice might want to try his hand at writing SAVE using a push-down stack instead of recursive calls to a procedure PROCESSN, and vice versa for RESTORE.

Data Structures and Subprograms

We of course use the dynamic string package presented first in Chapter 3. The basic data type is the tree, with the symbols stored in a binary search tree as before, and the a-list of LISP treated as a tree, type ATREE. The ATREE is a binary search tree, so each element has pointers to right and left children, rather than a single pointer to a successor which would have been the case if we had used a simple linked list (see Chapter 3). A pointer to a symbol is in the ID field, which is used, for example, for the ID of a frame itself, in which case the DATA is an ATREE of slots, or for the slot id, while the data itself is any number of facets for the slot. In the facet ATREEs, the ID field will contain the facet value and DATA will typically be unused.

Because the frame structure is defined recursively in terms of type ATREE, it is possible to have subfacets of facets, etc., to any desired depth. The user interface does not support this extension to the frame concept nor are the search routines designed to check for subfacets, but the SAVE and RESTORE procedures are general enough to handle them.

A push-down stack is used by the PROCESSN subprogram for the purpose of constructing the database from its representation as a list in a file.

SEARCH—searches the ATREE in an exactly analogous manner to the routine of the same name which searches the SYMBOL tree structure.

PUSH—had we used a pushes stack for PROCESSN.

POP—pops stack for PROCESSN.

RESTORE—had we used a reads in the database from a file. It has an exception handler for the possible errors, with the messages being self-explanatory (and more than a mere echoing of the name of the exception). For example, STATUS_ERROR is the exception which is typically raised if the file is not open, whereas NAME_ERROR is raised if the file could not be found to be opened. The operation of RESTORE is discussed above.

PROCESSN—is used by SAVE. Its operation is discussed above with that of RESTORE.

SAVE—does the file I/O and calls PROCESSN. It includes the exception handling associated with writing a file.

MAKEF—allocates a new ATREE for a frame element and initializes it. It then places the new frame in the frame ATREE structure.

FFIND—searches for an element in an ATREE, using SEARCH. It may therefore be used to locate a frame, or a given slot of a frame, or a given facet of a slot. It is used when data is added or deleted to a frame.

DELETE—is used to delete an element of an ATREE. It uses FFIND to locate the specified element.

ADD—inserts a value into an ATREE, in particular a facet value into a slot. It uses FFIND to find the member frame and the slot. It creates the slot if necessary.

PBT—does a preorder traversal of a binary tree and prints out the tree in the process.

IBT—is similar to PBT except it does an in-order traversal. This is a traversal of the form:

INORDER(NODE)

if NODE=null then return; end if;

INORDER(NODE.LEFTCHILD);

--process node

...

INORDER(NODE.RIGHTCHILD);

return;

end;

If we are processing a binary search tree, then the in-order traversal will process the elements in lexicographic order. We can thus get an alphabetized list of the elements of the tree. IBT is used for the "list members" function.

CBT—does an in-order traversal which is designed not to print the tree (as PBT) but to search for a value and print out a message if the appropriate value is located.

TBT—also does a preorder traversal, similar to CBT but is used to locate values via recursive calls to FINDQ.

FINDQ—searches for ATREE element value in response to a query. It employs SEARCH to locate the appropriate slot. If there is no specified target facet value, then IBT is used to list the facet values. Otherwise, CBT is used to search for and list member frames with matching slot/facet entries. If there are no matching slots, the demons come into play. Inheritance via the "isa" slot is used, if possible. This is done through recursion via TBT. This recursive structure provides the ability to inherit indirectly to any depth.

SBT—performs an in-order traversal search using FINDQ. It is used to search for member frames with given property.

FRAMES—is the main program. It is basically one large case statement to handle the user's input and queries.

Example

In addition to the program listing, we present the off-line (list) representation of a database of animal characteristics and a sample session.

References

1. C. J. Date, *An Introduction to Database Systems,* Vol. I, 4th ed. (Reading, Mass.: Addison-Wesley, 1986).

2. P. H. Winston and B. K. P. Horn, *LISP,* 2d ed. (Reading, Mass.: Addison-Wesley, 1984).

3. P. H. Winston, *Artificial Intelligence,* 2nd ed. (Reading, Mass.: Addison-Wesley, 1984).

4. C. Engleman and W. M. Stanton, in *Artificial and Human Intelligence* (A. Elithorn and R. Barnerji, ed.) (Amsterdam: Elsevier Sci. Publ., 1984), p. 141.

5. R. Fikes and T. Kehler, *Comm. ACM* 28, 904 (1985).

6. R. J. Baron and L. G. Shapiro, *Data Structures and their Implementation* (N.Y.: Van Nostrand Reinhold, 1980).

7. E. M. Reingold and W. J. Hansen, *Data Structures* (Boston: Little Brown, 1983).

Program Listing and Test Problem Output

```ada
-- Frames Database

with TEXT_IO; use  TEXT_IO;
with STRNG; use STRNG;
with LOGIC; use LOGIC;

procedure  FRAME is

package  INT_IO is  new  INTEGER_IO(NUM=> INTEGER);

subtype  PTRANGE is  INTEGER range  0..MAX_RULE_COUNT;

type  ATREE;
type  APTR is  access  ATREE;
type  ATREE is
    record
      ID:SYMPTR;
      DATA:APTR;
      LEFT:APTR;
      RIGHT:APTR;
    end  record ;

type  STACK;
type  STACKPTR is  access  STACK;
type  STACK is
    record
      DATA:APTR;
      DEPTH: INTEGER;
      LEFT: BOOLEAN;
      NEXT : STACKPTR;
    end  record ;

SLOTID,COMPV,WORD,IDENT,NAME,CPTR,PPTR:SYMPTR;
FRAME,FACET,SLOT,VALUE:APTR;
LENGTHIS,KTFRAMES,COMP:INTEGER;
CHAR:CHARACTER;
OUTFILE,FRAMEFILE:FILE_TYPE;
DROOT:SYMPTR;
```

```
FROOT:APTR;
CFPTR,PFPTR:APTR;
PFRAME:APTR;
SFRAME:APTR;
PREVIOUS:STACKPTR;
NTOKEN,ISATOKEN,IS2TOKEN:PHRASE;
IS2PTR,ISAPTR,NPTR:SYMPTR;
NEWF,ISA,FOUND:BOOLEAN;
TXT:STRING(1..LONGPHRASE_LENGTH);
STOP,SBTM:STACKPTR;

procedure PRINT( FRAMEFILE: in   FILE_TYPE;MSG: in PHRASE) is

I: INTEGER;
CHAR: CHARACTER;

begin
for  I in  1..STRINGLENGTH loop
  CHAR:=MSG(I);
  if (CHAR='$') then  return ; end if ;
  PUT(FRAMEFILE,CHAR);
end  loop ;
exception
    when  CONSTRAINT_ERROR=>
         return ;
end  PRINT;




procedure  SEARCH(CURPTR: in  out  SYMPTR;
           OPREVPTR: out  SYMPTR;
           STRNG: in  PHRASE;
           OFOUND: out  BOOLEAN) is

COMP:INTEGER;
FOUND: BOOLEAN;
PREVPTR: SYMPTR;
```

```
begin
FOUND:=FALSE;
loop
  PREVPTR:=CURPTR;
  COMP:=COMPAREPHRASES(STRNG,CURPTR.TOKEN);
  if COMP=0 then
    FOUND :=TRUE;
  elsif (COMP=-1) then
    CURPTR:=CURPTR.LEFT;
  else
    CURPTR:=CURPTR.RIGHT;
  end if ;
  if (FOUND or CURPTR=null) then
     exit ;
  end if ;
end loop ;
OFOUND:=FOUND;
OPREVPTR:=PREVPTR;
return ;
end SEARCH;

procedure SEARCH(CURPTR: in out APTR;
            OPREVPTR: out APTR;
            STRNG: in PHRASE;
            OFOUND: out BOOLEAN) is

COMP:INTEGER;
FOUND:BOOLEAN;
PREVPTR: APTR;

begin
FOUND:=FALSE;
PFRAME:=null;
loop
  PREVPTR:=CURPTR;
  COMP:=COMPAREPHRASES(STRNG,CURPTR.ID.TOKEN);
  if COMP=0 then
    FOUND :=TRUE;
```

```
  elsif (COMP=-1) then
    CURPTR:=CURPTR.LEFT;
  else
    CURPTR:=CURPTR.RIGHT;
  end if ;
  if (FOUND or CURPTR=null) then
    exit ;
  end if ;
  PFRAME:=PREVPTR;
end loop ;
OFOUND:=FOUND;
OPREVPTR:=PREVPTR;
return ;
end SEARCH;

procedure MAKESYM(PTR:in out SYMPTR; STRG: in PHRASE) is
NEWPTR: SYMPTR;

begin
NEWPTR:= new SYMBOL;
NEWPTR.TOKEN:=STRG;
NEWPTR.LEFT:=null;
NEWPTR.RIGHT:=null;
PTR:=NEWPTR;
end MAKESYM;

procedure READSYM(OSYM: out SYMPTR) is

TXT:STRING(1..80);
TEXT:LONGPHRASE;
SYMBOL: PHRASE;
SYM,DICTC,DICTP:SYMPTR;
COMP:INTEGER;
LENGTHIS:INTEGER;

begin
loop
  GET_LINE(TXT,LENGTHIS);
```

```
   if  LENGTHIS>0 then  exit ;end  if ;
end  loop ;
STRING_TO_PHRASE(TXT,TEXT,LENGTHIS);
LONGPHRASE_TO_PHRASE(TEXT,SYMBOL,1,LENGTHIS);
NEW_LINE;PRINT(SYMBOL);
DICTC:=DROOT;
SEARCH( DICTC,DICTP,SYMBOL,FOUND);
if FOUND then
   SYM:=DICTC;
   OSYM:=SYM;
   return ;
end  if ;
MAKESYM(SYM,SYMBOL);
COMP:=COMPAREPHRASES(DICTP.TOKEN,SYMBOL);
if COMP=1 then
   DICTP.LEFT:=SYM;
else
   DICTP.RIGHT:=SYM;
end  if ;
OSYM:=SYM;
return ;
end  READSYM;

procedure INSTALL_SYMBOL( SYMBOL: in SYMPTR) is
START,WHERE: SYMPTR;
FOUND: BOOLEAN;
COMP: INTEGER;

begin
START:=DROOT;
SEARCH( START,WHERE,SYMBOL.TOKEN,FOUND);
if not FOUND then
   COMP:=COMPAREPHRASES(WHERE.TOKEN,SYMBOL.TOKEN);
   if COMP=1 then
      WHERE.LEFT:=SYMBOL;
   else
      WHERE.RIGHT:=SYMBOL;
   end  if ;
```

```
end if;
end INSTALL_SYMBOL;

procedure PUSH (P:in  APTR;D:in  INTEGER;
          LEFT:BOOLEAN; S: in  out  STACKPTR) is

GLLS: STACKPTR;

begin

GLLS:= new  STACK;
GLLS.DATA:=P;
GLLS.DEPTH:=D;
GLLS.LEFT:=LEFT;
GLLS.NEXT:=S;
S:=GLLS;
return ;
end  PUSH;

procedure  POP(P:out  APTR ; D: out  INTEGER; LEFT:out  BOOLEAN;
               S:in  out  STACKPTR) is

begin
P:=S.DATA;
D:=S.DEPTH;
LEFT:=S.LEFT;
PREVIOUS:=S;
S:=S.NEXT;
return ;
end  POP;

procedure  RESTORE is

CHILD,FRAME:APTR;
TEXT:LONGPHRASE;
TXT:STRING(1..LONGPHRASE_LENGTH);
NULLP,NULLT:PHRASE;
WORD: PHRASE;
```

```
WPTR,CPTR,PPTR:SYMPTR;
STOP,SBTM: STACKPTR;
DEPTH,CDEPTH,PDEPTH,LINDEX:INTEGER;
LEFT,FOUND,ISNULL:BOOLEAN;
COMP:INTEGER;
ANSWER:CHARACTER;
FILENAME:STRING(1..10);
begin
FILENAME:="          ";
NEW_LINE;PUT(" ENTER FULL FILE NAME");NEW_LINE;
loop
   GET_LINE(FILENAME,LENGTHIS);--DEFAULT CONSOLE INPUT?
   if LENGTHIS>0 then exit;end if;
end loop;
NEW_LINE;PUT(" FILE TO BE READ IN IS ");PUT(FILENAME);
OPEN(FRAMEFILE,IN_FILE,FILENAME);
GET_LINE(FRAMEFILE, TXT,LENGTHIS);
DEPTH:=-1;
NEW_LINE;
PUT(" FRAME DATAFILE in use IS");
for LINDEX in  1..LENGTHIS loop
    PUT(TXT(LINDEX));
end  loop ;
STRING_TO_PHRASE(TXT,TEXT,LENGTHIS);
LONGPHRASE_TO_PHRASE(TEXT,WORD,1,LENGTHIS);
CPTR:=DROOT;
SEARCH(CPTR,PPTR,WORD,FOUND);
if not FOUND then
   COMP:=COMPAREPHRASES(WORD,PPTR.TOKEN);
   MAKESYM(CPTR,WORD);
   if COMP=-1 then
     PPTR.LEFT:=CPTR;
    else
     PPTR.RIGHT:=CPTR;
    end  if ;
end  if ;
FROOT:=NEW ATREE;
FROOT.ID:=CPTR;
```

```
FROOT.DATA:=null;
FROOT.LEFT:=null;
FROOT.RIGHT:=null;
FRAME:=FROOT;
LEFT:=TRUE;
STRING_TO_PHRASE("NULL$",NULLT,4);
STOP:=null;
SBTM:=null;
CDEPTH:=0;
PUSH(FROOT,CDEPTH,TRUE,SBTM);
STOP:=SBTM;
loop
  INT_IO.GET(FRAMEFILE,DEPTH);
--   PUT(" DEPTH=");INT_IO.PUT(DEPTH);--DEBUG
  SKIP_LINE(FRAMEFILE);--?? NEEDED
  GET_LINE(FRAMEFILE,TXT,LENGTHIS);
--   NEW_LINE;--DEBUG
--   for LINDEX in 1..LENGTHIS loop
--       PUT(TXT(LINDEX));
--   end loop ;
--   INT_IO.PUT(LENGTHIS);
  STRING_TO_PHRASE(TXT,NULLP,LENGTHIS);
  ISNULL:= (0=COMPAREPHRASES(NULLP,NULLT));
  STRING_TO_PHRASE(TXT,TEXT,LENGTHIS);
  LONGPHRASE_TO_PHRASE(TEXT,WORD,1,LENGTHIS);
  CPTR:=DROOT;
  SEARCH(CPTR,PPTR,WORD,FOUND);
  if not FOUND then
     COMP:=COMPAREPHRASES(WORD,PPTR.TOKEN);
     MAKESYM(CPTR,WORD);
     if COMP=-1 then
       PPTR.LEFT:=CPTR;
     else
       PPTR.RIGHT:=CPTR;
     end if ;
  end if ;
  if DEPTH=CDEPTH then
     if not ISNULL then
```

```
      CHILD:=NEW ATREE;
      CHILD.ID:=CPTR;
      CHILD.LEFT:=null;
      CHILD.RIGHT:=null;
      if LEFT then
        FRAME.LEFT:=CHILD;
      else
        FRAME.RIGHT:=CHILD;
      end if ;
      FRAME:=CHILD;
    end if ;
   LEFT:=NOT LEFT;
elsif DEPTH<CDEPTH then
  POP(FRAME,CDEPTH,LEFT,STOP);
   if not ISNULL then
     CHILD:=NEW ATREE;
     CHILD.ID:=CPTR;
     CHILD.LEFT:=null;
     CHILD.RIGHT:=null;
     if LEFT then
        FRAME.LEFT:=CHILD;
     else
        FRAME.RIGHT:=CHILD;
     end if ;
   end if ;
   LEFT:= not  LEFT;
   CDEPTH:=DEPTH;
else
   if not ISNULL then
     CHILD:=NEW ATREE;
     CHILD.ID:=CPTR;
     CHILD.RIGHT:=null;
     CHILD.LEFT:=null;
     FRAME.DATA:=CHILD;
     PUSH(FRAME,CDEPTH,LEFT,STOP);
     FRAME:=CHILD;
     CDEPTH:=DEPTH;
   end if ;
```

```
        LEFT:=TRUE;
   end  if ;
end  loop ;
CLOSE(FRAMEFILE);
return ;
exception
when  STATUS_ERROR=>
      NEW_LINE;PUT(" STATUS ERROR FILE not  OPEN");
      return ;
when  NAME_ERROR=>
      NEW_LINE;PUT(" NAME ERROR-FILE DOES not  EXIST");
      return ;
when  USE_ERROR=>
      NEW_LINE;PUT(" use  ERROR-PERHAPS DISK FULL/PROTECTED");
      return ;
when  DEVICE_ERROR=>
      NEW_LINE;PUT(" DEVICE ERROR-HARDWARE PBLM");
      return ;
when  DATA_ERROR =>
      NEW_LINE;PUT(" DATA ERROR ");
      return ;
when  END_ERROR =>
      NEW_LINE;PUT(" END OF INPUT FILE ENCOUNTERED");
      return ;
end  RESTORE;

procedure  PROCESSN(DEPTH:in  INTEGER; NODE: in  out  APTR) is

begin
if NODE=null then
  INT_IO.PUT(OUTFILE,DEPTH);NEW_LINE(OUTFILE);
  PUT(OUTFILE,"NULL");NEW_LINE(OUTFILE);
  return ;
lsif NODE=FROOT then
  PRINT(OUTFILE,NODE.ID.TOKEN);
  NEW_LINE(OUTFILE);
lse
  INT_IO.PUT(OUTFILE,DEPTH);NEW_LINE(OUTFILE);
```

```
    PRINT(OUTFILE,NODE.ID.TOKEN);NEW_LINE(OUTFILE);
    PROCESSN( (DEPTH+1) ,NODE.DATA);
end  if ;
PROCESSN(DEPTH,NODE.LEFT);
PROCESSN(DEPTH,NODE.RIGHT);
return ;
end  PROCESSN;

procedure  SAVE is
DEPTH:INTEGER;
FILENAME:STRING(1..10);

begin
DEPTH:=0;
FILENAME:="          ";
NEW_LINE;PUT(" ENTER FULL FILE NAME");NEW_LINE;
loop
    GET_LINE(FILENAME,LENGTHIS);--DEFAULT CONSOLE INPUT?
    if LENGTHIS>0 then exit;end if;
end loop;
CREATE(OUTFILE,OUT_FILE,FILENAME);
NEW_LINE;PUT(" FILE TO BE WRITTEN IN IS ");PUT(FILENAME);
PROCESSN(DEPTH,FROOT);
INT_IO.PUT(OUTFILE, 0 ); NEW_LINE(OUTFILE);
CLOSE(OUTFILE);
return ;
exception
when  STATUS_ERROR=>
      NEW_LINE;PUT(" STATUS ERROR CANNOT OPEN FILE");
      return ;
when  NAME_ERROR=>
      NEW_LINE;PUT(" NAME ERROR-FILE DOES not  EXIST");
      return ;
when  USE_ERROR=>
      NEW_LINE;PUT(" use  ERROR-PERHAPS DISK FULL/PROTECTED");
      return ;
when  DEVICE_ERROR=>
      NEW_LINE;PUT(" DEVICE ERROR-HARDWARE PBLM");
```

```
      return ;
when  DATA_ERROR =>
      return ;
when  END_ERROR =>
      return ;

end  SAVE;

procedure  MAKEF(ID: in  SYMPTR; DATA:in  APTR; WHERE:in  out  APTR;
                           OFRAME:out  APTR) is

COMP:INTEGER;
FRAME: APTR;

begin
FRAME:= new  ATREE;
FRAME.ID:=ID;
FRAME.DATA:=DATA;
FRAME.LEFT:=null;
FRAME.RIGHT:=null;
COMP:=COMPAREPHRASES(WHERE.ID.TOKEN,ID.TOKEN);
if COMP=1 then
  WHERE.LEFT:=FRAME;
else
  WHERE.RIGHT:=FRAME;
end  if ;
OFRAME:=FRAME;
return ;
end  MAKEF;

procedure  FFIND(ID:in  SYMPTR; STARTAT:in  APTR;
        F:out  APTR;
        OFOUND:out  BOOLEAN ) is

CPTR,PPTR:APTR;
FOUND: BOOLEAN;

begin
```

```
if STARTAT=null then
  FOUND:=FALSE;
  F:=null;
  PFRAME:=null;
  OFOUND:=FOUND;
  return ;
end if ;
CPTR:=STARTAT;
SEARCH(CPTR,PPTR,ID.TOKEN,FOUND);
if FOUND then
  F:=CPTR;
else
  F:=PPTR;
  PFRAME:=PPTR;
end if ;
OFOUND:=FOUND;
return ;
end  FFIND;

procedure  DELETE(ID:in  SYMPTR;STARTAT: in  out  APTR) is
P,C,Q,R: APTR;
COMP:INTEGER;
FIRST,FOUND:BOOLEAN;

begin
if STARTAT=null then
  NEW_LINE;PUT(" VACUOUS DELETE");
  return ;
end if ;
FFIND(ID,STARTAT,C,FOUND);
if not FOUND then
  NEW_LINE;PUT(" NO VALUE TO DELETE");
  return ;
end if ;
FIRST:= (STARTAT=C);
if not FIRST then
  COMP:=COMPAREPHRASES(ID.TOKEN,PFRAME.ID.TOKEN);
end if ;
```

```
if C.RIGHT=null then
  if FIRST then
    STARTAT:=C.LEFT;
  else
    if COMP=-1 then
      PFRAME.LEFT:=C.LEFT;
    else
      PFRAME.RIGHT:=C.LEFT;
    end if ;
  end if ;
  return ;
elsif C.LEFT=null then
  if FIRST then
    STARTAT:=C.RIGHT;
  else
    if COMP=-1 then
      PFRAME.LEFT:=C.RIGHT;
    else
      PFRAME.RIGHT:=C.RIGHT;
    end if ;
  end if ;
  return ;
end if ;
R:=C.RIGHT;
loop
  if R.LEFT=null then  exit ; end if ;
  R:=R.LEFT;
end loop ;
R.LEFT:=C.LEFT;
if FIRST then
  STARTAT:=C.RIGHT;
  return ;
end if ;
if COMP=-1 then
  PFRAME.LEFT:=C.RIGHT;
else
  PFRAME.RIGHT:=C.RIGHT;
end if ;
```

```
return ;
end DELETE;

procedure  ADD(VALUE:in  SYMPTR; SLOT: in  out  APTR;
                        ISA:in  BOOLEAN) is
FOUND:BOOLEAN;
CPTR,PPTR,PTR:APTR;
COMP:INTEGER;
begin
CPTR:=SLOT.DATA;
if CPTR/=null THEN
  SEARCH(CPTR,PPTR,VALUE.TOKEN,FOUND);
  if FOUND then
    NEW_LINE;PUT(" SLOT ALREADY HAS THIS VALUE");
  end  if ;
  MAKEF(VALUE,null,PPTR,CPTR);
else
  CPTR:=NEW ATREE;
  CPTR.ID:=VALUE;
  CPTR.DATA:=null;
  CPTR.RIGHT:=null;
  CPTR.LEFT:=null;
  SLOT.DATA:=CPTR;
end  if ;
return ;
end  ADD;

procedure  PBT(P:in  out  APTR) is
Q,R:APTR;
S:SYMPTR;
begin
if  P=null then  return ; end  if ;
S:=P.ID;
NEW_LINE;PUT(" VALUE ");PRINT(S.TOKEN);
PBT(P.LEFT);
PBT(P.RIGHT);
end  PBT;
```

```
procedure IBT(P:in out APTR) is
Q,R:APTR;
S:SYMPTR;
begin
if P=null then return ; end if ;
IBT(P.LEFT);
if P/=FROOT then
   NEW_LINE;PUT(" VALUE ");PRINT(P.ID.TOKEN);
end if ;
IBT(P.RIGHT);
end IBT;


procedure CBT(P:in out APTR;OFOUND:out BOOLEAN;CV:in SYMPTR) is

Q,R:APTR;
S:SYMPTR;
FOUND: BOOLEAN;

begin
if P=null then return ; end if ;
CBT(P.LEFT,FOUND,CV);
if CV=P.ID then
   NEW_LINE;PUT(" MEMBER ");PRINT(SFRAME.ID.TOKEN);
   PUT(" HAS VALUE DESIRED");
end if ;
CBT(P.RIGHT,FOUND,CV);
OFOUND:=FOUND;
return ;
end CBT;


procedure FINQ(SLOTID:in SYMPTR;FRAME:in APTR;
            COMPV:in SYMPTR;OGOT: out BOOLEAN) is

KOUNT:INTEGER;
CP,PP,SP:APTR;
GOT,FOUND:BOOLEAN;

procedure TBT(SLOT:in SYMPTR; P:in out APTR;OGOT:out BOOLEAN)is
```

```
Q,R:APTR;
S:SYMPTR;
GOT,FOUND:BOOLEAN;
begin
GOT:=FALSE;
if P=null then
  OGOT:=GOT;
  return ;
end if ;
R:=P.DATA;
if R=null then
  S:=P.ID;
  Q:=FROOT;
  SEARCH(Q,R,S.TOKEN,FOUND);
  if FOUND then
    FINQ(SLOT,R,null,GOT);
    if GOT then
      NEW_LINE;PUT(" VALUE VIA ISA ");PRINT(P.ID.TOKEN);
      PUT(" for  MEMBER ");PRINT(SFRAME.ID.TOKEN);
     end if ;
   end if ;
else
   NEW_LINE;PUT(" PROBLEM TBT ");PRINT(P.ID.TOKEN);
   OGOT:=GOT;
   return ;
end if ;
TBT(WORD,P.LEFT,GOT);
TBT(WORD,P.RIGHT,GOT);
OGOT:=GOT;
return ;
end TBT;

begin
GOT:=FALSE;
if FRAME=null then  return ; end if ;
SP:=FRAME.DATA;
if SP=null then
```

```
  OGOT:=GOT;
  return ;
end  if ;
CP:=SP;
SEARCH(CP ,PP,SLOTID.TOKEN,FOUND);
if FOUND THEN
  SP:=CP.DATA;
  if COMPV=null then
    IBT(SP);
    GOT:=TRUE;
    NEW_LINE;PUT(" for  MEMBER ");PRINT(SFRAME.ID.TOKEN);
   else
     CBT(SP,GOT,COMPV);
   end  if ;
else
   CP:=SP;
   SEARCH(CP,PP,ISATOKEN,FOUND);
   if not FOUND then
     CP:=SP;
     SEARCH(CP,PP,IS2TOKEN,FOUND);
   end if;
   if not FOUND then
     OGOT:=FALSE;
     return ;
   end  if ;
   PP:=CP.DATA;
   TBT(SLOTID,PP,GOT);
end  if ;
OGOT:=GOT;
return ;
end  FINQ;

procedure  SBT(STARTAT:in  APTR) is

GOT:BOOLEAN;

begin
 f  STARTAT=null then  return ; end  if ;
```

```
SBT(STARTAT.LEFT);
SFRAME:=STARTAT;
FINQ(SLOTID,SFRAME,COMPV,GOT);
SBT(STARTAT.RIGHT);
return ;
end SBT;

begin
NEWF:=TRUE;
FROOT:=null;
STRING_TO_PHRASE("isa$",ISATOKEN,3);
STRING_TO_PHRASE("ISA$",IS2TOKEN,3);
MAKESYM(ISAPTR,ISATOKEN);
MAKESYM(IS2PTR,IS2TOKEN);
DROOT:=ISAPTR;
INSTALL_SYMBOL(IS2PTR);
STRING_TO_PHRASE("null$",NTOKEN,4);
loop
<<MENU>>
if NEWF then
  NEW_LINE;
  PUT(" YOU MUST FIRST ENTER C or  R for  new  DATABASE");
end if ;
NEW_LINE;PUT(" MENU ENTER: ");
NEW_LINE;PUT(" Q TO QUIT SESSION ");
NEW_LINE;PUT(" C TO CREATE FRAME DATABASE");
NEW_LINE;PUT(" R TO RECALL FRAME DATABASE");
NEW_LINE;PUT(" E TO ENTER new  MEMBER ");
NEW_LINE;PUT(" A TO ADD TO DATA of  MEMBER ");
NEW_LINE;PUT(" L TO LIST MEMBERS");
NEW_LINE;PUT(" M TO LIST MEMBER SLOTS");
NEW_LINE;PUT(" D TO DELETE DATA of  MEMBER ");
NEW_LINE;PUT(" K TO KILL (DELETE)MEMBER");
NEW_LINE;PUT(" S TO SAVE DATABASE TO FILE");
NEW_LINE;PUT(" I for  INQUIRY");
NEW_LINE;PUT(" G for  GLOBAL SEARCH for  VALUE");
GET(CHAR);
if NEWF then
```

```
  if CHAR ='c' or CHAR='C' or CHAR='r' or CHAR='R' then
    null ;
  else
    NEW_LINE;PUT(" use C or R FIRST ");
    goto MENU;
  end if ;
end if ;
case CHAR is
     when 'q'|'Q'=>
      exit ;
     when 'c'|'C'=>
      NEW_LINE;PUT(" ENTER IDENTIFIER(FILENAME)");
      READSYM(WORD);
      FROOT:=NEW ATREE;
      FROOT.ID:=WORD;
      FROOT.DATA:=null;
      FROOT.RIGHT:=null;
      FROOT.LEFT:=null;
      NEWF:=FALSE;
     when 'r'|'R'=>
      RESTORE;
      NEWF:=FALSE;
     when 'e'|'E'=>
      NEW_LINE;PUT(" ENTER UNIQUE IDENTIFIER:");
      READSYM(WORD);
      CFPTR:=FROOT;
      SEARCH(CFPTR,PFPTR,WORD.TOKEN,FOUND);
      if FOUND then
        NEW_LINE;PUT(" IDENTIFIER ");
        PRINT(WORD.TOKEN);PUT(" USED PREVIOUSLY");
        goto MENU ;
      end if ;
      MAKEF(WORD,null,PFPTR,CFPTR);
     when 'a'|'A'=>
      NEW_LINE;PUT(" ENTER FRAME IDENTIFIER:");
      READSYM(WORD);
      FFIND(WORD,FROOT,FRAME,FOUND);
      if not FOUND then
```

```
        NEW_LINE;PRINT(WORD.TOKEN);
        PUT(" not  FOUND-USE E FIRST");
        goto  MENU;
     end  if ;
     NEW_LINE;PUT(" ENTER SLOT IDENTIFIER:");
     READSYM(WORD);
     ISA:= (WORD=ISAPTR or else WORD=IS2PTR);
     FFIND(WORD,FRAME.DATA,SLOT,FOUND);
     if not FOUND then
        NEW_LINE;PUT(" CREATING SLOT:");
        PRINT(WORD.TOKEN);
        if FRAME.DATA=null then
           SLOT:=NEW ATREE;
           SLOT.ID:=WORD;
           SLOT.DATA:=null;
           SLOT.LEFT:=null;
           SLOT.RIGHT:=null;
           FRAME.DATA:=SLOT;
         else
           MAKEF(WORD,null,SLOT,FACET);
           SLOT:=FACET;
         end  if ;
     end  if ;
     if WORD=ISAPTR then
        NEW_LINE;PUT(" ISA VALUE SHOULD BE FRAME ID");
     end  if ;
     NEW_LINE;PUT(" ENTER VALUE TO BE ADDED:");
     READSYM(WORD);
     ADD(WORD,SLOT,ISA);
  when  'd'|'D'=>
     NEW_LINE;PUT(" ENTER UNIQUE IDENTIFIER:");
     READSYM(WORD);
     FFIND(WORD,FROOT,FRAME,FOUND);
     if not FOUND then
        NEW_LINE;PUT(" NO FRAME");PRINT(WORD.TOKEN);
        goto  MENU;
     end  if ;
     NEW_LINE;PUT("ENTER SLOT ID");
```

```
    READSYM(WORD);
    FFIND(WORD,FRAME.DATA,SLOT,FOUND);
    if not FOUND then
       NEW_LINE;PUT(" NO SLOT ");
       PRINT(WORD.TOKEN);
       goto MENU;
    end if ;
       NEW_LINE;PUT("ENTER VALUE TO DELETE");
       READSYM(WORD);
       DELETE(WORD,SLOT.DATA);
when 'k'|'K'=>
    NEW_LINE;PUT(" ENTER UNIQUE IDENTIFER");
    READSYM(WORD);
    DELETE(WORD,FROOT);
when 's'|'S'=>
    SAVE;
when 'i'|'I'=>
    NEW_LINE;PUT(" ENTER UNIQUE IDENTIFIER");
    READSYM(WORD);
    FFIND(WORD,FROOT,FRAME,FOUND);
    if not FOUND then
       NEW_LINE;PUT(" NO ENTRY");PRINT(WORD.TOKEN);
    else
       NEW_LINE;PUT(" ENTER SLOT IDENTIFIER:");
       READSYM(WORD);
       SFRAME:=FRAME;
       FINQ(WORD,FRAME,null,FOUND);
    end if ;
when 'l'|'L'=>
    IBT(FROOT);
when 'm'|'M'=>
    NEW_LINE;PUT(" ENTER MEMBER ID");
    READSYM(WORD);
    FFIND(WORD,FROOT,FRAME,FOUND);
    if not FOUND then
       NEW_LINE;PUT(" NO MEMBER ");PRINT(WORD.TOKEN);
    else
       IBT(FRAME.DATA);
```

```
            end  if ;
      when  'g'|'G'=>
            NEW_LINE;PUT(" ENTER SLOT TO SEARCH ON");
            READSYM(SLOTID);
            NEW_LINE;PUT(" ENTER VALUE TO SEARCH FOR");
            READSYM(COMPV);
            SBT(FROOT);
      when  others  =>
            PUT(" I DON'T UNDERSTAND-REENTER");NEW_LINE;
end  case ;
if  CHAR='q' or  CHAR='Q' then  exit ;
end  if ;
end  loop ;
end  FRAME;
```

anim

0

NULL

0

lion

1

isa

2

mammal

3

NULL

2

NULL

2

NULL

1

NULL

1

NULL

0

NULL

0

tiger

1

NULL

0

mammal

1

gives

2

milk

3

NULL

2

NULL

2

NULL

1

NULL
1
NULL
0
NULL
0
NULL
0
NULL
0

YOU MUST FIRST ENTER C or R for new DATABASE

MENU ENTER:

Q TO QUIT SESSION

C TO CREATE FRAME DATABASE

R TO RECALL FRAME DATABASE

E TO ENTER new MEMBER

A TO ADD TO DATA of MEMBER

L TO LIST MEMBERS

M TO LIST MEMBER SLOTS

D TO DELETE DATA of MEMBER

K TO KILL (DELETE)MEMBER

S TO SAVE DATABASE TO FILE

I for INQUIRY

G for GLOBAL SEARCH for VALUE r

ENTER FULL FILE NAME

frame.dat

FILE TO BE READ IN IS frame.dat

FRAME DATAFILE in use ISanim

END OF INPUT FILE ENCOUNTERED

MENU ENTER:

Q TO QUIT SESSION

C TO CREATE FRAME DATABASE

R TO RECALL FRAME DATABASE

E TO ENTER new MEMBER

A TO ADD TO DATA of MEMBER

L TO LIST MEMBERS

M TO LIST MEMBER SLOTS

D TO DELETE DATA of MEMBER

K TO KILL (DELETE)MEMBER

S TO SAVE DATABASE TO FILE

I for INQUIRY

G for GLOBAL SEARCH for VALUE I

VALUE lion

VALUE mammal

VALUE tiger

MENU ENTER:

Q TO QUIT SESSION

C TO CREATE FRAME DATABASE

R TO RECALL FRAME DATABASE

E TO ENTER new MEMBER

A TO ADD TO DATA of MEMBER

L TO LIST MEMBERS

M TO LIST MEMBER SLOTS

D TO DELETE DATA of MEMBER

K TO KILL (DELETE)MEMBER

S TO SAVE DATABASE TO FILE

I for INQUIRY

G for GLOBAL SEARCH for VALUE i

ENTER UNIQUE IDENTIFIER lion

lion

ENTER SLOT IDENTIFIER: gives

gives

VALUE milk

for MEMBER lion

VALUE VIA ISA mammal for MEMBER lion

MENU ENTER:

Q TO QUIT SESSION

C TO CREATE FRAME DATABASE

R TO RECALL FRAME DATABASE

E TO ENTER new MEMBER

A TO ADD TO DATA of MEMBER

L TO LIST MEMBERS

M TO LIST MEMBER SLOTS

D TO DELETE DATA of MEMBER

K TO KILL (DELETE)MEMBER

S TO SAVE DATABASE TO FILE

I for INQUIRY

G for GLOBAL SEARCH for VALUE q

Chapter 6

Syntax and Semantics

Overview

In this chapter we discuss the basic (and controversial) ideas underlying natural language processing. The major issue is the role of syntax and semantics in the understanding of language. To what extent can syntactic processing proceed independently of semantic analysis? We discuss the formal theory of language, including phrase-structure grammars, the Chomsky hierarchy, and attribute and unification grammars, as a prelude to discussing an implementation of an augmented transition network approach in the next chapter.

UNDERSTANDING LANGUAGES

The study of language is conventionally divided into two major topics: *syntax* and *semantics*. The former specifies the structure of the language, the rules by which allowable utterances must abide. The latter specifies how meaning is to be attached to these utterances. The division between syntax and semantics is not clear-cut. This probably accounts for much of the controversy as to the role of semantics in understanding language.

One often-used example is the sentence "Time flies like an arrow." It is usually said that there are three interpretations of this sentence: (1) the noun *time*'s passage is compared to the flight of an arrow; (2) it is a command (*time* is an imperative verb) to use a stopwatch and measure the duration of the flight of insects of order *Diptera* (flies) in the same way as you would time the flight of an arrow, and (3) there is a species of fly, the Time fly, which thinks arrows are a tasty snack. I have not seen it noted that, strictly speaking, only the third interpretation is grammatically correct, because the others misuse the preposition *like* as a conjunction (as would be correct). Given the colloquial misuse of *like,* semantic information (understanding of, say, the various species of flies) would be required to resolve the ambiguity of the sentence and conclude that interpretation 1 was the "right" reading.

Regardless of philosophy, syntactic information is clearly vital. You must know what the verb is and what the subject and objects are to get any meaning out of the sentence. The issue is whether syntactic information is enough to parse a sentence for semantic analysis or whether the latter must be considered during the parse.

Regardless of how we believe languages are acquired (Chomsky and Piaget have filled a book with a debate on the subject), grammars are naturally described in terms of rules. The rules give the right and wrong to forming acceptable sentences. These rules are called production rules (as in Chapter 3) because they provide specifications on how to form valid utterances. The term generative grammar is also used to denote the same concept of providing a mechanism for generating valid sentences. This viewpoint underlies the formal approach to the theory of language. It also will lead naturally to a program for parsing and understanding sentences by a program rather similar to a rule-based expert system.

Most approaches to language understanding have followed from the formal theory of languages as developed by Post, Carnap, and others. In these theories, languages are considered as symbols (i.e., words) and the grammatical rules (syntax) for putting these symbols together into allowable sentences. Semantics was not considered in the earliest developments. Because of their fundamental importance, we consider these formal language theories and discuss how they have been adapted to the problem of real languages.

Syntax: Formal Language Theory

Post Productions and Phrase-Structure Grammar

A Post language consists of a finite set of symbols (the alphabet, corresponding to words in a natural language), a finite set of productions, a "vocabulary" of strings of the alphabet, and a finite subset of the vocabulary, called the axioms [2]. (See also the book by Rosenbloom cited in Chapter 1). The axioms serve as the starting points on which the productions operate to produce new, valid strings which are within the language generated.

A production is typically of the form $S \Rightarrow T$ where S and T are strings involving the symbols in the alphabet. A production basically states that it is allowed to generate or produce the string T from the string S.

We will concentrate on a special form of Post canonical language, the phrase-structure grammar. The concept of a phrase-structure grammar was introduced by the linguist Leonard Bloomfield well before Post's formalism. In this grammar, there is one particular symbol, <S>, which represents, in effect, any valid sentence in the language. It is the only axiom, called the start symbol. In the production language corresponding to first-order logic, S would represent a well-formed formula (wff). The other symbols of the alphabet divide into two classes—terminals and nonterminals. The former would correspond to English words in natural language processing, the latter to substructures which ultimately must be expanded into terminals symbols. Nonterminals are like variables, which must be bound to produce valid utterances. Although notations vary widely, one convention is to denote nonterminals as, say, <S>, while nonterminals are indicated by themselves without being enclosed in <>. We will denote strings of terminals and nonterminals by <<A>>. For example, consider the very simple language which would be defined by:

<S> ⇒ <NP><VP>
<NP> ⇒ <noun>
<det> ⇒ the
<noun> ⇒ John
<VP> ⇒ <verb> <object>
<verb> ⇒ hit
<object> ⇒ <det><noun>
<noun> ⇒ ball

Here we have used NP to denote noun phrase, VP to denote verb phrase, det to denote determiner (a type of adjective—typically an article—a, an, or the), while noun and verb permit nouns and verbs, respectively, to occur in their positions. One sentence which could be generated by such a grammar would be "John hit the ball." We can view the process as starting with the axiom S, from this producing <NP><VP>, then <noun><VP>, then John <VP>, then John <verb><object>, John <verb><det><noun>, John hit <det><noun>, John hit the <noun>, and finally John hit the ball. This sequence is not unique. The parse tree is unique, in this case and is shown in Fig. 6.1.

Each production can be viewed as a rule for transforming strings. A production of the form

<S>⇒<NP><VP>

can be viewed as a rule of the form if <NP>,<VP>, then <S>, interpreted to mean if you encounter a noun phrase, followed by a verb phrase, then you have encountered a valid sentence. A backward-chaining system would start by hypothesizing <S>, producing the subgoals <NP><VP>, etc., and would finally report success with the variable <verb> bound to hit, etc. (Note the two <noun> variables would standardize apart to different variables and

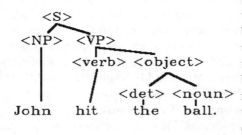

<S>
<NP> <VP>
<verb> <object>
<det> <noun>
John hit the ball.

Fig. 6.1 Typical parse tree.

bind to different "constants" John and ball). This approach to parsing a sentence is called *top-down* based upon the manner in which the parse tree is developed. (In computer science, trees grow downward from the root, in this case <S>.)

Alternatively, a forward-chaining system would match John to <noun>, etc., deducing that we had a valid <NP> and a valid <VP> and finally a valid sentence <S>. This approach is naturally called *bottom-up*. Both top-down and bottom-up parsers can be constructed. Our parser is primarily top-down, but incorporates some bottom-up features. Because of the flexibility and ambiguity of language, a top-down parser will often have to backtrack, having guessed wrongly as to which production rule to apply to generating any particular sentence. Similarly, a bottom-up parser generally needs to include "look-ahead" in order to predict which production rule applies.

The Chomsky Hierarchy

Noam Chomsky introduced a hierarchy of various restrictions on phrase-structure grammars. The general phrase-structure grammar we have briefly described is called a Type 0 grammar. If we limit the productions to the form A $\Rightarrow$ B where the length of string A is never less than that of string B, the grammar is called *context-sensitive,* or Type 1. The terminology arises because such a grammar can be described by a rewritten set of rules all of which are in the form a<A>b $\Rightarrow$ a<B>b. The symbols a and b define a context for the allowable substitution. The *context-free,* or Type 2 grammar, allows rules of the form <A> $\Rightarrow$ <<X>>. These may be put in the normal form of rules <A>$\Rightarrow$<B><C> or <A>$\Rightarrow$a. Substitutions are permitted without regard to the context. If the grammar is specified in such a manner, it is said to be in Chomsky Normal Form [3]. Such grammars may be put in Greibach Normal Form, in which all productions are of the form <A>$\Rightarrow$a<<X>> where <<X>> is a (possibly empty) string of variables. The most restrictive grammar, a regular or Type 3 grammar, allows only productions of the form <A>$\Rightarrow$a<B>.

Regular grammars may be parsed by fairly simple machines (or programs which emulate such machines) called *finite state automata* (FSA). They are so restrictive as to allowed sentences, however, that they are not of much interest in language processing. They are used in some pattern-matching algorithms such as the UNIX utility grep. If the alphabet includes a and b, then a pattern of the form a.MDSU/n.MDNM/b.MDSU/m.MDNM/ (meaning some number of a's followed by any number of b's) can be matched as a valid sentence in the language. The FSA may be diagrammed as a set of states with transition conditions. Thus, the accompanying illustration (Fig. 6.2) is a transition diagram between states. Each path or arc is labeled with the associated input symbol. Input strings beginning with b, or having a b followed by an a, would not be accepted by such a machine. The FSA (sometimes called FSM for finite-state machine) can be emulated by a simple program consisting of an infinite loop containing nested case statements. The outermost case statement could select for which state we are currently in, while for each state a case statement could select, on the basis of input symbol next encountered, which state we transition to. Of course, the nesting could be inverted, with the outer case statement selecting for different input symbols. This simple model assumes we have a deterministic FSA, which is no limitation, at least in theory.

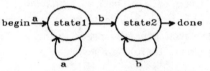

Fig. 6.2 Typical FSM transition network.

Context-Free Languages

The next level of generality is the Type 2 or context-free language. This type of language serves as the basis for most artificial languages, such as programming languages. It is possible to build efficient parsers for such languages [4,5,6]. With further restrictions, it is possible to build very efficient parsers, and this is usually what is done in practice. Of course, we do not have a similar luxury with a natural language. Theoretically, such languages can be processed by a push-down automata (PDA), which is similar to an FSA but possesses a memory of how it got to the present state (which an FSA does not) in the form of a push-down stack.

Context-free languages are sufficiently general that they can be ambiguous, i.e., that a sentence can have more than one valid parse tree. Of course, in designing artificial languages, this is avoided. Context-free languages may not be powerful enough for handling natural language, however [7]. One problem is in enforcing constraints such as subject-verb agreement. In principle, this might be done by defining a large number of subtypes of parts of speech, i.e., <masculine singular noun>, <masculine plural noun>, etc., and similarly for verbs, and writing appropriate productions for each pair. This is not a very practical or appealing approach. Another difficulty often raised is the case of a sentence of the form: "John and Jane gave their books to George and Mary, respectively." If one views the adverb *respectively* as modifying the semantics of the verb (*give* in this case) so as to establish a one-to-one correspondence between a list of items in the subject and a similar list in the object, then there is perhaps no problem. However, if you insist, as many people would, that a failure of the two lists to be of the same length, for example, be classed as a syntactic error, then it is difficult to see how a context-free grammar could establish the appropriate correspondence and test for such an error. The problem of treating correlative conjunctions, such as the pairs *either-or, neither-nor,* and *both-and,* is somewhat similar to that raised by *respectively.* Formally, they could be included in a context-free syntax, but this would require a variety of schema for compound subjects, objects, clauses, etc.

In Charniak and McDermott [8], it is argued that there is "probable agreement" that English is "weakly" context-free, in that there is a context-free grammar which would generate the same string of words (symbols), but no consensus on whether it is "strongly" context-free, meaning that it would in the example cited form the appropriate pairings.

The next step up in complexity is the context-sensitive language. It can theoretically be analyzed by a linear-bounded automata (LBA), a device of slightly less complexity than a Turing machine [3]. It is sufficiently daunting, however, that to my knowledge the full capability of a context-sensitive language to model all the features of natural language is still an open question, although I suspect most workers in the field would concede that, at least in principle, it is sufficiently general to do so. As a practical matter, however, the difficulties are enormous.

Inadequacy of Phrase-Structure Grammars

The foregoing suggests that while phrase-structure grammars might be powerful enough in principle, they leave something to be desired in practice. It is possible to consider approaches beyond this representation, some of which are reviewed below.

Transformational Grammar

One popular and controversial approach is called transformational grammar [9]. This is motivated largely by semantic consideration that the meaning of the sentence, "John gave the book to Jane," is essentially the same as the meaning of the sentence in the passive voice: "The book was given to Jane by John." Of course, there are often different shades of meaning implied when the passive voice is used, but in this example, at least, the meaning of both sentences is the same. The basic idea is that there is an underlying "deep structure" of which both sentences are different "surface" representations. In transformational grammar analyses, operations on the sentence are allowed to move and alter words. Thus, the passive voice might be recognized and altered into an active voice sentence prior to analysis of the deep sentence. The idea of deep structure leads naturally to the idea of semantic networks, discussed below. Work by Slobin, reported in [8], suggests that people in understanding passives do spend more time "processing" such sentences, but that the time difference cannot be simply explained by a syntactic transformation.

There are a few transformations commonly encountered. Aux-inversion is considered a method for generating a question from a declarative sentence pattern. Thus, the sentence "John is the boss" is transformed into "Is John the boss?" The question can be analyzed by applying the inverse transformation and then analyzing the declarative form, remembering that the transformation has been applied. Another transformation for producing questions is the "Wh-" transform: "Why is John the boss?" The passive formation is the last commonly encountered transformation rule: "John hit the ball" becomes "The ball was hit by John." Obviously, not every declarative sentence can be transformed this way. For example, the passive formation requires a verb taking a direct object. Finally, commands can be understood by "dropping" the implicit subject of the sentence into the sentence at the beginning. These transformations are all of interest in the theory of language and language acquisition [9] and form the basis of generative grammar. Their use in interpretation of language reduces somewhat the number of rules required for interpreting all forms of sentences.

Attribute Grammars and Unification Grammars

One can modify context-free languages, for example, with Donald Knuth's idea of attaching attributes to the various symbols. Thus, our noun could have attributes such as number (singular or plural), gender, case, and perhaps even semantic information as well. We could then incorporate relatively straightforward tests for subject-verb agreement, for example, into a context-free language by comparing attributes. This idea is used by unification grammars [10]. The concept of unification is related to that discussed with regard to matching predicate terms in Chapter 3. The idea is to match two terms by finding the "most general unifier" which subsumes each. If the subject noun's number is unspecified, then this will "unify" with a singular verb to produce a "binding" of its value to singular. If there is a subsequent reference to the noun as plural, this will generate an error as it will not be able to unify with that attribute pattern. There are a variety of approaches under the general heading of unification grammars, including generalized phrase-structure grammars, head-driven phrase-structure grammars, categorical grammars, etc. See note 10 for a survey of this area of current research.

In syntactic pattern recognition (see Chapter 1), a variety of grammars are used to represent features of images. The grammars discussed so far are useful to represent a string of symbols, i.e., a one-dimensional list. For representing multidimensional images or objects, it is often useful to have a more general structure. See note 11 for a discussion of tree, web, and plex grammars as examples of these higher-dimension grammars.

Semantics

We have mentioned above the possibility of including semantic information on a parse tree as attributes of elements of a grammar. Such information (syntactic as well as semantic) is said to "decorate" such a tree [5]. There are a number of questions currently open: whether semantic information is really needed at that stage to generate an appropriate parse tree, and once a parse tree is obtained, how to extract meaning (semantics) out of it. Some workers suggested on the basis of Slobin's work that semantic processing was being done almost independently of syntactic analysis [8]. The proper role of semantics in generating a parse is still quite controversial. The theory of "autonomous syntax" asserts that the parse can be done without regard to semantics. On the other hand, some workers in the field argue that while syntactic "clues" (word order, preposition placement, etc.) are necessary, a full parse need not be executed to extract meaning in most cases. With the flexibility of decorating our trees, however, we have a mechanism of testing for appropriate semantic agreement and rejecting inappropriate parses on that basis. It might be noted here that the frames discussed in the previous chapter would provide a useful mechanism for specifying the semantic and syntactic attributes of words and phrases, both in a dictionary and on the developing parse tree. Modified phrase-structure grammars which allow the use of semantic information are called semantic grammars. A simpler approach, called case grammars, is basically a template matching rather than a full syntactic analysis, the purpose being to extract the proper matches to a "deep structure."

The other side of the semantics issue is the extraction of meaning from a successfully parsed sentence. One approach is *conceptual dependency* (see the article by Schank in [12]). A number of primitive operations are defined: INGEST, POSS-BY, MTRANS, ATRANS, PTRANS, etc. They refer to basic conceptual relationships between objects. For example, MTRANS refers to the transfer of information or memory, while ATRANS refers to the physical transfer of possession of an object, and PTRANS to the change of location of an object. Various other primitives (MOVE, PROPEL, GRASP, EXPEL to name a few) exist.

The concept of semantic networks [12] (see, e.g., the article by Simmons in [13]) has also been popular for representing meaning as the relationship between various objects. The semantic network is generally described as a directed acyclic graph which can be used to represent conceptual dependency as discussed above (a variety of workers give somewhat differing definitions of semantic networks). The nodes of the graph (which typically represent objects) are connected by directed edges (called "links" or sometimes "arcs") which are labeled with the relationship involved (property-of, has, etc.). The graph is generally required to be acyclic; that is, there should be no circular self-references, as this could result in the usual infinite regress problems when trying to obtain a property of an object. The basic idea of conceptual dependency is similar to that of deep structure of Chomsky and similar ideas in language theory such as "thematic role" or "predicate argument structure" [14]. The principal virtue of the semantic network is its generality. The other side of this coin is that there is no algorithm for retrieving or modifying the information in such a network [15]. There is considerable range of opinion as to the construction and interpretation of such nets. Woods [16] in a well-known paper, "What's in a Link: Foundations for Semantic Networks" [16], suggested there should be two different categories of links. Brachman in a review article [17] suggests there are five different types of links, while Maida and Shapiro [18] suggest that there is really only one type of link.

Semantic nets may be represented using the frame data structure developed in the previous chapter. The slots can identify the relationship represented by the link, while the (unique) facet of that slot names the frame of the object pointed to by the link.

An extension of the idea of using frames to model semantic nets is the idea of a script. This is a data structure which has a number of "blanks" to be filled in with information as it is encountered in the text to be understood. As the data structure is static, a script is somewhat inflexible. Slots can be filled in with the appropriate information only if we have anticipated what information is of interest. Novel situations cannot be treated.

This chapter has laid the theoretical foundation for natural language processing. In the next chapter, we discuss the practice.

References

1. A. G. Oettinger, "The Uses of Computers in Science," originally in September 1966 *Scientific American* and reprinted in *Information* (San Francisco, Calif.: W. H. Freeman, 1966).

2. R. R. Korfhage, *Logic and Algorithms* (N.Y.: John Wiley, 1966).

3. J. E. Hopcroft and J. D. Ullman, *Introduction to Automata Theory, Languages, and Computation* (Reading, Mass.: Addison Wesley, 1979).

4. J.-P. Tremblay and P. G. Sorensen, *Theory and Practice of Compiler Writing* (N.Y.: McGraw-Hill Book Co., 1985).

5. C. N. Fisher and R. LeBlanc, Jr., *Crafting a Compiler* (Menlo Park, Calif.: Benjamin Cummings, 1988).

6. A. V. Aho, R. Sethi, J. D. Ullman, *Compilers* (Reading, Mass.:Addison-Wesley, 1986).

7. Klaus K. Obermeier, "Natural Language Processing," *BYTE,* December 1987, p. 225.

8. E. Charniak and D. McDermott, *Introduction to Artificial Intelligence,* (Reading, Mass.: Addison-Wesley, 1985).

9. T. Winograd, *Language as a Cognitive Process (Vol. I: Syntax)* (Reading, Mass.: Addison-Wesley, 1983).

10. Stuart M. Shieber, *An Introduction to Unification-Based Approaches to Grammar* (Stanford, Calif.: Center for the Study of Language and Information, 1986).

11. R. C. Gonzalez and M. G. Thomason, *Syntactic Pattern Recognition* (Reading, Mass.: Addison-Wesley, 1978).

12. M. R. Quillian, *Behavioral Sci.,* 12, 410 (1967).

13. *Computer Models of Thought and Language* (ed. R. C. Schank and K. M. Colby) (San Francisco, Calif.: W. H. Freeman, 1973).

14. R. Berwick, *The Acquisition of Syntactic Knowledge* (Cambridge, Mass.: MIT Press, 1985).

15. L. Bic and C. Lee, *ACM Trans. Prog. Lang. Systems,* 9, 618 (1987).

16. W. A. Woods, in *Representation and Understanding: Studies in Cognitive Science* (G. Bobrow and A. M. Collins, ed.) (N.Y.: Academic Press, 1975), p. 35.

17. R. J. Brachman, in *Associative Networks: Representation and Use of Knowledge by Computers* (N. V. Findler, ed.) (N.Y.: Academic Press, 1979), p. 3.

18. A. S. Maida and S. C. Shapiro, *Cognitive Sci.,* 6, 291 (1982).

Chapter 7

Augmented Transition Network Parser

Overview

We first discuss the augmented transition network (ATN) for the analysis of a sentence. We then describe an implementation which employs the basic structure of the top-down, backward-chaining expert system of Chapter 2 combined with a bottom-up construction of the parse tree. The bottom-up method contains some features similar to so-called wait-and-see parsers (WASP).

The ATN

In the previous chapter, we illustrated the parsing of simple regular grammars by finite-state machines (FSM) using simple-state transition diagrams. The next level of sophistication in the Chomsky hierarchy, context-free grammars, could be parsed by nondeterministic push-down automata (NPDA). Because recursive programs are implemented by means of a push-down stack, it should not be surprising that NPDA can be implemented by a recursive program (with backtracking). Our simple diagrams for finite-state machines can be generalized by viewing each arc as invoking a subprogram. In the FSM treatment of a regular grammar, arcs were effectively tests for a particular terminal symbol of the grammar. To parse more general grammars, we allow the arcs to perform a variety of tests, such as verifying that an appropriate nonterminal, such as a noun phrase, has been encountered. Unlike FSMs where the "road map" is given initially and is static, the analogous diagram for NPDAs consists of a number of partial diagrams, for <S>, <NP>, <VP>, etc., which invoke the appropriate subroutines. Hence

<S> ⇒ <NP><VP>

can be interpreted as verifying that a valid sentence has been supplied by first invoking a subprogram to verify that a noun phrase occurs, and then testing for a valid verb phrase, terminating successfully if that is true. Similar interpretations apply to the other production rules. This interpretation suggests a top-down implementation, but bottom-up procedures may be designed as well.

Additional generalizations are useful. First, rather than be required to specify individual words required to validly move from one "state" (sub-program) to another, it is useful to accept any word within a category, such as noun, verb, etc. It is useful to permit optional occurrences, either allow-ing a single occurrence (0 to 1 occurrences) or arbitrary numbers (0 to infinity) of occurrences. This is useful in allowing modifiers such as adjec-tives to appear in noun phrases, for example.

Finally, it is useful to permit there to be some global memory beyond the limited horizon of a push-down stack. This serves to give some of the flavor of context sensitivity. For example, it is useful to be able to remem-ber the characteristics of the previously encountered symbol.

Put these ideas together and you have the idea of an augmented transition network [1,2,3].

One feature often included is the ability to modify the input sentence. The motivation is that of transformational grammar, which moves components of the sentence around or inserts elements. This is inconvenient in the struc-ture-sharing approach we have followed, and is more appropriate to a struc-ture copying model.

Punctuation is often important. Consider, for example, the two sentences:

My sister who lives in Brooklyn is ill.
My sister, who lives in Brooklyn, is ill.

Both are valid English sentences, but they have different meanings. In the first sentence, the clause "who lives in Brooklyn" is restrictive. I presumab-ly have a number of sisters, and the clause modifies sister and specifies which one I am referring to. The same clause in the second sentence is nonrestrictive. I am supplying additional information about her, for some unspecified reason. A parser should be able to accept punctuation, such as the comma, as symbols containing information.

The process of building the parse tree has not been discussed yet. The pro-gram to be described builds the parse tree bottom-up, as it backs up to lower depths of recursion.

Global information, beyond the ken of the push-down stack (which can only access the top of the stack), is provided by a list to which tests can be inserted and postponed until parse tree generation has progressed sufficient-

ly to permit the test. In this the program is similar to the wait-and-see parser (WASP), such as discussed by Marcus [4].

Finally, there is the question of just what to do with the parse tree. This is
highly dependent upon the specific application. Our ATN program includes
a skeletal facility to analyze the parse tree upon completion of a successful
parse.

We have not considered the analysis of text consisting of a number of sentences. Resolving pronoun references can be a major difficulty.

The Program

ATN Operations

The ATN supports two classes of operations, namely those that act on elements of the sentence and those that act on the parse tree. The former include the following tests on the sentence

word __	Does the current word match __?
cat __	Is the current word in the specified category __?
parse __	Parse a phrase of type __.
peek __1 __2	
	Look ahead to next symbol __1 must be word or cat.
opt	The following term is optional (0–1).
opt*	The following term is optional (0–infinity).
ocat	The category of the preceding symbol

and the "transformational grammar" operations which modify the input
symbol string

detach	Delete the preceding symbol.
insert __	Insert the symbol __ into the input string.
push __	Push the parse tree node __ onto a "use" stack (and preventing node attachment to the tree). Uses the most recent matching node.
pushf __	Similar to push but takes first matching phrase that was encountered.
pop	Pop the "use" stack and insert the words (leaves of the subtree) into the sentence.

Some descriptions of ATNs discuss a "jump" which unconditionally trans-
fers to the next state. This can clearly be implemented via the opt operation.
The peek term is not necessary but can save considerable effort in prevent-

ing a failed parse attempt and the necessary backtracking which would follow. Similarly, opt is not absolutely necessary but economizes on the number of alternative rules which would have to be written.

Note that insert and detach do not act on the parse tree in any way, while push and pop do. Charniak and McDermott [1] discuss operations called save-last and use which are essentially the same as push and pop, respectively. They are the "unbounded movement" operators. They also define an operation called drop, which is the "bounded movement" operator and is equivalent to a push immediately followed by a pop.

In the latter category the operations on the parse tree include

> =   __1 __2 test (__1) (cat or word) on parse tree element __2
> :=   __1 __2 set the __1 node value to __2

Dictionary

Ada does not support sets or bit operations. This is a pity, because we would like to store information about words such as gender (masculine, feminine, neuter), number (singular, plural, either), tense (for verbs), case (for nouns, etc.), formal/familiar form (for languages other than English), etc. This information is not generally of a binary (yes or no) nature. (Meridian offers a Utility Library which includes Package Bit-Ops to perform bit-level functions, as does RR Software's JANUS/Ada UTIL package.)

The present program uses an enumerated type part_of_speech. This provides the most transparent code. A previous version used integers. A representation clause could be used to map the former onto the latter to provide a work around by storing all the information about the word or category in an integer. A binary system could be used in which certain bits are used to represent selected attributes. Such a method would more easily permit the ideas of unification grammar to be applied than some other approaches. For example, we could represent gender information by two bits, 1 being masculine, 2 feminine, 3 neuter. We could extract the gender field by **and**ing the code with a mask and then testing. To compare two constituents, we could use an and. The result of the operation would be zero if the comparison failed. If it is nonzero, then, following the ideas of unification grammar, it represents the value of the "most general unifier" of the two constituents. Each should be given this value on the parse tree. If one had been 3 and was compared to another with the value 1, both now have the value 1. In subsequent tests, both constituents would reflect the fact that only masculine (1) values are consistent with their status. In this way, the information on gender restriction is naturally propagated up the parse tree. Identical considerations apply to information about number, tense, etc. This technique is not coded in our model ATN but may easily be so incorporated.

Program Structure

A major change in the indexing of relevant (grammatical) rules is used for ATNs as compared to the expert system shells. Here, the .INDX pointer list is attached to the predicate term rather than to the symbol entry in the dictionary. This change is effected by alterations to MAKEPRED, IN-DEXHD, CHKGOAL, with GETRULE suitably altered to access the information. Otherwise, the change is transparent. It was done because, unlike the expert system shells, the "functors" of the ATN are reserved keywords such as cat and parse. Only parse statements are to be indexed, to parse statements of the same type. Thus, a rule of the form

if ... then parse pp,

should index only to rules with "parse pp" as an antecedent predicate term. The indexing procedures CHKGOAL and INDEXHD were changed to reflect this, and as the vast majority of the dictionary symbols require no index, it made sense to move the index to the predicate term. The STRNG package was kept general by permitting (at the cost of wasted storage) the use of either form of indexing. Variant records were not used to keep the programs uncluttered, The early versions of the JANUS/Ada compiler did not support them. There is no reason why the expert system shells of Chapters 3 and 4 could not attach index lists to the predicate terms directly instead of going through the symbol table. However, that would probably be less economical of storage in that case since each predicate would require a full list of all the other predicates it might unify with, resulting in considerable potential duplication compared to the indexing method presently used for rules.

To facilitate modifications to the sentence, type PREDICATE has an additional pointer so that the input sentence may be represented as a doubly-linked list.

The main program performs the requisite initialization, including loading the dictionary and the grammatical rules and calls DIAGNOSE after the sentence has been input by GETRULES. The presence of a question mark at the end of the sentence is noted (provision for an exclamation point would be simple to include in a similar manner if this is desired).

Procedure DIAGNOSE first initializes the pointer SENTHEAD to the first word in the sentence. It calls CHKGOAL to create and index the target goal "parse s" and pushes onto the goalstack this root goal as well as the "done" or end-of-sentence delimiter. (A sentence may, of course, have a number of clauses, and each should place a "parse s" on the goalstack. Parsing may be done by treating the clauses as sentences. The sentence value can easily be adjusted to indicate a subordinate clause, for example. At present this is not implemented, but the necessary alterations are easily made.) It then places "root" as the root of the parse tree on the parse tree.

Procedure VERIFY is relatively unchanged from the backward-chaining expert system shell in Chapter 3. It invokes procedure ATN to determine if the next predicate term is valid. ATN can recursively invoke VERIFY if it is given a predicate term of the form "parse ..." to evaluate. This mutual recursion is similar to that of the forward-chaining system of Chapter 4. One difference: in that case VERIFY was a subroutine of ASSERT, whereas now, because of the backward-chaining nature of our parser, ATN is a subroutine of VERIFY. ATN loops through the antecedents of the production rule, i.e., the right-hand side of the grammatical production. It calls verify whenever a parse operation is required. The parse processes phrases and clauses. If any term succeeds, ATN loops on to pop and then processes the next term. The opt and opt* operators are treated as any other term by the stack and by ATN. They set the appropriate flag (which defaults to REQUIRED if they do not precede a term). When the "done" term is encountered, we test to see if there are any unsatisfied tests remaining. If not, we have successfully parsed the sentence.

VERIFY will set the sentence value to interrogatory if the sentence ends with a question mark and if the sentence otherwise fits in this category. This choice was made because of examples such as "Who cares," which are not so much genuine inquiries as statements of personal opinion. Of course, "Who cares" might be punctuated with a final question mark. Readers with different tastes can easily modify this feature.

The operations on sentence constituents are all relatively straightforward. The parse tree operations are more complicated, in part because the parse tree is not generally fully formed when we wish to test or alter it. Thus, the parse tree operations are pushed onto a list for later action if the appropriate node for their action does not yet exist. The encounter of the final "done" on the goalstack forces out all of these tests and sets, with a failure if this is not possible. Note the following features:

1. Constituents are added to the parse tree automatically, by ATTACH. The location of attachment is not under user control. Rather, it is to the node at

the next highest level in the parse tree previously encountered. This should suffice for English, although separable prefix verbs in German, for example, might require other treatment or a prescan to establish such features. See the discussion in the previous chapter for the use of "respectively" and how it can be fit into this scheme. After an element is attached, the queued test and set operation list is checked to see if any are relevant to the new node.

2. The scope of the test (=) and set (:=) operators may be limited by user specification through the symbol value. The maximum difference in depth between the node and the depth at the time the test or set was inserted into the pending tree action list. If this depth-difference is zero, the scope is assumed global.

ANSWER performs a preorder traversal of the parse tree. It is similar to the preorder traversal routines in Chapter 5 (Frames), except that here the trees are general trees rather than binary trees. DROP is a modified ANSWER which prints the terminal symbols of the given tree into the sentence (list) it is given. It is used in the pop ("drop" or "use") action. Both ANSWER and DROP employ the convention that tree leaves are terminal symbols. For example, the noun phrase "the big blue book" is represented as a node of type "np" to which the noun *book* and the adjectives *the, big,* and *blue* are all attached. The word *the* is a special class of adjective, a "determiner." It might also be classed as the "definite article" adjective. This appears to be a universal convention in the formal analysis of sentences even though it is at variance with the method used in some elementary schools.

The implementation of the transformational operators (insert, push, pushf, pop, delete) should be considered provisional and modified to suit user needs.

Test Problem

The test problem illustrates a typical ATN grammar working on a simple declarative sentence. The diagnostic printouts are enabled to watch the process of parsing the sentence with a moderate amount of detail. Notice, for example, the backtracking after the failed attempt to parse a prepositional phrase.

Final Remark

It was remarked in the previous chapter, citing the text by Charniak and McDermott, p. 182 [1], that there is "probably agreement" that context-free syntax can describe English. If someone were to exhibit those production rules, there would no longer be any doubt. Therefore, it is clear no one has done so. Consequently, I cannot present here the production rules for a completely general English parser, any more than the expert system shells in previous chapters contained a perfectly general problem-solving expert system. As with those shells, the user will have to tailor his rule set to the application. The use of ideas from unification and case grammars, judicious use of semantic information to decorate the tree, and various other extensions from context-free treatment inherent in ATNs should make this task somewhat more practical. For a practical example of constructing semantic networks by parsing using a definite clause grammar (similar to the ATN approach given here), see [5].

References

1. E. Charniak and D. McDermott, *Introduction to Artificial Intelligence* (Reading, Mass.: Addison-Wesley, 1985).

2. T. Winograd, *Language as a Cognitive Process (Vol. I: Syntax)* (Reading, Mass.: Addison-Wesley, 1983).

3. R. Berwick, *The Acquisition of Syntactic Knowledge* (Cambridge, Mass.: MIT Press, 1985).

4. M. Marcus, *A Theory Of Syntactic Recognition For Natural Language* (Cambridge, Mass.: MIT Press, 1980).

5. R. F. Simmons and D. Chester, *Relating Sentences and Semantic Networks with Procedural Logic, Comm. ACM*, **25**,527 (1982).

Program Listing And Examples

--Augmented Transition Network (ATN) Parser


```
with TEXT_IO;use TEXT_IO;
with STRNG; use STRNG;
with GRAMMAR; use GRAMMAR;
with ATNSTK; use ATNSTK;
with ATNREAD; use ATNREAD;
with ATNINDEX;use ATNINDEX;
with REG;use REG;
with MATH;use MATH;
procedure ATN is
-- Structure copying method used to permit transformations

package INT_IO is new INTEGER_IO(NUM=>INTEGER);

--GLOBAL VARIABLES:
CURRENT_CLAUSE: LISTPTR;
ACTTOP,NODETOP: GOALSPTR;--ACTION,CHILDREN TO ADD STACKS
ACTIONS: TAPTR; -- PENDING TREE ACTIONS
CURRENTWORD,ENDP,DONEP: PREDICPTR;
SAVEUSE: LISTPTR;
--SAVEUSE stack for PUSHED/POPPED (DROP) CLAUSES and PHRASES
PARSETREE: TREEPTR;
NEWCAT,PREVCAT: PART_OF_SPEECH;
ATHEAD,AT_HEAD: BOOLEAN;
DETACHED_WORD: SYMPTR;

procedure VERIFY(CURRWORD:in out PREDICPTR;
            FATHER:in out TREEPTR;
            ANSWER: out BOOLEAN;
            DEPTH: in INTEGER) is

NEWSTRPTR: PTRANGE;
PREVRULE,CURRULNUM: RULERANGE;
CURGOAL: GOALSPTR;
ANTECED,TGTPRED,NEWPRED: PREDICPTR;
NEWPTR: SYMPTR;
```

```
CHILDNODE,DUMMYNODE: TREEPTR;
CLAUSES,CHILD,CURTAIL: LISTPTR;
ATHEAD,ANS,NOMORE,FOUND: BOOLEAN;
RULINDEX: INDEXPTR;
ARCTYPE: OCCUR;
LDEPTH: INTEGER;
SAVEPCAT: PART_OF_SPEECH;

procedure GETRULE(RUL: out RULERANGE;
            TARGET: in PREDICPTR;
            INDEX:in out INDEXPTR;
            FOUND: out BOOLEAN) is
-- FINDS THE NEXT  RELEVANT RULE
--  INDEXED
-- ENTER WITH : TARGET: INDEXED FIRST PREDICATE
--          INDEX: null  IF  FIRST,
--            ELSE  POINTER TO LAST INDEX ENTRY
-- EXIT : FOUND: IF  FOUND
--      RUL: NEXT  RELEVANT RULE NUMBER IF  FOUND IS  TRUE.
--      PRED: POINTER
begin
FOUND := TRUE;
if INDEX=null then
  -- FIND FIRST
  INDEX := TARGET.INDX;--PREDICATES ARE INDEXED,
  -- NOT SYMBOLS AS IN  EXPERT SHELLS
else
  INDEX := INDEX.NEXT;
end if ;
if INDEX=null then
  FOUND := FALSE;
  return ;
end if ;
-- RATHER THAN LOOPING THRU ALL  AND  STARTING AT
-- STARTRULE,NOW WE MUST START AT CURRENT RULE
RUL := INDEX.RULENUM;--WHICH IS  NEXT  RELEVANT RULE?
return ;
end GETRULE;
```

```
procedure GETPRED is

--enter with: global CURRULNUM is the rule in use: INTEGER
--            global NEWSTRPTR is the predicate desired: INTEGER
--on exit:  NOMORE:  if called with head
--            NEWPTR :SYMPTR
--            NEWPRED:PREDICPTR
--ALWAYS RETURNS TGTPRED, ETC. EVEN IF  NOMORE TRUE.
begin
-- finds next  PREDICATE in rule;
-- if none, returns NOMRESTR=HEAD=TRUE
-- NOTE: NEWSTRPTR IS  NOT AFFECTED BY THIS ROUTINE.
-- IF  CALLED WITH  HEAD, NOMORE:=
if NEWSTRPTR=RULEINDX(CURRULNUM+1)-1
  then
   --NO MORE PREDICATE ANTECEDENTS, head is next
  NOMORE := TRUE;
else
  NOMORE := FALSE;
end if ;
--@NEW_LINE;PUT(" NEXT  PREDICATE IS");
NEWPRED := RULES(NEWSTRPTR);--PREDICPTR
NEWPTR := NEWPRED.ITEM;--SYMPTR
return ;
end GETPRED;

procedure ATTACH( FATHER,CHILD:TREEPTR;
            DEPTH: in INTEGER;
            HEAD:in BOOLEAN; --AT HEAD ?
        OK:out BOOLEAN) is
PREV,TACT: TAPTR;
SIB,LIST1: LISTPTR;
DELTAD: INTEGER;
FINI: BOOLEAN;

begin
FINI := FALSE;
```

```
OK := TRUE;
--NEW_LINE;PUT(" ATTACHING NODE ");
--  PRINT(CHILD.NAME.TOKEN)
CHILD.PARENT := FATHER;
LIST1 := new LIST;
LIST1.NEXT := null;--IF FIRST CHILD OR TAIL (HEAD=FALSE)
LIST1.CHILD := CHILD;
CHILD.PARENT := FATHER;
if FATHER.CHILDR=null then
  --CREATE FIRST CHILD
  PUT(" FIRST CHILD");
  FATHER.CHILDR := LIST1;
  CURTAIL:=LIST1;
  LIST1.PREV:=null;
else
  -- THERE ARE ELEMENTS ALREADY THERE
  if HEAD then
    LIST1.PREV:=null;
    LIST1.NEXT := FATHER.CHILDR;
    CHILD.SIB := FATHER.CHILDR;
    FATHER.CHILDR := LIST1; --NEW HEAD
  else
    --TAIL
    SIB := FATHER.CHILDR;--SIB NOT null
    loop
      if SIB.NEXT=null then
         exit;
      end if;
      SIB := SIB.NEXT;
    end loop;
    SIB.NEXT := LIST1;
    LIST1.PREV:=SIB;
    CHILD.SIB := null;--NO RIGHT SIBLING
    SIB.CHILD.SIB := LIST1;
    CURTAIL:=LIST1;
  end if;
end if;
------------END OF ATTACHMENT.
```

```
if FATHER.VALUE=SENTENCE_ROOT then
   FINI := TRUE;
end if ;
-- CHECK ACTIONS
TACT := ACTIONS;
PREV := null;
loop
  if TACT=null then
    exit ;--NO MORE PENDING ACTIONS.
  end if ;
  if TACT.SVALUE= TEST
   then
   --TEST
    DELTAD := TACT.DEPTH-DEPTH;
    if TACT.DDEPTH=0
      then
        DELTAD := 0;
    end if;--GLOBAL SEARCH FLAG
    if TACT.TVALUE=FATHER.VALUE
        and DELTAD <= TACT.DDEPTH
      then
      -- CORRECT TYPE OF  NODE TO BE TESTED
      -- COULD INCLUDE TEST LOOP  HERE AS DISCUSSED UNDER SET
      -- TEST SUCCESS, REMOVE  IT
      if PREV/=null
        then
        --(SKIP IT-IT WASN'T ON TOP)
        PREV.NEXT := TACT.NEXT;
        -- PREV UNCHANGED
      else
        --MOVE HEAD OF  LIFO LIST (IT WAS TOP ITEM)
        ACTIONS := TACT.NEXT;
      end if ;
    else
      --ON TO NEXT?
      if FINI then
        OK := FALSE;
      end if ;
```

```
            -- WE HAVE DONE FINAL NODE ATTACH (TO ROOT)
            -- AND  STILL HAVE AN UNSATISFIED TEST.
            PREV := TACT;
          end if ;
      else
        --SET
        --@NEW_LINE;PUT(" SET? TVALUE,FATHER=");
        DELTAD := TACT.DEPTH-DEPTH;
        if TACT.DDEPTH=0 then
          DELTAD := 0;
        end if;--GLOBAL SEARCH FLAG
        if TACT.TVALUE=FATHER.VALUE and DELTAD <= TACT.DDEPTH
          then
          -- could include loop here to ensure backtrack possible
          -- from TACT.SOURCE to present node
          -- It is not generally necessary to do this,
          -- as parse tree builds upwards and actions stacked LIFO.
          FATHER.VALUE := TACT.SVALUE;
          --@NEW_LINE;PUT("PERFORMING QUEUED SET");
          -- SET PERFORMED, REMOVE  IT
          if PREV/=null then
            --(SKIP IT-IT WASN'T ON TOP)
            PREV.NEXT := TACT.NEXT;
            -- PREV UNCHANGED
          else
            --MOVE HEAD OF  LIFO LIST (IT WAS TOP ITEM)
            ACTIONS := TACT.NEXT;
          end if ;
        else
          --ON TO NEXT
          PREV := TACT;
        end if ;
      end if ;--TEST/SET DETERMINATION
      TACT := TACT.NEXT;
    end loop ;
    return ;
  end ATTACH;
```

```
procedure INSERT( WORD:in SYMPTR;LOCATION:in out PREDICPTR;
      WHERE: in out LISTPTR;ATTACH:in BOOLEAN)is
NEWWD: PREDICPTR;
WORD_TREE:TREEPTR;
NEW_WORD,PRECED,FOLLOW:LISTPTR;
begin
-- INSERT WORD BEFORE LOCATION, UPDATING LOCATION
NEWWD := new PREDICATE;
NEWWD.ITEM := WORD;
NEWWD.NEXT := LOCATION;
NEWWD.PREV := LOCATION.PREV;
LOCATION.PREV := NEWWD;
if NEWWD.PREV /= null then
   NEWWD.PREV.NEXT := NEWWD;
end if;
LOCATION := NEWWD;--UPDATE
if not ATTACH then return;end if;
-- now insert before previous word(WHERE) in tree
-- doubly-linked list. insert before where
WORD_TREE:= new TREE;
WORD_TREE.NAME:=WORD;
WORD_TREE.CHILDR:=null;
WORD_TREE.VALUE:=WORD.VALUE;
NEW_WORD:=new LIST;
NEW_WORD.CHILD:=WORD_TREE;
WORD_TREE.PARENT:=CHILDNODE;
PRECED:=CHILDNODE.CHILDR;
NEW_LINE;
if PRECED=null then--no words
  PRECED:=NEW_WORD;
  NEW_WORD.NEXT:=null;
  PUT(" INSERT ONLY WORD");
elsif WHERE=null then
  NEW_LINE;PUT(" WHERE=null");
elsif WHERE.PREV=null then
  --WHERE first word.
  PUT(" INSERT AS FIRST WORD before ");
  PRINT(WHERE.CHILD.NAME.TOKEN);
```

```
NEW_WORD.NEXT:=WHERE;
CHILDNODE.CHILDR:=NEW_WORD;
else
  WHERE.PREV.NEXT:=NEW_WORD;
  NEW_WORD.NEXT:=WHERE;
  WHERE.PREV:=NEW_WORD;
end if;
end INSERT;

procedure DETACH(DEADWORD: in PREDICPTR;CURTREE: in TREEPTR) is
DEBUG,WORDS_ATTACHED: LISTPTR;
WORD: TREEPTR;
FOUND: BOOLEAN;
DEAD_WORD:SYMPTR;
begin
FOUND:=FALSE;
DEAD_WORD:=DEADWORD.ITEM;
WORDS_ATTACHED:=CURTREE.CHILDR;--LIST OF CHILDREN
DEBUG:=WORDS_ATTACHED;
loop
if DEBUG=null then exit;end if;
PRINT(DEBUG.CHILD.NAME.TOKEN);
DEBUG:=DEBUG.NEXT;
end loop;
loop
  if WORDS_ATTACHED=null then exit; end if;
  WORD:=WORDS_ATTACHED.CHILD;--NODE OF WORD.
  if WORD.NAME=DEAD_WORD then
    --detach first occurance of word.
    -- this should usually suffice.
    FOUND:=TRUE;
    NEW_LINE;PUT(" DETACH word frm ");PRINT(CURTREE.NAME.TOKEN);
    if WORDS_ATTACHED.PREV/=null then
      WORDS_ATTACHED.PREV.NEXT:=WORDS_ATTACHED.NEXT;
    end if;
    if WORDS_ATTACHED.NEXT/=null then
      WORDS_ATTACHED.NEXT.PREV:=WORDS_ATTACHED.PREV;
    end if;
```

```
    if WORDS_ATTACHED=CURTREE.CHILDR then--first word
      PUT(" first word");
      CURTREE.CHILDR:=WORDS_ATTACHED.NEXT;
    end if;
    exit;
  end if;
  WORDS_ATTACHED:=WORDS_ATTACHED.NEXT;
end loop;
NEW_LINE;PUT(" FIRST CHILD NOW");
if CURTREE.CHILDR/=null then
PRINT(CURTREE.CHILDR.CHILD.NAME.TOKEN);
end if;
if FOUND then return; end if;
if CURTAIL/=null then
  NEW_LINE;PUT(" NOT FOUND TO DETACH");
  -- not yet attached to this parent node
  CURTAIL.ATTACH:=FALSE;
  return;
end if;
-- attached to previous node?
NEW_LINE;PUT(" word not detached-higher node");
end DETACH;


procedure DETACH_FROM_TREE(DEADNODE: in TREEPTR) is
WORDS_ATTACHED: LISTPTR;
WORD: TREEPTR;
FOUND: BOOLEAN;
begin
FOUND:=FALSE;
WORDS_ATTACHED:=DEADNODE.PARENT.CHILDR;
loop
  if WORDS_ATTACHED=null then exit; end if;
  WORD:=WORDS_ATTACHED.CHILD;
  if WORD=DEADNODE then
    FOUND:=TRUE;
    if WORDS_ATTACHED.PREV/=null then
      WORDS_ATTACHED.PREV.NEXT:=WORDS_ATTACHED.NEXT;
    end if;
```

```
  if WORDS_ATTACHED.NEXT/=null then
    WORDS_ATTACHED.NEXT.PREV:=WORDS_ATTACHED.PREV;
  end if;
  if WORDS_ATTACHED=DEADNODE.PARENT.CHILDR then--first word
    DEADNODE.PARENT.CHILDR:=WORDS_ATTACHED.NEXT;
  end if;
  exit;
 end if;
 WORDS_ATTACHED:=WORDS_ATTACHED.NEXT;
end loop;
if FOUND then return; end if;
if CURTAIL/=null then
  NEW_LINE;PUT(" inhibiting later attachment ");
  -- not yet attached to this parent node
  CURTAIL.ATTACH:=FALSE;
  return;
end if;
-- attached to previous node?
NEW_LINE;PUT(" node not detached-higher node");
end DETACH_FROM_TREE;


procedure DROP(TREE:TREEPTR;LOCATION: in out PREDICPTR;
    FIRST: in out PREDICPTR) is
--"PRINT"  words (leaves) from parse tree to sentence
-- DO  (PRE-ORDER) TRAVERSAL OF  PARSE TREE
NODE: TREEPTR;
WHERE,SIBLING: LISTPTR;
DUMMY: PREDICPTR;
begin
WHERE:=CURTAIL;
NODE := TREE;
FIRST:=LOCATION;
SIBLING := NODE.CHILDR;
if SIBLING=null then
--print terminals (leaves)
  NEW_LINE; PUT(" DROPPING "); PRINT(NODE.NAME.TOKEN);
  INSERT(NODE.NAME,LOCATION,WHERE,FALSE);
  FIRST:=LOCATION;
```

```
end if;
loop
  if SIBLING=null then exit;
  end if;
  DROP(SIBLING.CHILD,LOCATION,DUMMY);
  --pre-order traversal- don't want FIRST altered
  SIBLING := SIBLING.NEXT;
end loop;
FIRST:=LOCATION;
return;
end DROP;

procedure CLEAN_GOALSSTK is
ARCTYPE:OCCUR;
TARGET: PREDICPTR;
ATHEAD: BOOLEAN;
begin
loop
  POPGOAL(TARGET,ARCTYPE,ACTTOP,ATHEAD);
  if TARGET=ENDP  or else TARGET=null then return;
  end if;
end loop;
end CLEAN_GOALSSTK;


function QUOTED( SYM: in SYMPTR) return BOOLEAN is
begin
if( SYM.TOKEN(1) = '"') then return TRUE;
else return FALSE;
end if;
end QUOTED;

function ATN(CUWORD:in PREDICPTR;CUTREE: TREEPTR;
       DEPTH: INTEGER) return BOOLEAN is
SUBTREE,CURTREE: TREEPTR;
TARGET,NEWSENT,WRD,NEXTWRD,CURWORD,PREVWD: PREDICPTR;
SWORD,WORD,SYM,NEXTSYM: SYMPTR;
DOTOTREE: TAPTR;
```

```
ARCTYPE: OCCUR;
ATHEAD,ANS,OK: BOOLEAN;
KOUNT: INTEGER;
WHERE,ENTRY_PHRASES,SIBLING,USER: LISTPTR;
VAL: PART_OF_SPEECH;

begin
CURTREE := CUTREE;
CURWORD := CUWORD;
NEW_LINE;PUT(" in  ATN DEPTH=");INT_IO.PUT(DEPTH);
ENTRY_PHRASES:=PHRASES;--RETRACT TO HERE ON FAILURE
USER := CURRENT_CLAUSE;NEW_LINE;PUT(" CLAUSES:");
loop
  if USER=null then
     exit;
  end if;
  PUT(" ");
  PRINT(USER.CHILD.NAME.TOKEN );
  USER := USER.NEXT;
end loop;

KOUNT := 0;
if PREVCAT=CLAUSE  then
   PREVWD := null;
   WRD := null;WORD := null;
   NEWCAT := CURWORD.ITEM.VALUE;
   NEW_LINE;PUT(" PREVCAT=CLAUSE, NEWWORD:");
   PRINT(CURRWORD.ITEM.TOKEN);
end if;
loop
  USER := PHRASES;PUT(" PHRASES:");
  loop
    if USER=null then
       exit;
    end if;
    PUT(" ");
    PRINT(USER.CHILD.NAME.TOKEN );
    USER := USER.NEXT;
```

```
 end loop;
if ACTTOP=null then
   NEW_LINE;PUT(" ATN RETURNING TRUE ");
   PUSHPHRASE(CURTREE,DEPTH);
   return TRUE;--FINISHED PARSE
end if ;
POPGOAL(TARGET,ARCTYPE,ACTTOP,ATHEAD);
NEW_LINE;PRINTPRED(TARGET);
if ATHEAD then PUT(" ATHEAD");end if;
PUT(" atnREM. SENT.=");PRINTPRED(CURWORD);
NEW_LINE;PUT(" atn node=");PRINT(CURTREE.NAME.TOKEN);
if ARCTYPE=REQUIRED then
    PUT(" REQUIRED");
elsif ARCTYPE=OPTANY then
   PUT(" OPTANY");
else
  PUT(" OPT");
end if ;
SYM := TARGET.ITEM;
--PRED_OPTIONS WILL APPLY TO: PARSE,CAT ONLY
if SYM=DONEPTR then
    --DONE PLACED INTO STACK BY DIAGNOSE;
   if ACTTOP/=null then
    CLEAN_GOALSSTK;
    if CURWORD.NEXT=null then
       CURRENTWORD:=CURWORD;
       return TRUE;
     else
       PHRASES:=ENTRY_PHRASES;
       return FALSE;
     end if ;
   end if ;--CONTINUE LOOP  TO NEXT  ACTION
 elsif SYM=ENDPHPTR then
   CURRENTWORD:=CURWORD;
   PUSHPHRASE(CURTREE,DEPTH);
   NEW_LINE;
   PUT(" PUSHING PHRASE ");PRINT(CURTREE.NAME.TOKEN);
   PUT(" DEPTH=");INT_IO.PUT(DEPTH);
```

```
    return TRUE;
-- TESTS ON SENTENCE
elsif QUOTED(SYM) then
   if not REGISTER(TARGET.NEXT) then
      CLEAN_GOALSSTK;
      PHRASES:=ENTRY_PHRASES;
      return FALSE;
      -- if TRUE, continue
   end if;
 elsif SYM =PARSEPTR then
   WRD := TARGET.NEXT;--SYMPTR
   WORD := WRD.ITEM;
   <<PAGAIN>>
   if CURWORD=null then
      -- no more
      CLEAN_GOALSSTK;
      if ARCTYPE=REQUIRED  then
         PHRASES:=ENTRY_PHRASES;
         return FALSE;
      end if;
      --else
      CURRENTWORD:=CURWORD;
      return TRUE;
   end if;
   SWORD := CURWORD.ITEM;
   PUSHGOAL(TARGET,ARCTYPE,ACTTOP,ATHEAD);
   --PARSE
   -- CREATE NEW "SENTENCE" FROM CURWORD-
   OK := TRUE;
   WRD := null;
   loop
      if CURWORD = null then exit;
      end if;
      TARGET := new PREDICATE;
      if OK then
         NEWSENT := TARGET;
         OK := FALSE;
      end if;--HEAD OF LIST
```

```
TARGET.ITEM := CURWORD.ITEM;
TARGET.PREV := WRD;
TARGET.NEXT := null;--DEFAULT
CURWORD := CURWORD.NEXT;
if WRD /= null then
   WRD.NEXT := TARGET;
end if;
WRD := TARGET;
end loop;
NEW_LINE;PUT(" verify sent=");PRINTPRED(NEWSENT);
CURWORD := NEWSENT;
CURRENTWORD:=NEWSENT;
VERIFY(NEWSENT,CURTREE,ANS,DEPTH+1);
CURWORD:=NEWSENT;
PUT(" IN ATN AFTER VERIFY ");PRINTPRED(CURWORD);
if not ANS and ARCTYPE=REQUIRED then
 NEW_LINE;
 PUT(" IN ATN VERIFY FAILURE FOR REQUIRED ARC parse ");
 PRINT(CURTREE.NAME.TOKEN);PUT(" DEPTH=");INT_IO.PUT(DEPTH);
 CURTREE.CHILDR:=null;--discard bindings
 CLEAN_GOALSSTK;
 loop
   if PHRASES=null then exit; end if;
   if PHRASES.DEPTH<DEPTH then exit; end if;
   NEW_LINE;PUT(" POPPING PHRASE ");
   PRINT(PHRASES.CHILD.NAME.TOKEN);
   PHRASES:=PHRASES.NEXT;
 end loop;
 return FALSE;
elsif ANS and ARCTYPE=OPTANY
 then
   if CURWORD/=null then
     goto PAGAIN;
   end if ;
   -- ELSE,EITHER:
   -- NOT ANS, OPTIONAL OR OPTANY- CONTINUE
   -- ANS, OPTIONAL OR REQUIRED - CONTINUE
end if ;
```

```
elsif SYM= CATPTR then
  WRD := TARGET.NEXT;
  WORD := WRD.ITEM;
  PREVCAT := NEWCAT;
  NEWCAT := WORD.VALUE;
  <<CAGAIN>>
  if CURWORD=null then
    if ARCTYPE=REQUIRED then
      CLEAN_GOALSSTK;
      PHRASES:=ENTRY_PHRASES;
      return FALSE;
    end if;
  else
    SWORD := CURWORD.ITEM;
    -- IN  GENERAL, WOULD HAVE TO TEST FOR  MORE THAN
    -- MERE EQUALITY AS BELOW:
    -- EG NP COULD BE NOMINATIVE OR  OBJECTIVE OR  POSSESSIVE
    --    VERB COULD BE TENSLESS, PRESENT, SING. OR  PLURAL.ETC.
    ANS := (WORD.VALUE= SWORD.VALUE);
    if ANS then
      -- ATTACH IT
      SUBTREE := new TREE;
      SUBTREE.NAME := SWORD;
      SUBTREE.CHILDR := null;
      SUBTREE.VALUE := SWORD.VALUE;
      ATTACH( CURTREE,SUBTREE,DEPTH,FALSE,OK);
      if not OK then
        CLEAN_GOALSSTK;
        PHRASES:=ENTRY_PHRASES;
        return FALSE;
      end if ;
      NEW_LINE;PUT(" CAT ATTACHING "); PRINT(SWORD.TOKEN);
      PREVWD := CURWORD;
      CURWORD := CURWORD.NEXT;
    end if ;
    --@NEW_LINE;PUT(" CAT PROCESSING");
    if not ANS and ARCTYPE=REQUIRED
      then
```

```
    --@PUT(" FALSE,REQUIRED");
    CLEAN_GOALSSTK;
    PHRASES:=ENTRY_PHRASES;
    return FALSE;
  elsif ANS and ARCTYPE=OPTANY
    then
    if CURWORD/=null
      then
      goto CAGAIN;
    end if ;
    -- ELSE,EITHER:
    -- NOT  ANS, OPTIONAL OR  OPTANY- CONTINUE
    -- ANS, OPTIONAL OR  REQUIRED - CONTINUE
    end if;
  end if;
elsif SYM=PEEKPTR then
  -- ONLY ALLOW CAT,WORD TESTS TO FOLLOW
  -- SEE COMMENTS UNDER CAT TEST.
  -- WOULD MOST GENERALLY CALL SUBROUTINES WHICH
  -- DO  CAT OR  WORD TEST.
  WRD := TARGET.NEXT;
  WORD := WRD.ITEM;
  NEXTWRD := WRD.NEXT;
  NEXTSYM := NEXTWRD.ITEM;
  if CURWORD=null or else CURWORD.NEXT=null then
    CLEAN_GOALSSTK;
    PHRASES:=ENTRY_PHRASES;
    return FALSE;
  end if;
  SWORD := CURWORD.NEXT.ITEM;
  if WORD=CATPTR
    then
    if NEXTSYM.VALUE/=SWORD.VALUE
      then
      CLEAN_GOALSSTK;
      PHRASES:=ENTRY_PHRASES;
      return FALSE;
    end if ;
```

```
    else
      -- WORD=WORDPTR IS  ASSUMED, NOT  CHECKED
      if NEXTSYM/=SWORD then
        CLEAN_GOALSSTK;
        PHRASES:=ENTRY_PHRASES;
        return FALSE;
      end if ;
    end if ;
  elsif SYM=INSERTPTR then
    --BEFORE CURRENT WORD (AND BECOME CURRENT WD)
    WHERE:=CURTAIL;
    INSERT(TARGET.NEXT.ITEM,CURWORD,WHERE,FALSE);
  elsif SYM=INSERTDPTR then
    --BEFORE CURRENT WORD (AND BECOME CURRENT WD)
    WHERE:=CURTAIL;
    if DETACHED_WORD= null then
      NEW_LINE;PUT(" NO DETACHED WORD ");
    else
      INSERT(DETACHED_WORD,CURWORD,WHERE,FALSE);
      -- might want DETACHED_WORD:=null here
    end if;
  elsif SYM=DETACHPTR then
    --THROW AWAY CURRENT WORD FROM SENTENCE
    DETACHED_WORD:=CURWORD.ITEM;
    PUT(" DETACHING ");PRINT(DETACHED_WORD.TOKEN);
    --THROW AWAY FROM TREE. singly linked list. ITS TAIL
    DETACH(CURWORD,CURTREE);
    if CURWORD.NEXT/=null then
      CURWORD.NEXT.PREV := CURWORD.PREV;
    end if;
    PREVWD:=CURWORD.PREV;
    CURWORD := CURWORD.NEXT;
  elsif SYM=BACKUPPTR then
    if CURWORD.PREV/=null then
      CURWORD:=CURWORD.PREV;
      PREVWD:=CURWORD.PREV;
    else
      NEW_LINE;PUT(" CANNOT BACKUP WITHIN PHRASE");
```

```
    end if;
elsif SYM=SKIPPTR then
   PREVWD:=CURWORD;
   CURWORD:=CURWORD.NEXT;--DO NOT ATTACH
elsif SYM=PUSHPTR or SYM=PUSHFPTR
   then
   WORD := TARGET.NEXT.ITEM;--GET PHRASE MATCHING TARGET
   VAL := WORD.VALUE;
   OK := FALSE;
   SIBLING := PHRASES;
   loop
      if SIBLING=null then  exit;
      end if;
      if SIBLING.CHILD=null then
         exit;
      end if;
      NEW__LINE;PUT(" PUSH(F) PHRASE=");
PRINT(SIBLING.CHILD.NAME.TOKEN);
      if SIBLING.ATTACH then PUT(" attachable");end if;
      if VAL = SIBLING.CHILD.VALUE
         and then SIBLING.ATTACH then
            --FOUND
            USER := SIBLING;
            OK := TRUE;
            if SYM=PUSHPTR then exit;
            end if;
      end if;
      SIBLING := SIBLING.NEXT;
   end loop;
   if not OK then
      CLEAN_GOALSSTK;
      PHRASES:=ENTRY_PHRASES;
      return FALSE;
   end if;
   -- REMOVE FROM PHRASE LIST AND DETACH AND STACK IT
   SIBLING := USER;
   DETACH_FROM_TREE(USER.CHILD);
   if SIBLING.PREV/=null then
```

```
      SIBLING.PREV.NEXT:=SIBLING.NEXT;
   end if;
   if SIBLING.NEXT/=null then
      SIBLING.NEXT.PREV:=SIBLING.PREV;
   end if;
   USER := new LIST;
   USER.NEXT := SAVEUSE;
   SAVEUSE := USER;
   USER.CHILD := SIBLING.CHILD;
elsif SYM=POPPTR
   then--POP SAVEUSE, DROP IT IN
   DROP(SAVEUSE.CHILD,CURWORD,NEWPRED);
   SAVEUSE := SAVEUSE.NEXT;
   CURWORD:=NEWPRED;
elsif SYM=OCATPTR then
   -- NEW- TEST OLD CATEGORY. OPT OR REQUIRED
   WORD := TARGET.NEXT.ITEM;
   ANS := WORD.VALUE = PREVCAT;
   if not ANS and ARCTYPE=REQUIRED
      then
      CLEAN_GOALSSTK;
      PHRASES:=ENTRY_PHRASES;
      return FALSE ;
   end if;
elsif SYM= WORDPTR then
   --REQUIRED ONLY ALLOWED
   PREVWD := CURWORD;
   CURWORD := CURWORD.NEXT;
   if CURWORD=null or else CURWORD.NEXT=null then
      CLEAN_GOALSSTK;
      PHRASES:=ENTRY_PHRASES;
      return FALSE;
   end if;
   SWORD := CURWORD.ITEM;
   WRD := TARGET.NEXT;
   WORD := WRD.ITEM;
   PREVCAT := NEWCAT;
   NEWCAT := WORD.VALUE;
```

```
  if WORD/=SWORD
    then
    CLEAN_GOALSSTK;
    PHRASES:=ENTRY_PHRASES;
    return FALSE;
  end if ;
    --WORD IS  OK ATTACH IT
    SUBTREE := new TREE;
    SUBTREE.NAME := SWORD;
    SUBTREE.CHILDR := null;
    SUBTREE.VALUE := SWORD.VALUE;
    ATTACH( CURTREE,SUBTREE,DEPTH,FALSE,OK);
    if not OK then
      CLEAN_GOALSSTK;
      PHRASES:=ENTRY_PHRASES;
      return FALSE;
    end if ;

-- ACTIONS ON PARSETREE
elsif SYM= TESTPTR
  then
  --BACK UP TREE TO APPRPRIATE NODE TYPE
  WORD := TARGET.NEXT.ITEM;-- EG, NOUNPTR,SPTR
  SUBTREE := CURTREE;
  loop
    if (WORD.VALUE=SUBTREE.VALUE)
      then
      exit ;
    elsif WORD.VALUE/=SUBTREE.VALUE
      then
      CLEAN_GOALSSTK;
      PHRASES:=ENTRY_PHRASES;
      return FALSE;
    elsif (SUBTREE.VALUE= SENTENCE_ROOT
          or SUBTREE.PARENT=null)
      then
      --@NEW_LINE;PUT(" SEACH FOR  = FAILED");
      --CAVEAT: TREE MAY NOT  YET BE BUILT UP ENOUGH TO FORM
```

```
        --LINK BACK TO NODE TESTED.
        -- PUT TEST REQUEST ON LIST.  ATTACH SHOULD
        -- THEN  PERFORM TEST IF  NODE(FATHER) ATTACHING
        -- IS  THE ONE DESIRED. ATTACH WILL THEN  RETURN
        -- A TRUE/FALSE.
        DOTOTREE := new TREEACT;
        DOTOTREE.NEXT := ACTIONS;
        ACTIONS := DOTOTREE;
        ACTIONS.SVALUE := TEST;
        VAL := WORD.VALUE;
        ACTIONS.TVALUE := VAL;--INTEGER VALUE
        ACTIONS.SOURCE := CURTREE;
        ACTIONS.DEPTH := DEPTH;
        ACTIONS.DDEPTH := 0;  -- DELTA-DEPTH LIMIT 0=>ANY.
      end if ;
      SUBTREE := SUBTREE.PARENT;
    end loop ;
  --TEST VALUE IN EFFECT DONE
  elsif SYM=SETPTR
    then
    --BACK UP TREE TO APPRPRIATE NODE TYPE-
    -- WILL NOT,CURRENTLY, CHECK SIBLINGS -
    -- ONLY NODE VALUES ON DIRECT BACKTRACK
    -- SEE COMMENTS ABOVE ON TESTPTR. SIMILAR,EXCEPT
    -- ATTACH WOULD THEN  DO  THE SET ON THE PARENT NODE.
    -- would need to generalize to test, e.g.,SUBJ-VERB agreement
    WORD := TARGET.NEXT.ITEM;-- EG, NOUNPTR,SPTR
    SUBTREE := CURTREE;
    loop
      if (WORD.VALUE=SUBTREE.VALUE)
        then
        exit ;
      elsif (SUBTREE.VALUE=SENTENCE_ROOT
          or SUBTREE.PARENT=null)
        then
        --@NEW_LINE;PUT(" SEACH FOR  := FAILED");
        DOTOTREE := new TREEACT;
        DOTOTREE.NEXT := ACTIONS;
```

```
        ACTIONS := DOTOTREE;
        ACTIONS.TVALUE := WORD.VALUE;
        ACTIONS.SVALUE := TARGET.NEXT.NEXT.ITEM.VALUE;
        ACTIONS.SOURCE := CURTREE;
        ACTIONS.DEPTH := DEPTH;
        ACTIONS.DDEPTH := 0;--0 FOR UNIVERSAL
        --@NEW_LINE;PUT(" QUEUING SET TO");
        goto GIVEUP;
      end if ;
      SUBTREE := SUBTREE.PARENT;--ON TO NEXT
    end loop ;
    --SET VALUE
    -- ONLY IF  PRESENTLY UNSET
    if SUBTREE.VALUE=CLAUSE
      then
      SUBTREE.VALUE := TARGET.NEXT.NEXT.ITEM.VALUE;
    --ELSE MIGHT WARN
    else
      NEW_LINE;PUT(" ATTEMPT TO RESET VALUE");
    end if ;
    <<GIVEUP>> null ;-- DO  NOTHING IF  NOT  FOUND
  else
    NEW_LINE;PUT(" TROUBLE in  ATN-");PRINTPRED(TARGET);
    CLEAN_GOALSSTK;
    PHRASES:=ENTRY_PHRASES;
    return FALSE;
  end if ;
end loop ;
CLEAN_GOALSSTK;
PHRASES:=ENTRY_PHRASES;
return FALSE;
end ATN;

begin
--VERIFY (THAT SENTENCE IS  VALID)
NEW_LINE;PUT(" in verify sent.=");PRINTPRED(CURRWORD);
-- END OF PUSH ONTO PHRASE LIST
if ACTTOP=null
```

```
then
--SUCCESS  ANSWER;
ANSWER := TRUE;
return ;-- ABSOLUTE TRUTH NOTHING LEFT!
else
--WORK ON TOPMOST GOAL
  LDEPTH := DEPTH;
  CURGOAL := ACTTOP;
  POPGOAL(TGTPRED,ARCTYPE,ACTTOP,ATHEAD);
  -- get target from actions
  PRINTPRED(TGTPRED);
  --SHOULD BE: PARSE X
  -- X=S FIRST TIME. X=S,NP,VP,PP.
  if TGTPRED.ITEM=DONEPTR
    then
      -- DONE ENCOUNTERED -THIS PROB. SHOULD NOT HAPPEN HERE.
    if CURRWORD/=null then
        PHRASES := PHRASES.NEXT;--POP
        ANSWER := FALSE;
        return ;
    else
        ANSWER := TRUE;
        return ;
      end if ;
  elsif TGTPRED.ITEM/=PARSEPTR
    then
      PUT(" VERIFY CALLED with  ");PRINTPRED(TGTPRED);
      ANSWER := FALSE;
      PHRASES := PHRASES.NEXT;--POP
      return ;
  end if ;
  -- MAKE NEW  NODE FOR  CONSTITUENT TO BE PARSED-
  CHILDNODE := new TREE;
  CHILDNODE.CHILDR := null;
  CHILDNODE.NAME := TGTPRED.NEXT.ITEM;-- S,S_CLAUSE,NP,VP,PP
  CHILDNODE.PARENT := FATHER;
  NEW_LINE;
  PUT(" verify will attempt child:");PRINT(CHILDNODE.NAME.TOKEN);
```

```
PUT(" to father:");PRINT(FATHER.NAME.TOKEN);
if TGTPRED.NEXT.ITEM =SPTR
  or else TGTPRED.NEXT.ITEM=S_CLAUSEPTR
  then
   PUSHCLAUSE(CHILDNODE,CURRENT_CLAUSE);
   --sentence(clause):mood unknown
   CHILDNODE.VALUE := CLAUSE;
   if QMARK and CHILDNODE.VALUE=SENTENCE_ROOT
     then
     CHILDNODE.VALUE := QUESTION;--INTERROGATORY SENTENCE
   end if ;
elsif TGTPRED.NEXT.ITEM =PPPTR
  then
    CHILDNODE.VALUE := PREPPHRASE;
elsif TGTPRED.NEXT.ITEM =VPPTR
  then
    CHILDNODE.VALUE := VERBPHRASE;
elsif TGTPRED.NEXT.ITEM =NPPTR
  then
    CHILDNODE.VALUE := NOUNPHRASE;
else
  PUT(" TROUBLE in  VERIFY CASE");PRINTPRED(TGTPRED);
  ANSWER := FALSE;
  --PHRASES := PHRASES.NEXT;--POP
  --CURRWORD:=null;
  return ;
end if ;
RULINDEX := null;
GETRULE(CURRULNUM,TGTPRED,RULINDEX,FOUND);
if not FOUND then
-- GIVE UP!
  ANSWER := FALSE;
  NEW_LINE;PUT(" NO RELEVANT ARCS FOR");
  PRINTPRED(TGTPRED);
  --CURRWORD:=null;
  return;
end if ;
loop-- OVER RELEVANT HEADS
```

```
NEWSTRPTR := RULEINDX(CURRULNUM+1)-1;
NUMSTRRULES := RULEINDX(CURRULNUM);
GETPRED;
CURGOAL := ACTTOP;--SAVE
SAVEPCAT := PREVCAT; --SAVE
PUSHGOAL(ENDP,REQUIRED,ACTTOP,TRUE);
AT_HEAD:=FALSE;
loop-- PUSH ANTECEDENTS
  if NEWSTRPTR<=NUMSTRRULES
    then
    exit ;
  end if ;
  NEWSTRPTR := NEWSTRPTR-1;
  --PUSH LAST FIRST, SO FIRST DONE FIRST
  ANTECED := RULES(NEWSTRPTR);
  PUSHGOAL(ANTECED,PRED_OPTIONS(NEWSTRPTR),ACTTOP,
 AT_HEAD);
  --AT_HEAD:=FALSE;--ALL FALSE
end loop ;--ANTECEDENT PUSH LOOP
if ATN(CURRWORD,CHILDNODE,LDEPTH) then
--SUCCESS-ATTACH NEW  NODE TO ENTRY  NODE!
  NEW_LINE;PUT(" VERIFY ATTACHING");
  CURRWORD:=CURRENTWORD;
  --TOPMOST CLAUSE ON STCK-DON'T POP YET.
  if CHILDNODE.VALUE=CLAUSE or else
    CHILDNODE.VALUE=SUBORD_CLAUSE
    then
    --TIME TO MOVE TO PARENT
    POPCLAUSE(DUMMYNODE,CURRENT_CLAUSE);
  end if ;
  if PHRASES.ATTACH
    then
    ATTACH(FATHER,CHILDNODE,LDEPTH,ATHEAD,ANSWER);
    PRINT(CHILDNODE.NAME.TOKEN);PUT(" TO ");
    PRINT(FATHER.NAME.TOKEN);
    --ANSWER:=TRUE;--NOW SET IN  ATTACH
  end if;
  NEW_LINE;
```

```
    PUT(" VERIFY CURRWORD ");PRINTPRED(CURRWORD);
    return ;
  end if ;--    ATN TRUE
  --OTHERWISE, GO ON TO NEXT  POSSIBLE RULE
  NEW_LINE;PUT(" VERIFY FAILURE");
  ACTTOP := CURGOAL;--RESTORE
  PREVCAT := SAVEPCAT;--RESTORE
  CHILDNODE.CHILDR := null;-- DISCARD ANY WRONG "BINDINGS"
  NEW_LINE;PUT(" VERIFY NOT CLEARING(PA):");
  PRINT(CHILDNODE.NAME.TOKEN);PUT(" CHILD=");
  PRINT(FATHER.NAME.TOKEN);
  GETRULE(CURRULNUM,TGTPRED,RULINDEX,FOUND);
  if not FOUND then
     exit ;-- DROP THRU TO RETURN  FALSE
  end if ;
 end loop ;
end if ;
ANSWER := FALSE;
--PHRASES := PHRASES.NEXT;
--CURRWORD:=null;
return;
end VERIFY;


procedure ANSWER(TREE:TREEPTR) is
--PRINT SALIENT INFO FROM PARSE TREE
-- DO  (PRE-ORDER) TRAVERSAL OF  PARSE TREE
NODE: TREEPTR;
SIBLING: LISTPTR;
begin
NODE := TREE;
if NODE.VALUE=SENTENCE_ROOT then
   NEW_LINE;PUT(" SENTENCE RESULTS");
else
   NEW_LINE; PRINT(TREE.NAME.TOKEN);
   case TREE.VALUE is
      when NOUN => PUT(" noun");
      when VERB => PUT(" verb");
      when DETERMINER => PUT(" determiner(adj) ");
```

```
      when PREPOSITION => PUT(" preposition");
      when ADJECTIVE => PUT(" adjective");
      when ADVERB => PUT(" adverb");
      when WH_WORD => PUT("wh-word");
      when COMMA => PUT("(comma)");
      when NOUNPHRASE => PUT(" noun phrase");
      when VERBPHRASE => PUT(" verb phrase");
      when PREPPHRASE => PUT(" prepositional phrase");
      when CONJUNCTION => PUT(" conjunction");
      when CLAUSE => PUT(" clause ");
      when QUESTION =>PUT(" question(interrogatory) ");
      when COMMAND =>PUT(" command(imperative) ");
      when DECLARATION =>PUT(" declarative  ");
      -- ETC.
      when others => null;
    end case;
    if NODE.CHILDR= null  then
      PUT(" IS LEAF (TERMINAL SYMBOL)");
    end if;
end if ;
SIBLING := NODE.CHILDR;
loop
  if SIBLING=null then
     exit ;
  end if ;
  ANSWER(SIBLING.CHILD);
  SIBLING := SIBLING.NEXT;
end loop ;
return ;
end ANSWER;


procedure DIAGNOSE is
TARGET: PREDICPTR;
CURRWORD: PREDICPTR;
CURRTREE: TREEPTR;
ANS: BOOLEAN;
SENTN: INTEGER;
```

```
begin
--DIAGNOSE BODY
QMARK := FALSE;
DETACHED_WORD:=null;
INDEX_RULES;-- INDEX ARCS IN ATN.
INDEX_SENTENCE(TARGET);-- INDEX "PARSE S"
for SENTN in 1..NUMGOALS loop
   SENTHEAD := SENTPTR(SENTN);
   NEW_LINE;PUT(" SENTENCE=");PRINTPRED(SENTHEAD);
   -- COULD EASILY PROCESS UP TO TEN SENTENCES, LOOPING IN
   -- DIAGNOSE OVER NUMGOALS
   ACTTOP := null;
   ACTIONS := null;
   SAVEUSE := null;
   PHRASES := null;
   PUSHGOAL(DONEP,REQUIRED,ACTTOP,TRUE);
   PUSHGOAL(TARGET,REQUIRED,ACTTOP,TRUE);
   --INITIALIZE
   CURRWORD := SENTHEAD;-- START AT TOP OF SENTENCE
   CURRTREE := new TREE;
   CURRTREE.VALUE := SENTENCE_ROOT;--ROOT
   CURRTREE.NAME := ROOTPTR;--ensure name is defined.
   CURRTREE.PARENT := null;--TOPS NO PARENT EVER
   CURRTREE.SIB := null;--NO SIBLINGS EVER
   CURRTREE.CHILDR := null; -- NOT YET ANY CHILDREN
   --ROOT AT TOP OF CLAUSETREE STACK
   PUSHCLAUSE(CURRTREE,CURRENT_CLAUSE);
   PREVCAT := CLAUSE;
   PUSHPHRASE(CURRTREE,0);
   VERIFY(CURRWORD,CURRTREE,ANS,0);
   if ANS then
      ANSWER(CURRTREE);
      -- "ARGUMENT" IS GLOBAL AGENDA STACK
   else
      NEW_LINE;
      PUT(" SENTENCE not RECOGNIZED");
   end if ;
end loop ;
```

```
end DIAGNOSE;

begin
--ATN
-- INITIALIZE
PARSETREE := null;
NODETOP := null;
DONEP := new PREDICATE;-- MAKE A PREDICATE DONE FOR
-- INSERTION ONTO ACTION STACK.
DONEP.ITEM := DONEPTR;
DONEP.NEXT := null;
DONEP.INDX := null;
ENDP := new PREDICATE;-- MAKE A PREDICATE DONE FOR
-- INSERTION ONTO ACTION STACK.
ENDP.ITEM := ENDPHPTR;
ENDP.NEXT := null;
ENDP.INDX := null;
LOADDICT;--INPUT DICTIONARY
GETRULES; --INPUT 1)ATN RULES 2) SENTENCE
DIAGNOSE;--BUILD PARSE TREE
end ATN;
```

```
-- Type Definitions for ATN
-- Similar to LOGIC Package for Expert System Shells)

with STRNG; use STRNG;

package GRAMMAR is

type OCCUR is (OPT,OPTANY,REQUIRED);

type PART_OF_SPEECH is (SENTENCE_ROOT,CLAUSE, QUESTION,
COMMAND,DECLARATION,TEST,SUBORD_CLAUSE,ENDPHRASE,
NOUNPHRASE,VERBPHRASE,PREPPHRASE,
WH_WORD,COMMA,NOUN,PRONOUN,VERB,ADJECTIVE,
DETERMINER,ADVERB,PREPOSITION,CONJUNCTION,SUBORD_CONJ);

MAX_RULE_COUNT: constant :=100;
MAX_SENTENCES: constant:=10;

subtype RULERANGE is INTEGER range 0..MAX_RULE_COUNT;
subtype PTRANGE is INTEGER range 0..MAX_RULE_COUNT ;
subtype GOALRANGE is INTEGER range 0..MAX_SENTENCES;

type  INDEX;--dynamically-allocated linked-list
type  INDEXPTR is access INDEX;

type SYMBOL;
type SYMPTR is access SYMBOL;
type SYMBOL is
  record
    TOKEN: PHRASE;
    LEFT:  SYMPTR;
    RIGHT: SYMPTR;
    VALUE: PART_OF_SPEECH;
  end record ;

type PREDICATE;-- WILL BE for  RULE, FACT, or  GOAL.
type PREDICPTR is access PREDICATE;
type PREDICATE is
```

```
record
   ITEM: SYMPTR;--POINT TO LIST WHICH is  PREDICATE
   NEXT : PREDICPTR;--FOR next  SYMBOL in  PREDICATE
   INDX: INDEXPTR;--FOR ATN
   PREV: PREDICPTR;--for atn doubly-linked list
   DELTA_DEPTH: INTEGER; --USED FOR TEST/SET PREDICATES
end  record ;

type LIST;
type LISTPTR is access LIST;

type TREE;
type TREEPTR is access TREE;
type TREE is
   record
      NAME: SYMPTR;-- WORD IF  ANY
      VALUE: PART_OF_SPEECH;-- node's function in sentence
      PARENT: TREEPTR;--for backtracking up parse tree
      SIB: LISTPTR;--for backtracking to siblings to the right
      CHILDR: LISTPTR;-- LINKED LIST OF  CHILDREN
   end record ;

type LIST is
   record--DOUBLY-LINKED LIST
      CHILD: TREEPTR;
      NEXT : LISTPTR;
      PREV : LISTPTR;
      ATTACH: BOOLEAN;--FOR PHRASE LIST
      DEPTH: INTEGER;--FOR PHRASE LIST
   end record ;

type  INDEX is
   record
      RULENUM: PTRANGE;-- RULE with appropriate head
      NUMSTR: INTEGER;-- WHICH PREDICATE
      NEXT : INDEXPTR;
   end  record ;
```

```
type TREEACT;
type TAPTR is access TREEACT;
type TREEACT is
 record
   TVALUE: PART_OF_SPEECH;-- TARGET (TEST) VALUE
   SVALUE: PART_OF_SPEECH;-- IF SET, VALUE TO USE. ELSE  0
   DEPTH,DDEPTH: INTEGER;
   SOURCE: TREEPTR;-- SOURCENODE
   NEXT : TAPTR;
 end record ;

type GOALS;-- PUSH-DOWN STACK- FOR ACTIONS, AGENDA
type GOALSPTR is access GOALS;
type GOALS is
 record
   DATA: PREDICPTR;--BINDING ITSELF
   NEXT : GOALSPTR;--LINKED-LIST LIFO IMPLEMENTATION
   ATYPE: OCCUR;--REQUIRED OR OPTIONAL
   ATTCHPT: BOOLEAN;--ATTACH TO NODE HEAD?
 end record ;

ROOT: SYMPTR;-- symbol table root

procedure PRINTPRED (P: in PREDICPTR);

end GRAMMAR;
```

-- Types and Support Routines for ATN

```
with TEXT_IO; use TEXT_IO;
with STRNG; use STRNG;

package body GRAMMAR is

procedure  PRINTPRED(P:in  PREDICPTR) is
PP:PREDICPTR;
begin
PP:=P;
loop
   if  PP=null then  exit ;end  if ;
   PUT(" ");PRINT(PP.ITEM.TOKEN);
   PP:=PP.NEXT;
end  loop ;
return ;
end  PRINTPRED;

end GRAMMAR;
```

```
--ATN Stack Processing

with GRAMMAR; use GRAMMAR;
with STRNG; use STRNG;

package ATNSTK is

PHRASES: LISTPTR;

procedure PUSHGOAL (P:in PREDICPTR; ATYPE:OCCUR;
        STACK:in out GOALSPTR;
    AT_HEAD: in BOOLEAN) ;

procedure POPGOAL(P:out PREDICPTR ; ATYPE:out OCCUR;
        STACK:in out GOALSPTR;
    AT_HEAD: out BOOLEAN) ;

procedure PUSHCLAUSE (P:in TREEPTR;
        STACK:in out LISTPTR);

procedure POPCLAUSE(P:out TREEPTR ;
        STACK:in out LISTPTR) ;


procedure PUSHPHRASE(CURRTREE: in TREEPTR;
    DEPTH: in INTEGER);

end ATNSTK;
```

```
-- Stack Operations for ATN

with GRAMMAR; use GRAMMAR;
with STRNG; use STRNG;

package body ATNSTK is

procedure PUSHGOAL (P:in PREDICPTR; ATYPE:OCCUR;
            STACK:in out GOALSPTR;
        AT_HEAD: in BOOLEAN) is

GLLS: GOALSPTR;
-- GOALTOP SHOULD BE INITIALIZED TO null
begin
GLLS := new GOALS;
GLLS.DATA := P;
GLLS.ATYPE := ATYPE;
GLLS.ATTCHPT:=AT_HEAD;
GLLS.NEXT := STACK;--POINT TO PREVIOUS (PUSH-DOWN STACK)
STACK := GLLS;
return ;
end PUSHGOAL;

procedure POPGOAL(P:out PREDICPTR ; ATYPE:out OCCUR;
            STACK:in out GOALSPTR;
        AT_HEAD: out BOOLEAN) is

OLD: GOALSPTR;

begin
OLD := STACK;
P := STACK.DATA;
ATYPE := STACK.ATYPE;
AT_HEAD:=STACK.ATTCHPT;
STACK := STACK.NEXT;
-- IF  WE ARE NOT  USING AUTOMATIC GARBAGE COLLECTION,
--COULD CALL FREE(OLD);
return ;
```

```
end POPGOAL;

procedure PUSHCLAUSE (P:in TREEPTR;
            STACK:in out LISTPTR) is

GLLS: LISTPTR;
-- GOALTOP SHOULD BE INITIALIZED TO null
begin

GLLS := new LIST;
GLLS.CHILD := P;
GLLS.NEXT := STACK;--POINT TO PREVIOUS (PUSH-DOWN STACK)
STACK := GLLS;
return ;
end PUSHCLAUSE;

procedure POPCLAUSE(P:out TREEPTR ;
            STACK:in out LISTPTR) is

OLD: LISTPTR;

begin
OLD := STACK;
P := STACK.CHILD;
STACK := STACK.NEXT;
-- IF  WE ARE NOT  USING AUTOMATIC GARBAGE COLLECTION,
--COULD CALL FREE(OLD);
return ;
end POPCLAUSE;

procedure PUSHPHRASE(CURRTREE: in TREEPTR;DEPTH: in INTEGER) is
CLAUSES: LISTPTR;
begin
-- PUSH ONTO PHRASES LIST
CLAUSES := new LIST;
CLAUSES.CHILD := CURRTREE;
CLAUSES.ATTACH := TRUE;
CLAUSES.NEXT := PHRASES;
```

```
PHRASES := CLAUSES;
return;
end PUSHPHRASE;

end ATNSTK;
```

```
-- Index ATN

with GRAMMAR; use GRAMMAR;
with STRNG; use STRNG;
with TEXT_IO; use TEXT_IO;

package ATNINDEX is

procedure INDEX_RULES;

procedure INDEX_SENTENCE(TRGET:out PREDICPTR);

end ATNINDEX;
```

```
-- Index ATN

with GRAMMAR; use GRAMMAR;
with STRNG; use STRNG;
with ATNREAD; use ATNREAD;
with TEXT_IO; use TEXT_IO;

package body ATNINDEX is

package INT_IO is new INTEGER_IO(NUM=>INTEGER);
procedure INDEX_RULES is

PPTR: PREDICPTR;
HDS,STRG: PHRASE;
HYP2,HYP: SYMPTR;
HEADNUM,RULE,SOURCE,PREDICATE: RULERANGE;
HEAD: PTRANGE;
IND,OLD: INDEXPTR;
KOUNT: INTEGER;
-- LOOP  OVER SYMBOLS  IN  ANTECEDENT PREDICATES.
-- IF  THE HEAD OF  ANY RULE CAN UNIFY WITH
-- THAT PREDICATE, INDEX IT
begin
for SOURCE in 1..NUMRULES loop
  -- LOOP  OVER RULE ANTECEDNT PREDICATES
  PREDICATE := RULEINDX(SOURCE);
  HEADNUM := RULEINDX(SOURCE+1)-1;
  if HEADNUM=PREDICATE then
    NEW_LINE;PUT(" RULE ");INT_IO.PUT(SOURCE);PUT(" is  A FACT");
  else
    loop
    --OVER PREDICATES WITHIN RULE
    --CHANGED FOR  CLAUSE FORM
      if PREDICATE>= HEADNUM then
        exit ;
      end if ;-- DONE WITH  RULE
      PPTR := RULES(PREDICATE);
      if PPTR.ITEM=PARSEPTR then
```

```
HYP := PPTR.NEXT.ITEM;--SYMPTR TO UNIFY WITH  HEADS
STRG := HYP.TOKEN;
-- WE WILL ASSUME ALL  HEADS ARE OF  FORM PARSE X AND
-- ATTEMPT TO MATCH X
--IF (PPTR.INDX=null) THEN  PREDICATES,NOT SYMBOLS INDEXED
KOUNT := 0;
OLD := null;
for RULE in 1..NUMRULES loop
   HEAD := RULEINDX(RULE+1)-1;
   -- THE LAST PREDICATE,THUS THE CONSEQUENT OR  HEAD
   HYP2 := RULES(HEAD).NEXT.ITEM;--POINTER TO SYMBOL
   HDS := HYP2.TOKEN;
   if HYP=HYP2 then
      if SOURCE=RULE then
         NEW_LINE;PUT(" WARNING-SELF-REFERENCE RULE ");
         INT_IO.PUT(RULE);
      end if ;--SELF-REFERENCE WARNING
      IND := new INDEX;
      IND.RULENUM := RULE;
      IND.NEXT := null;
      if PPTR.INDX=null then
         PPTR.INDX := IND ;
      else
      -- NOT  THE FIRST-ADD IT TO END  OF  INDEX LIST
         OLD.NEXT := IND;
      end if ;--=null TEST
      OLD := IND;
      KOUNT := KOUNT+1;
     end if ; --HIT
   end loop ;-- FOR  RULE:HEADS TO RESOLVE WITH.
   NEW_LINE;PUT(" ANTECEDENT "); PRINT(STRG);
PUT(" UNIFIES with  ");
   INT_IO.PUT(KOUNT);PUT(" RULES");
   -- =null HAS SYMBOL BEEN INDEXED YET?
--PREDICATES, NOT SYMBOLS INDEXED
 end if ; --IS IT OF  FORM PARSE X ?
 PREDICATE := PREDICATE+1;
end loop ;--LOOP OVER PREDICATES
```

```
  end if ;--TEST IF  FACT OR  ELSE  NEEDS TO INDEX
end loop ;-- RULES
end INDEX_RULES;

procedure INDEX_SENTENCE(TRGET:out PREDICPTR) is

TARGET,PPTR,HDPTR,NEXTPTR: PREDICPTR;
KOUNT,RULE: INTEGER;
HEAD: RULERANGE;
STRG: SYMPTR;
IND,OLD: INDEXPTR;

begin
----@NEW_LINE;PUT(" INDEX_SENTENCE");
KOUNT := 0;
OLD := null;
-- CREATE THE GOAL "PARSE S" (BOTH SYMBOLS SHOULD EXIST)
TARGET := new PREDICATE;
TARGET.ITEM := PARSEPTR;
PPTR := new PREDICATE;
PPTR.ITEM := SPTR;
TARGET.NEXT := PPTR;
PPTR.NEXT := null;-- TARGET IS  NOW: PARSE S
TARGET.INDX := null;-- FOR  ATN, INDEX FIRST TERM IN  PREDICATE.
-- INDEX IT TO RULES (ARCS)HEADS
for RULE in 1..NUMRULES loop
   HEAD := RULEINDX(RULE+1)-1;
   HDPTR := RULES(HEAD);
   STRG := HDPTR.ITEM;--SYMPTR
   if STRG/=PARSEPTR then
      NEW_LINE;PUT(" BAD HEAD:");
   PRINTPRED(HDPTR);INT_IO.PUT(RULE);
   end if ;
   -- WE REUSE POINTER PPTR. NEXT-DATA NOT  AFFECTED
   PPTR := HDPTR.NEXT;
   STRG := PPTR.ITEM;
   if STRG=SPTR then
      IND := new INDEX;
```

```
      IND.RULENUM := RULE;
      IND.NEXT := null;
      KOUNT := KOUNT+1;
      if TARGET.INDX=null then
        TARGET.INDX := IND;
      else
        OLD.NEXT := IND;--ADD TO TAIL OF  INDEX LIST
      end if ;
        OLD := IND;
    end if ;--SECOND PRED ITEM IS  S
end loop ;
--@NEW__LINE;PUT(" There are ");INT__IO.PUT(KOUNT);
--@PUT(" Parse Sentence Arcs.");
TRGET := TARGET;
return ;
end INDEX_SENTENCE;

end ATNINDEX;
```

```
-- Input for ATN

with GRAMMAR; use GRAMMAR;
with STRNG; use STRNG;

package ATNREAD is

DONEPTR,PARSEPTR,CATPTR,WORDPTR,PEEKPTR: SYMPTR;
CONJPTR,PPPTR,NPPTR,VPPTR,SPTR,VERBPTR,NOUNPTR: SYMPTR;
ROOTPTR,PNOUNPTR,PREPPTR,ADJPTR,ADVPTR: SYMPTR;
COMMAPTR,OCATPTR,DETPTR,WHPTR,DECLPTR,IMPERPTR,
ENDPHPTR,S_CLAUSEPTR,S_CONJPTR,QPTR,SETPTR,TESTPTR: SYMPTR;
INSERTPTR,INSERTDPTR,DETACHPTR,SKIPPTR,BACKUPPTR,
PUSHPTR,PUSHFPTR,POPPTR: SYMPTR;


QMARK : BOOLEAN;
SENTHEAD: PREDICPTR;
-- RULES POINTS TO PREDICATES OF  RULES
RULES: array (1..MAX_RULE_COUNT) of PREDICPTR;
-- IS  PREDICATE ARC OPTIONAL?
PRED_OPTIONS: array (1..MAX_RULE_COUNT) of OCCUR;
SENTPTR: array (1..MAX_SENTENCES) of PREDICPTR;
-- POINT TO FIRST PREDICATE OF  EACH SENTENCE
NUMGOALS: GOALRANGE;
NUMRULES: RULERANGE;
RULEINDX: array (1..MAX_RULE_COUNT) of INTEGER;
-- GIVES INDEX OF  RULE FIRST PREDICATE
NUMSTRRULES : RULERANGE;

procedure LOADDICT;

procedure GETRULES;

IFTOKEN,THENTOKEN,NOTTOKEN,OPTTOKEN,OPANYTOKEN:
                PHRASE;

end ATNREAD;
```

```
-- Input for ATN


with STRNG; use STRNG;
with GRAMMAR; use GRAMMAR;
with TEXT_IO; use TEXT_IO;

package body ATNREAD is

package INT_IO is new INTEGER_IO(NUM=>INTEGER);


procedure SEARCH(CURPTR: in out SYMPTR;
           PREVPTR: out SYMPTR;
           STRNG: in PHRASE;
           OFOUND: out BOOLEAN) is
--PUT NEW  PREDICATES INTO MEMORY
-- STORED AS STRINGS IN  BINARY SEARCH TREE FOR  EFFICIENCY
-- IF  NOT  THERE, PREVPTR RETURNED
COMP: INTEGER;
FOUND: BOOLEAN;

begin
FOUND := FALSE;
loop
   PREVPTR := CURPTR;
   COMP := COMPAREPHRASES(STRNG,CURPTR.TOKEN);
   if COMP=0 then
     FOUND := TRUE;
   elsif (COMP=-1) then
     CURPTR := CURPTR.LEFT;
   else
     CURPTR := CURPTR.RIGHT;
   end if ;
   -- GIVE UP IF  FOUND OR  UNFINDABLE
   if (FOUND or CURPTR=null) then
     exit ;
   end if ;
```

```
end loop ;
OFOUND := FOUND;
return ;
end SEARCH;

procedure MAKESYM(PTR:out SYMPTR; STRG: in PHRASE) is
-- CREATE A NEW  SYMBOL FOR  NEW  PREDICATE
NEWPTR: SYMPTR;

begin
NEWPTR := new SYMBOL;
NEWPTR.TOKEN := STRG;
NEWPTR.LEFT := null;
NEWPTR.RIGHT := null;
NEWPTR.VALUE := CLAUSE;--DEFAULT AS KEYWORD
PTR := NEWPTR;
end MAKESYM;

procedure INTSYM(SYMBOL:in STRING; PTR:out SYMPTR;
    LENGTH: in INTEGER) is

DUMMY: PHRASE;
CUR,PREV,POINTR: SYMPTR;
FOUND: BOOLEAN;
COMP: INTEGER;

begin
if LENGTH>0 then
  STRING_TO_PHRASE(SYMBOL,DUMMY,LENGTH);
else
  STRING_TO_PHRASE(SYMBOL,DUMMY);
end if;
if ROOT=null then
  MAKESYM(ROOT,DUMMY);
  CUR := ROOT;
else
  CUR := ROOT;
  SEARCH(CUR,PREV,DUMMY,FOUND);
```

```
  if not FOUND then
    MAKESYM(CUR,DUMMY);-- RETURNS NEW  CUR
    COMP := COMPAREPHRASES(PREV.TOKEN,DUMMY);
    if COMP=1 then
      PREV.LEFT := CUR;
    else
      PREV.RIGHT := CUR;
    end if ;
  end if ;-- DO  NOTHING IF  FOUND (SHOULD NOT  BE FOUND)
end if ;
PTR := CUR;--POINTER TO SYMBOL.
return ;
end INTSYM;

procedure INTSYM(SYMBOL:in STRING; PTR:out SYMPTR) is

begin
INTSYM(SYMBOL,PTR,-1);
end INTSYM;


procedure INTSYM(SYMBOL:in STRING;
  PTR:out SYMPTR; PART: in PART_OF_SPEECH) is
begin
INTSYM(SYMBOL,PTR);
PTR.VALUE:=PART;
end INTSYM;

procedure INIT_TOKEN is
begin
STRING_TO_PHRASE("if$",IFTOKEN);
STRING_TO_PHRASE("then$",THENTOKEN);
STRING_TO_PHRASE("not$",NOTTOKEN);
STRING_TO_PHRASE("opt$",OPTTOKEN);
STRING_TO_PHRASE("opt*$",OPANYTOKEN);
end INIT_TOKEN;

procedure INIT_GRAMMAR is
```

```
begin
INTSYM("parse$",PARSEPTR);
INTSYM("cat$",CATPTR);
INTSYM("word$",WORDPTR);
INTSYM("peek$",PEEKPTR);
INTSYM("done$",DONEPTR);
INTSYM("root$",ROOTPTR);
INTSYM("ocat$",OCATPTR);
INTSYM("insert$",INSERTPTR);
INTSYM("detach$",DETACHPTR);
INTSYM("insertd$",INSERTDPTR);
INTSYM("push$",PUSHPTR);
INTSYM("pushf$",PUSHFPTR);
INTSYM("pop$",POPPTR);
INTSYM("skip$",SKIPPTR);
INTSYM("backup$",BACKUPPTR);
INTSYM("endphrase$",ENDPHPTR);
-- TREE MANIPULATION
INTSYM(":=$",SETPTR);
INTSYM("=$",TESTPTR);
-- TREE NODE ATTRIBUTES
INTSYM("decl$",DECLPTR, DECLARATION);
INTSYM("quest$",QPTR, QUESTION);--INTERROGATORY (QUESTION)
INTSYM("imper$",IMPERPTR,COMMAND);
-- QUALIFIERS OF PARSE,CAT,ETC.
INTSYM("det$",DETPTR, DETERMINER);
INTSYM("wh-wd$",WHPTR, WH_WORD);
INTSYM("pp$",PPPTR, PREPPHRASE);
INTSYM("np$",NPPTR, NOUNPHRASE);
INTSYM("vp$",VPPTR,VERBPHRASE);
INTSYM("s$",SPTR,CLAUSE);--UNKNOWN VALUE
INTSYM("verb$",VERBPTR, VERB);
INTSYM("noun$",NOUNPTR, NOUN);
INTSYM("pronoun$",PNOUNPTR,PRONOUN);
INTSYM("prep$",PREPPTR, PREPOSITION);
INTSYM("adj$",ADJPTR,ADJECTIVE);
INTSYM("conj$",CONJPTR, CONJUNCTION);
INTSYM("adv$",ADVPTR, ADVERB);
```

```
INTSYM(",$",COMMAPTR, COMMA);
INTSYM("subord_conj$",S_CONJPTR);
INTSYM("subord_clause$",S_CLAUSEPTR);
end INIT_GRAMMAR;

function LOCATE(SOURCE,TARGET: in PHRASE;
    SOURCELENGTH: in INTEGER)
                  return BOOLEAN is
TARGETLENGTH: INTEGER;
begin
--SOURCELENGTH:=PHRASE_LENGTH(SOURCE);
TARGETLENGTH:=PHRASE_LENGTH(TARGET);
return  (FIND_PHRASE(TARGET,SOURCE,
 SOURCELENGTH,TARGETLENGTH)/=0);
end LOCATE;

procedure LOADDICT is
--USES MAKESYM,SEARCH AS DOES GETRULES, INTSYM.
DICT: FILE_type ;
WORDCOUNT,LENGTH: INTEGER;
WORD,CATEGORY: STRING(1..STRINGLENGTH);
--SDUM: STRING(1..1);
TEXT: PHRASE;
SYMBOL: LONGPHRASE;
PTR: SYMPTR;
begin
WORDCOUNT:=0;
OPEN(DICT,in_FILE,"DICT.DAT");
loop
  GET_LINE(DICT,WORD,LENGTH);
  if LENGTH<1 then
    return ;
  end if ;
  INTSYM(WORD,PTR,LENGTH);
  GET_LINE(DICT,CATEGORY,LENGTH);
  STRING_TO_PHRASE(CATEGORY,SYMBOL,LENGTH);
  LONGPHRASE_TO_PHRASE(SYMBOL,TEXT,1,LENGTH);
  if LOCATE(TEXT,NOUNPTR.TOKEN,LENGTH) then
```

```
      PTR.VALUE:=NOUN;
   elsif LOCATE(TEXT,VERBPTR.TOKEN,LENGTH) then
      PTR.VALUE:=VERB;
   elsif LOCATE(TEXT,ADVPTR.TOKEN,LENGTH) then
      PTR.VALUE:=ADVERB;
   elsif LOCATE(TEXT,ADJPTR.TOKEN,LENGTH) then
      PTR.VALUE:=ADJECTIVE;
   elsif LOCATE(TEXT,PREPPTR.TOKEN,LENGTH) then
      PTR.VALUE:=PREPOSITION;
   elsif LOCATE(TEXT,COMMAPTR.TOKEN,LENGTH) then
      PTR.VALUE:=COMMA;
   elsif LOCATE(TEXT,PNOUNPTR.TOKEN,LENGTH) then
      PTR.VALUE:=PRONOUN;
   elsif LOCATE(TEXT,CONJPTR.TOKEN,LENGTH) then
      PTR.VALUE:=CONJUNCTION;
   elsif LOCATE(TEXT,WHPTR.TOKEN,LENGTH) then
      PTR.VALUE:=WH_WORD;
   elsif LOCATE(TEXT,DETPTR.TOKEN,LENGTH) then
      PTR.VALUE:=DETERMINER;
   else
      PUT(" PROBLEM- UNKOWN PART OF SPEECH:");PRINT(TEXT);
   end if;
   WORDCOUNT:=WORDCOUNT+1;
end loop ;
exception
   when CONSTRAINT_ERROR =>
      return;
   when END_ERROR =>
      NEW_LINE;PUT(" NUMBER OF WORDS KNOWN=");
      INT_IO.PUT(WORDCOUNT);
      return ;
end LOADDICT;

procedure GETRULES is
RULEFILE: FILE_type ;
TXT: STRING(1..LONGPHRASE_LENGTH);
TEXT: LONGPHRASE;
KOUNT,LENGTHIS: INTEGER;
```

```
GOALS: PHRASE;
CHAR: CHARACTER;

procedure LOADRULES(SYMBOL: in LONGPHRASE;
              RULE: in BOOLEAN ) is

--LENGTH:INTEGER;
I,P,OLDP,COMP: INTEGER;
CHAR: CHARACTER;
PRED: PHRASE;
FOUND,ISNOT,NEGATED,ISIF,ISOPT,ISTHEN: BOOLEAN;
ARCTYPE: OCCUR;

procedure MAKEPRED(OLDP:in INTEGER;I:in INTEGER;
              RULE:in BOOLEAN) is
-- PREDICATE IS SERIES OF  STRINGS SEP BY SPACES.
-- FORM INTO LINKED LIST

POINTER,OLDPTR: PREDICPTR;
COUNTER,LOCALP: INTEGER;
C: CHARACTER;
CURPTR,PREVPTR: SYMPTR;
--PART: PHRASE;
begin
--@NEW_LINE; PUT(" MAKEPRED");PUT(OLDP);PUT(I);
POINTER := new PREDICATE;
POINTER.PREV := null;--for DOUBLY-LINKED LIST. MODIFY SYMBOL
POINTER.INDX := null;--PREDICATES,NOT SYMBOLS,INDEXED.
if (RULE) then
  RULES(NUMSTRRULES) := POINTER;
  PRED_OPTIONS(NUMSTRRULES) := ARCTYPE;
else
  -- ITS SENTENCE
  NUMGOALS := NUMGOALS+1;
  -- SENTENCE SHOULD NOT  BE NEGATED, AND
  --  THERE SHOULD ONLY BE ONE.
  SENTPTR(NUMGOALS) := POINTER;
end if ;
```

```
POINTER.NEXT := null;
OLDPTR := null;
LOCALP := OLDP;
for COUNTER in OLDP..(I) loop
  --INCLUDE FINAL COMMA
  --FORM SYMBOLS
  C := SYMBOL(COUNTER);
  -- IF SENTENCE, ACCEPT , AS A TOKEN "WORD"
  if (C=' ' or (C=',' and RULE ) or C='.' or C='?' or C='!')
    then
    -- SYMBOL TERMINATOR IS  C
    LONGPHRASE_TO_PHRASE(SYMBOL,
     PRED,LOCALP,COUNTER-1);
    LOCALP := COUNTER+1;
    if ROOT=null then
      MAKESYM(ROOT,PRED);--place in empty symbol table
      CURPTR := ROOT;
    else
      --FIND WHERE TO PUT IT
      CURPTR := ROOT;
      SEARCH(CURPTR,PREVPTR,PRED,FOUND);
      if not FOUND then
        MAKESYM(CURPTR,PRED);
        COMP := COMPAREPHRASES(PREVPTR.TOKEN,PRED);
        if COMP=1 then
          PREVPTR.LEFT := CURPTR;
        else
          PREVPTR.RIGHT := CURPTR;
        end if ;
        --FOUND  DON'T NEED TO INSERT IT
      end if ;-- NOT  FOUND  TEST
    end if ;--ROOT=null
    if OLDPTR/=null then
      --NOT FIRST SYMBOL IN  PREDICATE
      POINTER := new PREDICATE;
      POINTER.NEXT := null;
      OLDPTR.NEXT := POINTER;
      POINTER.PREV := OLDPTR;--DOUBLY LINKED LIST
```

```
      end if ;-- /=null
      POINTER.ITEM := CURPTR;
      OLDPTR := POINTER;
    end if ;-- , OR  SPACE- NEW  TOKEN IN  PREDICATE
  end loop ;-- GO TO NEXT  CHARACTER
  end MAKEPRED;

begin
--LOADRULES BODY
P := 1;
ARCTYPE := REQUIRED;
NEGATED := FALSE;ISNOT := FALSE;ISOPT := FALSE;
-- SCAN INPUT LINE TO OBTAIN PREDICATE STRINGS FROM RULE
--LENGTH:= LENGTHS(SYMBOL);
for I in 1..LONGPHRASE_LENGTH loop
   CHAR := SYMBOL(I);
   if CHAR='$' then
      exit ;
   end if ;-- STRING TERMINATOR FOUND
   -- AS LINE ENDS WITH  , LAST PRED (HEAD) WILL BE FORCED OUT
   if CHAR=',' or CHAR='.' or CHAR='?'  then
   -- WE HAVE FOUND END  OF  THE PREDICATE
     if CHAR='?' then
        QMARK := TRUE;
     end if ;
     LONGPHRASE_TO_PHRASE(SYMBOL,PRED,P,I-1);
     OLDP := P;P := I+1;
     ISIF := (COMPAREPHRASES(PRED,IFTOKEN)=0);
     ISTHEN := (COMPAREPHRASES(PRED,THENTOKEN)=0);
     -- TOKEN OF  FORM NOT,  NEGATES FOLLOWING PREDICATE
     if COMPAREPHRASES(PRED,NOTTOKEN)=0 then
        NEGATED := TRUE; ISNOT := TRUE;
     end if ;-- IF  ROOT=null TEST
     if COMPAREPHRASES(PRED,OPTTOKEN)=0
        then
        ARCTYPE := OPT;
        ISOPT := TRUE;
     elsif COMPAREPHRASES(PRED,OPANYTOKEN)=0
```

```
        then
          ARCTYPE := OPTANY;
          ISOPT := TRUE;
        end if ;
        --WE HAVE FOUND A PHRASE DELIMITED BY ,
        -- IS  IT A NEW  RULE,BEGINNING WITH  IF?
        if ISIF
          then
          -- ONLY HAPPEN IF  RULE
          --@NEW_LINE;PUT(" IF  FOUND");
          -- PUT(NUMRULES);PUT(NUMSTRRULES);
          RULEINDX(NUMRULES) := NUMSTRRULES;
          NUMRULES := NUMRULES+1;
          -- NUMRULES WILL BE ONE MORE THAN ACTUAL NUMBER OF
          --  IF PHRASES ENCOUNTERED
        end if ;-- IF  TOKEN TEST
        -- PREDICATE -
        if not (ISNOT or ISIF or ISTHEN or ISOPT)
          then
          MAKEPRED(OLDP,I,RULE);
          -- BUMP COUNT OF  PREDICATES
          --@IF PRED_OPTIONS(NUMSTRRULES) THEN
          if RULE then
            NUMSTRRULES := NUMSTRRULES+1;
          end if ;
          ARCTYPE := REQUIRED;
          -- RESET SO NEXT  PRED NOT  NEGATED
          NEGATED := FALSE;
          -- IF  GOAL, NO NEED TO DO  ANYTHING??
         end if ;--NOT ISNOT
      end if ;-- CHAR=',' TEST
      ISOPT := FALSE;-- ARCTYPE WILL REMEMBER
      ISNOT := FALSE;
      -- RESET ALWAYS. NEGATED WILL REMEMBER IF  NECESSARY
  end loop ;-- END  OF  FOR  LOOP
  exception
    when CONSTRAINT_ERROR =>
      return ;
```

```
end LOADRULES;

begin
-- GETRULES
--OPEN FILE, GET GOALS
OPEN(RULEFILE,in_FILE,"ATN.DAT");
NUMGOALS := 0;
--
GET_LINE(RULEFILE, TXT,LENGTHIS);
NEW_LINE;PUT(" AUGMENTED TRANSITION NETWORK in use is");
NEW_LINE;STRING_TO_PHRASE(TXT,TEXT,LENGTHIS);
PRINT(TEXT);
NUMRULES := 1;
NUMSTRRULES := 1;
--GET RULES
loop
  GET_LINE(RULEFILE,TXT,LENGTHIS);
  -- CAVEAT: NON-STANDARD BELOW-
  if LENGTHIS<1 then
    exit ;
  end if ;
  STRING_TO_PHRASE(TXT,TEXT,LENGTHIS);
  LOADRULES(TEXT,TRUE);
end loop ;
RULEINDX(NUMRULES) := NUMSTRRULES;-- CLOSE OFF RULES
NUMRULES := NUMRULES-1;-- ACTUAL NUMBER OF RULES
NEW_LINE;PUT(" NUMBER OF ARC RULES =");
INT_IO.PUT(NUMRULES);
SENTHEAD := null;
loop-- GET SENTENCE
  -- INPUT SAME AS GOAL (HYPOTHESIS) BUT NOT UNIFIED W. RULES
  GET_LINE(RULEFILE, TXT,LENGTHIS);
  STRING_TO_PHRASE(TXT,TEXT,LENGTHIS);
  --EMPTY LINE USED TO DELIMIT END OF GOALS
  --NEW_LINE;PUT(" SENT=");PRINT(TEXT);
  --PUT(" LENGTH ");INT_IO.PUT(LENGTHIS);
  if LENGTHIS<1 then
    exit ;
```

```
  else
    LOADRULES(TEXT,FALSE);
  end if ;
  LENGTHIS := 0;
end loop ;
NEW_LINE;
PUT(" NUMBER of  SENTENCES=");INT_IO.PUT(NUMGOALS);
CLOSE(RULEFILE);
end GETRULES;


begin           -- INITIALIZE
INIT_GRAMMAR;
INIT_TOKEN;
end ATNREAD;
```

-- (Floating-Point) Register for ATN

with GRAMMAR; use GRAMMAR;

package REG is

function REGISTER(INFIX_EX: in PREDICPTR)return BOOLEAN;

end REG;

```
-- (Floating-Point) Register for ATN

with STRNG; use STRNG;
with GRAMMAR; use GRAMMAR;
with LOGIC;
with MATH; use MATH;


package body REG is

function REGISTER(INFIX_EX: in PREDICPTR)return BOOLEAN is
PRED_TERM: GRAMMAR.PREDICPTR;
XFORMED_TERM,PREVIOUS_TERM: LOGIC.PREDICPTR;
XFORMED_SYMPTR: LOGIC.SYMPTR;
OBJECT: PHRASE;
RESULT: FLOAT;
NOT_FIRST: BOOLEAN;

begin
PRED_TERM:=INFIX_EX;
PREVIOUS_TERM:=null;
NOT_FIRST:=FALSE;
loop
  if PRED_TERM=null then exit; end if;
  XFORMED_TERM:= new LOGIC.PREDICATE;
  OBJECT:= PRED_TERM.ITEM.TOKEN;
  XFORMED_SYMPTR:= new LOGIC.SYMBOL;
  XFORMED_SYMPTR.TOKEN:=OBJECT;
  XFORMED_TERM.ITEM:=XFORMED_SYMPTR;
  if NOT_FIRST then
    PREVIOUS_TERM.NEXT:=XFORMED_TERM;
  else
    NOT_FIRST:=TRUE;
  end if;
  PREVIOUS_TERM:=XFORMED_TERM;
  PRED_TERM:=PRED_TERM.NEXT;
end loop;
RESULT:=MATHD(XFORMED_TERM);
```

```
if RESULT= 0.0 then
   return FALSE;
else
   return TRUE;
end if;
end REGISTER;

end REG;
```

the
det
boy
noun
is
verb
tall
adj
he
pronoun
eats
verb
spam
noun
whether
conj
very
adv
John
noun
because
conj
to
prep
what
wh-wd
go
verb
heck
noun
you
pronoun

----- simple atn declarative sentence------
if,cat prep,parse np,then,parse pp,
if,cat verb,parse np,opt*,parse pp,parse vp,
if,cat verb,opt*,cat adv,cat adj,parse vp,
if,cat det,opt*,cat adj,cat noun,opt*,parse pp,parse np,
if,cat pronoun,parse np,
if,parse np,parse vp,:= s decl,parse s,
if,cat verb,parse np,:= s imper,parse s,
if,parse vp,parse pp,:= s imper,parse s,
if,cat verb,backup,insert you,skip,skip,parse vp,

the boy is tall.

NUMBER OF WORDS KNOWN= 16
AUGMENTED TRANSITION NETWORK in use is
----- simple atn declarative sentence------
NUMBER OF ARC RULES = 9
NUMBER of SENTENCES= 1
ANTECEDENT np UNIFIES with   2 RULES
ANTECEDENT np UNIFIES with   2 RULES
ANTECEDENT pp UNIFIES with   1 RULES
ANTECEDENT pp UNIFIES with   1 RULES
ANTECEDENT np UNIFIES with   2 RULES
ANTECEDENT vp UNIFIES with   3 RULES
ANTECEDENT np UNIFIES with   2 RULES
ANTECEDENT vp UNIFIES with   3 RULES
ANTECEDENT pp UNIFIES with   1 RULES
SENTENCE= the boy is tall
in verify sent.= the boy is tall parse s
verify will attempt child:s to father:root
in ATN DEPTH= 0
CLAUSES: s root
PREVCAT=CLAUSE, NEWWORD:the PHRASES: root
parse np atnREM. SENT.= the boy is tall
atn node=s REQUIRED
verify sent= the boy is tall
in verify sent.= the boy is tall parse np
verify will attempt child:np to father:s
in ATN DEPTH= 1
CLAUSES: s root
PREVCAT=CLAUSE, NEWWORD:the PHRASES: root
cat det atnREM. SENT.= the boy is tall
atn node=np REQUIRED FIRST CHILD
CAT ATTACHING the PHRASES: root
cat adj atnREM. SENT.= boy is tall
atn node=np OPTANY PHRASES: root
cat noun atnREM. SENT.= boy is tall
atn node=np REQUIRED
CAT ATTACHING boy PHRASES: root
parse pp atnREM. SENT.= is tall

atn node=np OPTANY
verify sent= is tall
in verify sent.= is tall parse pp
verify will attempt child:pp to father:np
in ATN DEPTH=   2
CLAUSES: s root PHRASES: root
cat prep atnREM. SENT.= is tall
atn node=pp REQUIRED
VERIFY FAILURE
VERIFY NOT CLEARING(PA):pp CHILD=np IN ATN AFTER VERIFY is tall PHR
endphrase ATHEAD atnREM. SENT.= is tall
atn node=np REQUIRED
PUSHING PHRASE np DEPTH=   1
VERIFY ATTACHING FIRST CHILDnp TO s
VERIFY CURRWORD is tall IN ATN AFTER VERIFY is tall PHRASES: np root
parse vp atnREM. SENT.= is tall
atn node=s REQUIRED
verify sent= is tall
in verify sent.= is tall parse vp
verify will attempt child:vp to father:s
in ATN DEPTH=   1
CLAUSES: s root PHRASES: np root
cat verb atnREM. SENT.= is tall
atn node=vp REQUIRED FIRST CHILD
CAT ATTACHING is PHRASES: np root
parse np atnREM. SENT.= tall
atn node=vp REQUIRED
verify sent= tall
in verify sent.= tall parse np
verify will attempt child:np to father:vp
in ATN DEPTH=   2
CLAUSES: s root PHRASES: np root
cat det atnREM. SENT.= tall
atn node=np REQUIRED
VERIFY FAILURE
VERIFY NOT CLEARING(PA):np CHILD=vp
in ATN DEPTH=   2
CLAUSES: s root PHRASES: np root

cat pronoun atnREM. SENT.= tall
atn node=np REQUIRED
VERIFY FAILURE
VERIFY NOT CLEARING(PA):np CHILD=vp IN ATN AFTER VERIFY tall
IN ATN VERIFY FAILURE FOR REQUIRED ARC parse vp DEPTH=   1
POPPING PHRASE np
VERIFY FAILURE
VERIFY NOT CLEARING(PA):vp CHILD=s
in ATN DEPTH=   1
CLAUSES: s root PHRASES: root
cat verb atnREM. SENT.= is tall
atn node=vp REQUIRED FIRST CHILD
CAT ATTACHING is PHRASES: root
cat adv atnREM. SENT.= tall
atn node=vp OPTANY PHRASES: root
cat adj atnREM. SENT.= tall
atn node=vp REQUIRED
CAT ATTACHING tall PHRASES: root
endphrase ATHEAD atnREM. SENT.=
atn node=vp REQUIRED
PUSHING PHRASE vp DEPTH=   1
VERIFY ATTACHINGvp TO s
VERIFY CURRWORD IN ATN AFTER VERIFY PHRASES: vp root
:= s decl atnREM. SENT.=
atn node=s REQUIRED PHRASES: vp root
endphrase ATHEAD atnREM. SENT.=
atn node=s REQUIRED
PUSHING PHRASE s DEPTH=   0
VERIFY ATTACHING FIRST CHILDs TO root
VERIFY CURRWORD
SENTENCE RESULTS
s declarative
np noun phrase
the determiner(adj) IS LEAF (TERMINAL SYMBOL)
boy noun IS LEAF (TERMINAL SYMBOL)
vp verb phrase
is verb IS LEAF (TERMINAL SYMBOL)
tall adjective IS LEAF (TERMINAL SYMBOL)

Chapter 8

Conclusion

Overview

The common thread of pattern matching in AI techniques are reviewed. The integration and application of the various programs presented above are discussed.

Pattern Recognition, Language, and Rules

Intelligence is quite possibly sophisticated pattern matching. In the introduction, we paraphrased a definition of AI as sophisticated searching of a sophisticated database. A search is, of course, an attempt to match a pattern. As discussed in the first chapter, the chess master extracts the relevant pattern from the chessboard, compares it to his stored database, and conceives of his plan. The production rule formulations of expert system shells are attempts to find a sequence of matches to antecedent predicate terms to attain the goal. The matching process, unification, is a search which allows variable substitution but is otherwise a simple attempt to form a match.

Syntactic pattern recognition is discussed briefly in Chapter 1. Grammar rules are essentially prescriptions for matching (one-dimensional) sequences, or strings, of symbols. These prescriptions are not simple templates, but are rather complicated, requiring agreement between distant symbols in the string. This complication requires treatment by an approach such as context sensitivity, unification grammar, etc. This, in turn, means that tests for agreement cannot generally be performed immediately but must be postponed until the entire sentence is "in view."

Because of this unifying thread, the expert system shells and ATN language processor have similar structure. It is plausible that any advance in pattern recognition would therefore impact all these and similar areas of AI. Conversely, the methods discussed here are applicable to many pattern recognition problems when suitably (syntactically) expressed.

Integration, Blackboarding

Chapter 5 discusses a frames database. This can be used to hold rules (syntactic or production) for the systems of Chapters 3, 4, or 7, as well as dictionary information for Chapter 7. Currently, SQL as a relational database interface is rapidly becoming a standard, and there are a number of efforts to integrate Ada and SQL. It would make sense to make use of such interfaces rather than writing your own B-tree package if one wished to use external storage. Otherwise, just use the internal binary search tree storage. Chapter 4 discusses the possible integration of the forward- and backward-chaining systems of Chapter 3 and that chapter, and the appropriate modifications of these systems for optimized use in embedded real-time applications.

A blackboard is a temporary, subsidiary database which is used in common by a number of interacting systems. Blackboards were pioneered by the HEARSAY speech recognition system developed at Carnegie-Mellon University. For example, one expert system might post its conclusions on the blackboard for the use of other systems. Another system might interrogate the blackboard to select the most appropriate "view" (see Chapter 4), i.e., the best assumptions to employ to treat its part of the problem. A frames database should be quite suitable for such a purpose. Ada should simplify the coding of a blackboard system by permitting the problem to be coded as a number of interacting tasks, thereby simplifying issues of mutual exclusion during file operations.

Extensions

The methods presented in this book may be applied to a variety of problems beyond expert systems.

Constraint Programming

The usual programming language, such as Ada, is *procedural,* i.e., the programmer specifies precisely what the computer is to do. In constraint programming, only the desired result is specified and the means of achieving this result are left to the program. Rule-based systems are an example of constraint programming, and the methods of one are those of the other.

Planning

A planning problem is a backward-chaining problem with one goal. The attention is focused on the precise path or paths which may achieve this goal. Rather than generate a confidence factor for the goal based upon a number of alternate paths, it is more important to save each alternative, along with information about the path's cost, etc. It may be desirable to determine an optimal path. In a situation involving uncertainty or an adversary, it may be useful to generate and save a variety of choices.

Discrete Event Simulation

Simulation typically involves studying the behavior of a system specified by a set of rules. In continuous simulation, these rules are differential equations. In discrete event simulation, these rules are more like the rules of an expert system. The classic example is that of a supermarket checkout counter with customers arriving at some probabilistic rate. Different queuing systems can be modeled and the best compromise between cost, average serving time, etc., can be determined given assumptions about the expected arrival rate, duration of service, etc. Typically, such simulations are written in special-purpose languages such as SIMSCRIPT, GASP, or SIMULA.

I have seen a system developed at Los Alamos National Laboratory, using KEE, to automate such simulations. Such simulations obviously lend themselves to specification in terms of rules or constraints. Events can trigger other events just as rules can fire other rules by establishing facts. Active values or demons (see Chapter 5) are used to ensure that all appropriate actions occur when conditions warrant.

Conclusion

I hope that readers will use the programs here as a foundation to build on in developing not just "AI" applications, but other Ada programs. I would enjoy hearing from readers about such attempts along with comments.

The development of Ada was motivated in part by "life-cycle" issues. Ada was conceived of as an approach to reducing life-cycle costs of maintenance and upgrade as well as improving initial program development. A computer program must be thought of as a dynamic, living entity which evolves and grows. A program which no one wishes to modify is almost certainly not perfect, but moribund. Please think of the programs presented here in this light. I hope that the use of Ada has made the methods of artificial intelligence accessible to a wider audience and that this audience will take the computer code presented here and shape it to their own designs.

INDEX

INDEX

AIE, 36
ALS, 36
ALSN, 36
Antinomy, Cretan, 39
APSE, 35
Arc, 274, 278
ARIADNE, 37
Atkin, L., 11
Attribute grammar, 276
Attribute-value system, 39
Autonomous syntax, 277
Aux-inversion, 276

Backward chaining, 40
Baker, L., 35
Barnes, G. J. P., 28
Bayesian, 42
Berliner, H., 12
Binary search tree, 238
Blackboard, 354
Bottom-up parser, 273
Bounded movement, 284
Breadth-first search, 41
Bucket hashing, 52
Burns, A., 33
Buzzard, G. D., 35

Carnap, R., 271
Chomsky, N., 271, 273
Chomsky hierarchy, 273
Church, A., 37, 39
Church's theorem, 37, 47
Circularity check, 50
Closed-world model, 48
Cognitive dissonance, 4
Completeness, 48
Complexity explosion, 4
Conceptual dependency, 277
Confidence factors, 42

Consistency, 48
Constraint programming, 354
Context, 61
Context-free grammar, 273
Context-free language, 274
Context-sensitive grammar, 273
Cut, 50

Decorated tree, 277
Demon, 235
Depth, 61
Depth-first search, 41
Determiner, 272
Dijkstra, E., 33
Dreyfus, H., 7
Dreyfus, S., 7
Dynamic string, 54

EMYCIN, 63

Facet, 234
Factoring, 49
Feigenbaum, E. A., 5
Festinger, L., 4
Finite state automata, 274
Finite-state machine, 274, 281
First-order logic, 38
Forward chaining, 41, 149
Frame, 233
Fuzzy sets, 42

General Problem Solver, 1
Generative grammar, 271
Gentzen, G., 50
Gödel, K., 39
Good, I. J., 43
GPS, 1, 4
Grammar:
   attribute, 276

Grammar (*Cont.*):
  context-free, 273
  context-sensitive, 273
  definite clause, 288
  generative, 271
  phrase-structure, 271
  regular, 274
  semantic, 277
  transformational, 275
  unification, 277
Greibach Normal Form, 273
Guarded Horn clause, 45

Haberman, A. N., 28
Hash table, 44, 56
  bucket, 52
HEARSAY, 354
Herbrand sentence, 149
Heuristic:
  strong, 155
  weak, 155
Heuristic search, 41
Hierarchical database model, 233
Hitech, 12
Hoare, C. A. R., 33
Hopfield, J. J., 10
Horn, A., 45
Horn clause, 45
  definite, 45
Hough transform, 15

Ichbiah, J. D., 33
Indexing, 48
Inheritance, 233, 234
Isa slot, 234

Jerardi, T., 62

KAPSE, 35

Levy, D., 8
Lewis, C. I., 43
Linear-bounded automata, 275
Link, 278
List, linked, 51
Literals, 45

MAPSE, 35
Marcus, D., 283
Marr, D., 13
Metaknowledge, 154
Modal logic, 43
Mudge, T. N., 35

MYCIN, 63

Negation as failure, 48
Network database model, 233
Nielson, K., 33
Non-Horn clause, 49
Nonmonotonic logic, 157
NP-completeness, 4

Object-attribute-value system, 39
"Occurs" test, 45
OPS5, 40, 149, 154, 156, 157

Parse tree, 273
Pascoe, G., 35
Pask, G., 1
Perry, D. E., 28
Phrase-structure grammar, 271, 275
Piaget, J., 4, 271
Plex grammar, 277
Polish notation, 150
Post, E., 271
Post Algebra, 43
Post language, 271
Post production, 271
Predicate logic, first-order, 38
Primal sketch, 13
Production, 271
PROLOG, 37, 41, 45, 46, 48, 50, 62
Push-down automata, 274

Queue, 52

R-1, 157
Regular grammar, 274
Relational database model, 233
Resolution, 46
  binary, 46
RETE, 157
Rich, E., 1
Robinson, J., 46
Russell, B., 38

Schank, R., 278
Script, 278
Semantic grammar, 277
Semantic network, 278
Shumate, K., 33
Simon, H. A., 1, 5
Slate, D., 11
Slot, 234
Soundness, 48
SQL, 354

Stack, 52
Standardizing apart, 47, 56
String, dynamic, 54
Structure sharing, 44
Subjective contours, 14
Symbolic logic, 37

Terminal symbol, 272
Top-down parser, 273
Transformational grammar, 275
Tree, 51
  binary, 52
  binary search, 238
Truth-maintenance, 157
Turing machine, 275

Unbounded movement, 284
Unification, 44
Unification grammar, 284

View, 157

Wait-and-see parsers (WASP), 281
Web grammar, 277
Wegmann, L., 35
Wh-transformation, 276
World, 157

XCON, 149, 157

Zadeh, L., 42

ABOUT THE AUTHOR

Louis Baker, Ph.D., is a senior researcher at Mission
Research Corporation in Albuquerque, New Mexico. Prior
to this, he held positions at Sandia National Laboratories
and the Naval Research Laboratory in Washington, D.C.
Dr. Baker has written numerous articles on
electromagnetic field propagation, computer interfacing,
AI, and computer simulation.

VERITAS

MDCCXL

Given In Memory Of
Dr. Robert U. Drinkard

By

Dr. Perry E. Gresham